Longman Modular Geography Series

URBAN AND RURAL SETTLEMENTS

Harold Carter

Emeritus Professor of Human Geography,
The University College of Wales, Aberystwyth

Longman
London and New York

Contents

Preface

This modular series of nine separate but inter-locking geography texts is designed primarily for sixth form students in the 1990s in the UK. The series is written by a team of authors who, with the Joint Editors, are Chief Examiners and Moderators for a number of GCE Examining Boards, and have been actively involved with sixth form teaching of geography at GCE 'A', and now 'A/S' Levels, as well as at college and university level.

In any modular system, self-standing parts are complementary to each other and to the series as a whole which caters, in its full range of systematic studies, for the needs of any conventional UK geography 'A' Level syllabus. In this series, there are nine texts: three physical and three human, together with three which focus on the interfaces (a) within physical geography, (b) within human geography and (c) between physical and human geography. Thus, the traditional compartmentalisation of the subject is challenged and new interdisci-plinary syllabus and educational developments anticipated. Moreover, real case-studies on global and local scales abound throughout, providing a continuing, but ordered and necessary, real-world perspective. Assignments of varying types are to be found in each chapter, providing stimulating work at the sixth form level as well as maintaining the spirit and approaches of GCSE.

Above all, this series offers a representative range of geography books, covering most of the subject, from which individuals may select their own combination for study. A combination of selected physical, human or interface texts can be tailored to suit any teaching programme and designed to meet the special requirements of a specific 'A' or 'A/S' Level syllabus, including those 'A/S' Levels which concentrate on physical or human topics alone. Again, the available expertise and preferences in any given sixth form centre could govern the selection of texts adopted for study. Such selections could favour specialisation (either in physical or human geography) or the interdisciplinary approach (based primarily on the interface volumes). The choice is yours.

Geography is a changing academic subject in a changing world, a changing society and a changing environment, creating great interest and new challenges at all educational levels. The inquisitive and illustrative style of these texts will provide sixth formers with the oppor-tunities to learn, by self-discovery, how theory matches practice and how the local, or distant, geographies can come alive in the classroom. Geography is in a unique position, straddling the humanities and the sciences, yet main-taining a strong academic and professional identity of its own. This series of texts serves to promote and advance that identity, in both the pure and applied senses, providing a contri-bution to training for good citizenship, and environmental awareness, as well as perspec-tives on human opportunities and environmental issues the world over.

B. P. Price
J. A. Taylor
(Joint Editors)

1

Urban and Rural Populations

INTRODUCTION: THE DISTINCTION OF VILLAGE AND TOWN

The first classification which is made by geographers when considering settlement is into two apparently totally contrasted types, urban and rural. This is also, of course, the immediate contrast used in everyday life when people refer to towns and villages. At this stage, it must be noted that Americans use the word city as a direct equivalent of the English word town and throughout the literature of urban geography city appears with that connotation and not as in Britain where it refers to a special status granted by the Crown, and by implication, although it is not always so, to a somewhat larger settlement. In this book, therefore, city and town must be taken as synonymous since that is nearest to current international usage.

The implication of the use of the two terms, city or town and village, is that there is a fundamental and easily defined distinction which can be made between them. Of course, there are settlements smaller than the village such as the hamlet, and settlements larger than the town, such as the conurbation and metropolis, but along that scale of size it is implied that there is a point where a significant change in the fundamental nature of the settlement occurs. The first question to be asked, therefore, is whether that concept can be validated.

In simple descriptive and functional terms, it is possible to maintain the validity of the distinction on the basis that the village is made up of population primarily engaged in agriculture. Nucleation has come about for agricultural reasons, such as the availability of water supply. In contrast, the town is characterised by a population engaged in non-agricultural pursuits, especially the provision of centrally or accessibly located facilities, such as shops, banks and professional services. But such a simple distinction is not tenable. The village offers central and accessible services, traditionally, for example, the blacksmith (although now it would be a garage). The village inn is part of the tradition also, whilst the village shop offers a wide range of low cost, immediately necessary goods. Moreover, the growth of commuting means that many city workers live in what are commonly called villages so that the primarily agricultural nature of employment becomes greatly modified. The clear break is, therefore, lost or misted over and the distinction becomes one of degree rather than of kind.

ASSIGNMENT

1. As a preliminary exercise, review the settlement pattern in an area known to you and consider whether you can, without difficulty, divide the nucleated settlements into towns and villages. Do you need to introduce supplementary terminology such as hamlet or metropolis?

CRITERIA FOR DEFINITION OF URBAN AND RURAL

Faced with these difficulties it is not surprising that the countries of the world have arrived at no uniform or standardised method of distinguishing between urban and rural populations. The boundary line between them must of necessity be arbitrary. Table 1.1 lists a selection of some of the definitions employed.

The first point to note is the considerable variation in the complexity of definition, and the second is that careful analysis will show how the criteria which were briefly introduced in the discussion above have been used. There are four types of definition but, of course, they are not exclusive and can overlap.

Table 1.1 *Definition of urban – UN Demographic Yearbook 1983*

Argentina
Populated centres with 2000 or more inhabitants.

Iraq
The area within the boundaries of Municipality Councils (Al Majlis Al-Baldei).

Israel
All settlements of more than 2000 inhabitants, except those where at least one third of the heads of households, participating in the civilian labour force, earn their living from agriculture.

Japan
City (*shi*) having 50 000 or more inhabitants with 60 per cent or more of the houses located in the main built-up areas and 60 per cent or more of the population (including their dependants) engaged in manufacturing, trade or other urban type of business. Alternatively, a *shi* having urban facilities and conditions as defined by the prefectural order is considered as urban.

Norway
Localities of 200 or more inhabitants.

Czechoslovakia
Large towns, usually of 5000 or more inhabitants, having a density of more than 100 persons per hectare of built-up area, three or more living quarters in at least 15 per cent of the houses, piped water and a sewage system for the major part of the town, at least five physicians and a pharmacy, a nine-year secondary school, a hotel with at least twenty beds, a network of trade and distributive services which serve more than one town, job opportunities for the population of the surrounding area, the terminal for a system of bus lines and not more than 10 per cent of the total population active in agriculture; small towns, usually of 2000 or more inhabitants, having a density of more than seventy-five persons per hectare of built-up area, three or

more living quarters in at least 10 per cent of the houses, piped water and a sewage system for at least part of the town, at least two physicians and a pharmacy, other urban characteristics to a lesser degree and not more than 15 per cent of the total population active in agriculture; agglomerated communities which have the characteristics of small towns in regard to size, population density, housing, water supply and sewage, and the percentage of the population active in agriculture, but which lack such town characteristics as educational facilities, cultural institutions, health services and trade and distributive services, because these facilities and services are supplied by a town in the vicinity.

India
Towns (places with municipal corporation, municipal area committee or cantonment board); also all places having 5000 or more inhabitants, a density of not less than 1000 persons per square mile or 390 per square kilometre, pronounced urban characteristics and at least three quarters of the adult male population employed in pursuits other than agriculture.

---

1. A minimum population. This is the simplest, most direct and effective basis but the real problem follows from the introductory discussion for there is no agreement on the figure to be used. It varies, as Table 1.1 shows, from 200 in Norway to 50 000 in Japan. Real difficulties arise from the nature of the settlement pattern itself, cultural tradition and perception of what is urban. A very thinly peopled area with extensive *tracts* of remote territory will tend to have a low threshold population, hence Norway's figure of 200. A similar definition is used in Iceland. A very intensively developed country with high densities of agricultural populations will adopt a high figure, hence Japan's 50 000, although it is partly modified in the full definition. The United Nations have attempted to introduce some standardisation and have requested governments to provide data on the basis of common size ranges, the lowest, and presumably the minimum urban size, being 2000. Often associated with a minimum population is a minimum population density as a measure of the compactness of settlement, but it is difficult to use as an isolated and sole measure. Another way of ensuring nucleation or compactness is to specify a minimum distance between houses. Thus the Swedish definition is 'Built-up areas with at least 200 inhabitants and usually not more than 200 metres between houses'. Again, this is always associated with a minimum population.

2. Administrative areas designated urban. A clear break is introduced when a country, by legislative process, specifically designates settlements as urban. Until 1974, Britain had an unequivocal division based on local government areas where all county boroughs, municipal boroughs and urban districts constituted the urban element, regardless of size. The 1974 reorganisation of local government introduced considerable difficulty, for those specifically urban areas were subsumed into the new 'Districts'. The *Preliminary Report for Towns* of the 1981 census had to admit that 'post-1974 local authority boundaries rarely provide even a crude definition of towns or an approximate urban-rural division' (p. 5) and hence it had to revert to the presentation of figures on the pre-1974 basis with a series of modifications which required extensive explanation in an Appendix. To show the use of this type of definition, although in a different culture context, the example of Iraq has been included in Table 1.1.

3. Employment in agriculture. This basis for definition takes up the distinction in role which was identified at the outset of this chapter. It depends on the necessary occupational data being available. Israel has a basic numerical qualification for a town of 2000 people but then deletes as urban those areas where, though the population is over 2000, at least one third of the heads of household in the civilian labour force earn their living from agriculture. The Netherlands has a similar procedure including municipalities below 2000 where *not more* than 20 per cent of the economically active male population is engaged in agriculture. This qualification is clearly intended to pick up suburban or commuter municipalities and place them in the urban category.

4. Urban functions or facilities. The fourth basis for recognition of the urban population is the identification of characteristic urban functions. The very complex Czechoslovak definition is included in Table 1.1 as an example. In contrast, some definitions add an undefined qualification to a minimum population. Thus Honduras adopts a definition which reads, 'Localities of 2000 or more inhabitants having essentially urban characteristics'. The essentially urban characteristics are given a full interpretation in the Czech definition.

If the definition used by India is now reviewed (Table 1.1) it can be seen that all four of the bases are brought into play, and, indeed, a fifth, the density of population is added. The result of this review of the formal distinction between what is urban and what is rural is to highlight the plethora of non-standardised definitions which are used. Two further problems need to be added. The first is that many of the figures are estimates based on censuses which are unreliable, especially censuses for the less developed countries. The second is that even where censuses are reliable, the figures given refer to administratively defined areas and there is no guarantee that the boundaries used actually coincide with the physical extent of the settlement itself. The area included may be much greater than the settlement – a situation referred to as *overbounded* – or it may be less extensive, leaving much of the settlement outside the limit taken – a situation referred to as *underbounded*. These anomalies are usually the result of lags in the adjustment of defined area to settlement growth or decline. The urban history of nineteenth century Britain and the USA is characterised by the continuous attempts of cities to extend their boundaries in order to take in their growing suburbs.

This process, as well as problems of contemporary definition, are very well illustrated by the Standard Metropolitan Statistical Area (SMSA) in the United States. These are extended areas including both central city, or cities because there may be more than one, and the dependent suburbs.

This is the formal definition:

Table 1.2 *United States – Standard Metropolitan Statistical Areas 1960*

Except in New England, the criteria used to delineate an SMSA pertain to county units. An SMSA is a county or group of contiguous counties that contains at least one city of 50 000 inhabitants or more, or twin cities with a combined population of at least 50 000. To qualify as twin cities, two cities must have contiguous boundaries and must constitute, for general social and economic purposes, a single community with a combined population of at least 50 000; the smaller place must have a population of at least 15 000.

In addition to the county or counties containing such a city or cities, contiguous counties are included in an SMSA if they are essentially metropolitan in character and are socially and economically integrated with the central city.

Criteria of metropolitan character (1) At least 75.0 per cent of the labour force of the county must be in the nonagricultural labour force. (2) In addition to criterion 1, the county must meet at least one of the following conditions: (a) it must have 50.0 per cent or more of its population living in contiguous minor civil divisions with a density of at least 150 persons per square mile, in an unbroken chain of minor civil divisions with such density radiating from a central city in an area. (b) The number of non-agricultural workers employed in the county must equal at least 10.0 per cent of the number of non-agricultural workers employed in the county containing the largest city in the area (the central city); or the outlying county must be the place of employment of at least 10 000 non-agricultural workers. (c) The non-agricultural labour force living in the county must equal at least 10.0 per cent of the non-agricultural labour force living in the county containing the central city; or the outlying county must be the place of residence of a non-agricultural labour force of at least 10 000.

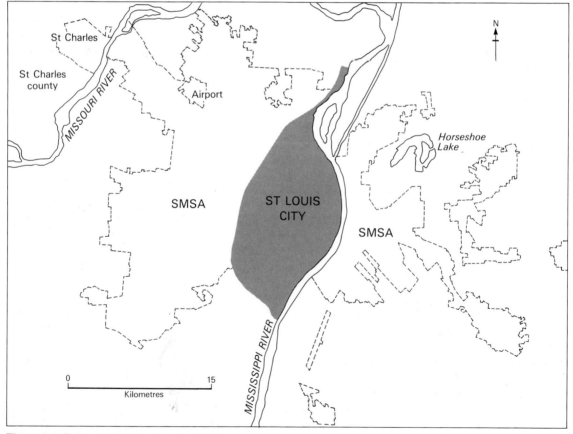

Figure 1.1 *St Louis City showing the SMSA*

Criteria of integration A county is regarded as integrated with the county or counties containing the central city or cities if either of the following criteria is met: (1) If 15.0 per cent of the workers living in the outlying county work in the county or counties containing the central city or cities of the area. (2) If 25.0 per cent of those working in the outlying county live in the county or counties containing the central city or cities of the area.

Only where data for criteria 1 and 2 are not conclusive are other related types of information used, for example newspaper circulation reports, per cent of the population in the county located in the central city telephone exchange area, or delivery areas of retail stores in central cities, and so on.

Central cities Although there may be several cities of 50 000 or more inhabitants in an SMSA, not all are necessarily central cities. The central city or cities are determined by the following criteria: (1) The largest city in an SMSA is always the central city. (2) One or two additional cities may be secondary central cities if each has (a) at least 250 000 inhabitants, (b) a population of one-third of that of the largest city and a minimum population of 25 000. When the criteria for twin cities is met, then both cities are considered to be central cities.

For historical reasons there is some variation in New England.

It is now possible to summarise the material considered up to this point by asserting that there are three basic reasons why urban proportions of a country's population need to be treated with the greatest care and to stress that one is not dealing with standard and comparable situations. The reasons are:

1. Variations in definition.
2. The unreliability of censuses.
3. The problem of under and overbounding.

ASSIGNMENTS

2. List the various methods of identifying metropolitan populations and relate them to the different bases outlined earlier in this chapter.
3. Try to obtain copies of the Census 1981 Preliminary Report for Towns and/or the appropriate census volume(s) for your area. How effectively are settlements identified? What sort of variation occurs when different definitions are used?

WORLD CONTRASTS IN THE URBAN PROPORTION OF THE POPULATION

A review of all the urban proportions which appear in the United Nations Demographic Yearbook, accepting the inevitable inaccuracies due to the reasons reviewed, suggests that three groupings can be derived which can be equated with the so-called three worlds: the developed, capitalist west; the socialist countries of eastern Europe; the less developed countries or Third World. This is no more than an oversimple division of convenience. Thus Third World countries are both capitalist and communist in politico-economic structure and cut across the initial division. Again, the degree of development varies greatly and a fourth group, Latin American countries, has been added to indicate how they could be considered to make up a regional group on their own, breaking across the other three groups. These groupings are set out in Table 1.3 and can be used as the basis for discussion.

Table 1.3 *Urban proportions of total population*

		Percentage	Date	Source
Group 1	Belgium	94.6	1976	estimate
	UK	76.9	1981	census
	USA	73.7	1980	census
	France	73.4	1982	census
Group 2	Czechoslovakia	66.7	1974	estimate
	USSR	63.6	1981	estimate
	Poland	59.0	1981	estimate
	Hungary	53.2	1980	census
Group 3	Burma	23.9	1983	census
	India	23.3	1981	census
	Sudan	20.2	1983	census
	Mozambique	13.2	1980	census
Group 4	Argentina	82.9	1980	estimate
	Brazil	68.3	1982	estimate
	Bolivia	46.4	1983	estimate
	Ecuador	44.5	1982	estimate

The developed west: the capitalist countries

These countries register high urban proportions, generally above 70 per cent. They are closely associated with industrialisation in the nineteenth and early twentieth centuries and a very low employment proportion in agriculture. Three phases which have led to the present situation can be identified.

1. Conurbation. The word was devised as late as 1915 by Patrick Geddes in his book '*Cities in Evolution*', but it effectively summarises the predominant process during the last century. The proportion of urban dwellers in the United Kingdom had risen from 33.8 per cent in 1801 (compare this figure with those for contemporary Third World countries in Table 1.3) to 78 per cent in 1901. There were three major reasons.

The first was the growth of manufacturing industry and the coming of mass production. That inevitably involved the assembly of large numbers of workers at single points and, given the limitations of transport, meant their living *en masse* close to the centres of production. Moreover, *external linkages*, the advantages gained from associated activities being proximate, demanded that the centres of production themselves be located physically near to each other, thus increasing the related workforces and settlement size. It is significant that between the two major reorganisations of local government in Britain in 1888 and 1974, many of these areas, which were not older boroughs, carried the name Urban District.

The second reason is very closely associated and can be called economic development and the *division of labour*. Any advance from a purely subsistence economy is inevitably based on an increasingly complex division of labour or high specialisation in occupation. These specialisms are mutually supporting. Thus a teacher needs builders and painters to erect a house and a whole gamut of specialists to produce the house's equipment. The specialists, in turn, need vans to deliver material and the vans need mechanics to service them. But the *friction of distance*, that is the drag exerted in the form of time and cost to get about, means that all these specialists have to be spatially associated. This is the crux of Lampard's succinct summary, 'city growth is simply the concentration of differentiated but functionally integrated specialisms in rational locales'.

The third reason is termed *agglomeration economies* or *economies of scale*. From the two reasons set out, it is apparent that a characteristic of the nineteenth century was concentrated, mass producing industry distributing its goods by a national network of railways. This replaced the old trades and crafts which had been present in every town. In turn, that industry attracted not only labour but services, or a growing *infrastructure* which is the word used to denote the whole range of support from schools and hospitals to roads, railways, water supply and sewage systems. These in turn, because of the advantages they gave, attracted new investment thereby initiating cumulative growth. Further, innovation characterised these buoyant areas stimulating even more development. Advantages, therefore, accrued to size. In Britain in 1801, towns of between 2500 and 10 000 population accounted for 19.1 per cent of the urban population but the figure had fallen to 11.4 per cent in 1901. In contrast, towns of over 100 000 in 1801 (there was only one, London) accounted for 32.6 per cent of the urban population but 56 per cent by 1901 (when there were 33).

It is important, however, not to overemphasise urbanward migration. Certainly it was significant, but the greater part of the urban gain was from *natural increase*.

2. Suburbanisation. This was apparent in the eighteenth century in Britain, was a major feature of the nineteenth century and the predominant process in the twentieth century. The reasons for its increasing significance are not difficult to identify. City centres became increasingly dirty, noisy and dangerous, the perils resulting both from the prevalence of disease as well as physical disturbance. To that condition was added the growing problem of access as congestion became more and more characteristic. The consequence was to push those who could afford it out to the town periphery at a time when the development of mass transit systems, at first the tram, then the railway, made the journey to work possible. A resultant characteristic has already been noted, the constant attempt by towns to extend their boundaries to take in the new settlement, and the revenue from the rates which it produced.

3. Counterurbanisation. The present predominant trend, most apparent in the USA but clearly identifiable in Britain, is an extended rejection of city living and a desire to live beyond the urban limits, in areas which are primarily rural. The technology of the private motor car allied to the construction of urban expressways or motorways makes for easier physical movement, whilst the telephone and modern micro-electronic devices provide wide-ranging communication (note the word) link-ups without any physical movement at all. Table 1.4 sets out recent population changes (a) in England and Wales and (b) in selected USA cities. There is clear evidence of metropolitan and inner city decline and of major growth taking place in small towns and the countryside. The result of this is a new dispersal of population over extensive areas, building up into large scale metropolitan regional systems, virtually dispersed cities.

The following is an extract from the *New York Times* consequent upon the mid-decade (1985) population estimates.

Table 1.4 a) *England and Wales 1961–1981, population: percentage changes*

	1961–1971	**1971–81**
England	5.9	0.4
Wales	3.3	2.2
Conurbations	−4.3	−8.1
Greater London	−6.8	−10.1
Merseyside	−8.5	−11.0
SE Lancs.	−1.4	−6.2
Tyneside	−5.9	−9.2
West Midlands	−0.3	−5.4
West Yorks.	1.4	−3.0
Towns outside conurbations	8.7	2.5
Over 100 000	2.6	−1.6
50 000–100 000	9.4	2.2
Under 50 000	13.0	5.5
Rural areas	17.9	9.7

b) *USA 1970–1980, population: percentage changes*

	Central city	Suburbs
Chicago	−11.4	+12.9
Detroit	−20.0	+7.7
St Louis	−27.6	+5.9
Cleveland	−23.7	+0.8
Houston	+27.6	+72.0
San Diego	+25.4	+49.1
USA	−4.9	+16.0

St Charles County, Mo, on the outer ring of the St Louis metropolitan area provides an example of the latest large development around the largest population centres.

St Charles County is beyond the heavy layers of suburbs that surround the old city, beyond the airport, beyond the Interstate 270 beltway and beyond the Missouri River which in the past had served as a practical and psychological barrier between the St Louis area and farmland beyond.

Since 1980 the city of St Louis lost another 6 per cent of its population, leaving it with about 426 000, half of what it was in 1950. St Louis County which contains most of the suburbs but not the city of St Louis grew less than 1 per cent in the last five years to about 983 000 people. The new growth went mostly to St Charles which gained almost 14 per cent to 164 000 and other peripheral counties.

St Charles County is becoming increasingly independent. General Motors has a new plant in the town of Wenzville, 40 miles from St Louis and industrial parks are springing up throughout the county . . .

In another sense, however, the county has no centre. Its population is spread over a broad matrix of exclusive housing developments, old towns and villages and new subdivisions of all sizes, interspersed with shopping malls, forests and farms. (See Fig. 1.1.)

A term has been coined for the situation epitomised in the last paragraph, *counterurbanisation*, which is producing an urban civilisation without cities, as appropriate a comment on contemporary process as was conurbation some seventy years ago. The comparison in Britain is especially relevant to south-east England, where the growth of industrial parks, office parks, out-of-town shopping centres and metropolitan villages has created a composite regional system in which hobby farming and the demand for recreational use of land also plays a part.

All this ultimately poses a single question. Is it now possible or meaningful to make any distinction between what is urban and what is rural? It would seem that the two are so intertwined in the composite regional system that separation, with which this chapter began, makes little sense. It follows that a situation has been reached where the old free-standing town, completely in contrast to the surrounding countryside, represents a situation which has long disappeared. If so, the concept of an urban percentage of the population also lacks real meaning. Certainly such a situation is not universally true in the western world, but it represents the condition to which most countries and regions are moving. Even the remotest areas are becoming characterised by the second homes or summer homes of urban dwellers and are thus brought into the metropolitan orbit, into the metropolitan regional system.

Socialist countries or countries of centralised control

The critical criterion for separating these countries is that it is presumed that free market conditions do not exist and hence urban growth can be constrained by state direction. The constraint can, in fact, come from the political left or the political right. Thus, until its relaxation in 1986, influx control was the main means of preventing mass migration from the black Homelands to the cities of South Africa. All blacks were assumed to be nationals of the Homelands and, therefore, not citizens of South Africa. They were only allowed temporary and controlled residence in cities, based on the notorious pass book. It is instructive to draw a comparison with the Soviet *propiska*. This is a sort of visa which every urban inhabitant must have and which gives the right to live in a specific city. James Bater in his book *The Soviet City* writes, 'The propiska denotes whether residence is permanent or temporary. In theory, one cannot live in a city without such documentation. In practice, most major cities attract sizeable numbers of illegal, unregistered residents. If detected, illegal residents are either prosecuted, deported, or both. Registered migrants are normally permitted a three-month temporary residence during which time they must secure a job if they arrived without one in hand.' The aims of both South Africa and the USSR are fundamentally the same, to control urbanward migration, although in the South African case it is selective of a certain group of people.

The situation in the capitalist west and that in the socialist east is not, however, as polarised as might be assumed. Throughout the west, there are planning constraints of greater or lesser severity which constitute limitations on the free operation of the market. The statutory Green Belts about British towns are a good example. It is worth noting that attempts to control urban growth in Britain are not new and the products of recent planning ideas. As early as 1580, the first Queen Elizabeth had issued a proclamation which read, 'The Queene's Majestie perceiving the state of the Citie of London . . . and the suburbs and confines thereof to incth indaily, by accesse of people to inhabite the same . . . her Majestie . . . doth charge and straightly command all manner of Persons, of what qualitie soever they be, to desist and forebear from any new buildings of any house or tenement within three miles from any of the gates of the saide Citie of London, to serve for Habitation or Lodging for any person where no former house hath been knowen to have been in the memorie of such as are now living'. This problem recurred continually but came to a head with the rapid suburban extension of London after the First World War. In response, the Green Belt (London and Home Counties) Act was passed in 1938. The purpose of the Green Belt was much the same as in the Proclamation of 1580, to set up a ring of land around the city within which development was very strictly controlled. After the Second World War it was seen that the problem was wider in scope, affecting many large cities, so that Statutory Green Belts were established in 1955 by the then Ministry of Housing and Local Government for the largest British cities. The reasons were to check the continued growth of large built-up areas, to prevent neighbouring towns merging (literally conurbation) and to preserve the special character of towns. In addition, the taking-up of good quality agricultural land, the need to preserve green spaces for recreation and the desire to retain traditional rural scenery were all cited. The resultant Green Belts are effective checks on urban extension and part of the set of constraints on unlimited development which are typical in western democracies. Freer market forces do not rule without restriction.

This brief treatment of Green Belts occurs here under the apparently anomalous heading of socialist countries since it is indicative of the way in which controls operate, even in countries not usually given that designation. It is even more interesting that the legislation was not introduced by a socialist government. Further treatment will be found in Chapter 10, page 178.

If the western democracies have erected constraints on development, the control system in many socialist states is bureaucratic and ineffective. However, there are extremes of coercion which have been recorded. The Government of Vietnam actually reduced the population of Ho Chi Minh City (Saigon) from 4.5 million in 1975 to 3.1 million in 1982 by means of compulsory deportation. Given the natural increase of the population, that is a much more substantial removal than the bare figures suggest. The most spectacular and notorious example was the action of the Khmer Rouge in Kampuchea (Cambodia) in 1975 when the national and provincial capitals were emptied by force and some three million people dispersed to work in the countryside. It has been estimated that between one and two million people died during the process. Another example of strict regulation is Cuba where Havana's urban population seems to have changed little under Fidel Castro.

But such extremes are exceptional. The Soviet Union has shown a fairly standard pattern of increase from 32 per cent in 1939, to 48 per cent in 1959 and to a majority of the population becoming urban residents in 1961. The figure rose to 62.3 per cent in 1979 and to an estimated 64.1 per cent by 1982. Even so, anomalies do lie at the heart of these changes. On both a regional and an individual basis, socialist systems aim for equality, by developing regional specialisation and self-sufficiency on the one hand and removing inequalities by the spread of the benefits of socialism. These can only be achieved by the central direction of capital investment and of labour, the problem already discussed. But urban growth, and especially metropolitan development, presents a major ideological problem in socialist countries. Cities are places which grow by competition: the successful grow most quickly. But this necessarily introduces differential access to facilities, and hence inequalities. For example, the resident of the largest metropolis in a core area is always going to have easiest access to specialist hospital facilities. On another level, the Bolshoi Ballet does not spread its performances evenly over the whole country; they are not equally accessible to all Soviet citizens. A hierarchically ordered set of cities is necessarily an expression of inequalities. It is from these bases that the argument arises for the incompatibility of socialist equality and urbanisation. These ideological hesitations have generally been set aside, apart from the extreme cases noted above. It is not unreal, therefore, to place the constraints exercised by socialist countries on a continuum with those exercised in non-socialist countries, and relate the percentage of urban population to measures of economic development. When this is done the socialist states do not in any way stand out as anomalous (see Chapter 8).

The less developed or Third World countries

The urban proportions of these countries show two characteristics. The first is a low percentage living in cities (Table 1.3) whereas the second is a strong and rapid urbanisation process at work. That process is, indeed, more rapid than that which characterised Europe in the nineteenth century. Between 1800 and 1850 the world's urban population grew by 22.5 per cent per decade; in the decade 1960–1970 it grew by 40.8 per cent. To this the developed world contributed but little, indeed there was some actual decline. The major proportion of the growth took place in the cities of the less developed world. The reasons for that growth in Third World countries, which has quite properly been called frightening, are very varied but the more important can be listed:

1. Demographic. These countries are still characterised by massive increases in population related to very rapidly lowered death rates but persistent high birth rates. Kenya's population in 1948 was 5.4 million; at the 1959 census it was 15.3 million and estimated to be 18.78 million in 1983, with a growth rate of some 4 per cent per annum. The World Bank estimates its population will be 40 million by the year 2000. The present urban proportion is only 15 per cent but it is increasing massively: the population of Nairobi doubled between 1970 and 1980.

2. The break-up of colonialism. Most, though not all, of the Third World countries experienced a period when they were under direct control by western states. That control was exploitative and extractive. There was little attempt to develop industry within the colonies themselves but rather raw materials were extracted for processing or manufacture in the home territory. Two consequences followed. The first was that exploitation was best accomplished in a political, social and economic system which was held absolutely rigid. The second was an absence of industrial development. The break-up of the colonial constraints under the added stimulus of new nationalisms resulted in less stable and much more fluid conditions. It also raised expectations both in relation to standards of living and to opportunities for advancement. These have all triggered off an urbanward migration, for it is in the cities that the new expectations are most likely to be met. But the lack of indigenous industrial and economic development has meant that employment chances are limited and the drift to the towns is not accompanied by the meeting of the hopes engendered by the new nationalisms and the new freedoms.

3. Economic change. If the early phase of western colonialism was one of exploitation by the extraction of raw materials from Third World countries, the present situation is one of domination by the export of manufactured goods to them. Western countries are urgently seeking new markets and finding them in less developed countries. The goods they export replace the crafts of the villages, destroying what has been called the *bazaar economy*. The result is a total undermining of traditional craft occupations and a disruption of the rural economy. The displaced population moves to the cities.

4. Agricultural change. It has been characteristic of much rural development that it was based on relatively high technology and high capital input. Once again labour is displaced. Moreover, as Third World nations try to meet the burden of debt to western bankers incurred to promote development or even to offset disaster, they find themselves pushed to concentrate on cash crops for sale on world markets in order to generate revenue. To compete, such crops have to be produced on a large scale and as cheaply as possible so that yet again labour is displaced. When the west urbanised, two revolutions went on alongside each other, an industrial and an agricultural revolution; they were closely related. In present less developed countries, agricultural change pushes population towards the cities where there is only limited industrial development to support them.

5. Information flows. A consequence of the improvement of communications has been a massively increased awareness of urban living standards and the possibility of travelling to share in them. Television has been particularly important since it is widely available even in the poorest slums of the poorest countries. It is by no means unusual in the Third World countries to find a television set in the meanest of dwellings where electricity is available, whilst even if individual families do not have sets village community centres provide the facility. Because of cost and limited production capacity, indigenous programmes are inevitably limited and schedules are filled out with western soap operas, situation comedies and the like. These bring to rural populations, the illusions of the urban consumer society, indeed they usually exaggerate the glamour and attractiveness of city living. They bring home, literally, the possibilities of a much more secure and affluent life style. Television, along with the other media, especially magazines, breaks down localisms, widens horizons and generates discontent with the immediate environment and what it has to offer. New aspirations are aroused. And once one migrant has left and established himself (it is usually a male) he will encourage members of an extended family to join him. Return visits will spread the news and so a whole cityward chain of migration is established.

Because of this large urbanward flow the countries of the developing world face immense problems. Three of these can be noted as of especial significance.

1. Over-urbanisation, primacy and the dominance of core regions. These three descriptions are not necessarily three different ways of looking at the same phenomenon yet they are closely related. *Over-urbanisation* refers to large populations being built up in towns but without the concomitant economic growth to support them. *Primacy* refers to that large urban population being concentrated in one city, nearly always the capital city, which becomes over dominant in size. The dominance of core regions is similar to primacy except that the reference is to a region rather than a city. Thus, in British terms, the city would be London, the core region the south-east. All these situations present real problems. Thus, in Panama, the proportion of the population living in and about the capital rose from 31 per cent in 1950 to 46 per cent in 1980. In Indonesia the metropolitan area of the capital Jakarta has risen from 6.7 million in 1961 to over 13 million in 1981. Such massive growth demands excessive investment. Thus it is estimated that to provide an adequate supply of water for Jabotabek (the Jakarta metropolitan area) will take up 60 per cent of the total national allocation for water supply over the next five years. And the greater the investment in infrastructure, the greater the drawing power of the metropolis. This process has gone under a number of names: the exploding metropolis; the rise of the insatiable *megacity (The Times.* 4 July, 1986). Estimates of growth suggest that by 2000 AD Mexico City will have a population of some 26.3 million (a figure of 35 million has even been suggested), São Paulo of 24 million, Calcutta and Bombay of 16 million.

2. Squatter settlement. The rapid and immense growth of these cities means that the responsible municipal authorities find it totally impossible to provide standard services, above all to provide housing. The urban immigrants, therefore, build themselves the crudest of shelters, lacking all services such as water supply, sewage system or electricity, on the least wanted sites, usually at the urban periphery. Such settlements have a wide variety of names: spontaneous settlements is one, but the term *squatter* is most appropriate, since the critical issue is the lack of legal rights to the occupied land. These types of occupation account for some 46 per cent of the total population in Mexico City, 45 per cent in Istanbul, 33 per cent in Calcutta and 25 per cent in Jakarta.

3. *The informal sector and shared space.* The consequence of immigration accompanied by limited development is very high unemployment. A dual economy tends to develop. One circuit is concerned with formal transactions, trading, banking and administration. The other, totally informal, characterises the squatter settlements and slums, and consists of individuals making small objects for sale, recycling discarded goods picked up from rubbish heaps, carrying out minor services like hair cutting. Milton Santos has called this the *shared space* since two very different economic systems share the same space. Nowhere is it more spectacularly illustrated than in the new capital of Brazil, Brasilia. About the magnificent and monumentally planned buildings of the capital have accumulated huge and miserable squatter camps. The contrasts epitomise the shared space.

Latin America

The overlap with the developing world is apparent in that the last example, Brasilia, is in Latin America, as is the prime example of the mega-city, Mexico City. Even so, the history of colonialism in Latin America was very different from that of Asia and Africa and more in line with the occupation of North America. It is true that many more of the colonial inheritances remain, as in the persistence of the haciendas, the very large rural estates. There is also a much more mixed cultural inheritance. But, also, development has been more significant so that some countries, like Argentina, seem to have achieved a form of stability with a high urban proportion (Table 1.3). The Latin American countries, therefore, are different in degree rather than kind.

ASSIGNMENTS

4. Consider the distinction of the area in which you live into discrete urban and rural parts. How did local government reorganisation in 1974 in Britain relate to the same problem of the separation of urban from rural? Consider the changes in an area known to you.

5. Attempt to make a list of British cities with approved Green Belts. Either examine the detail of any one in a city near to you or, if you do not live near a large city with a Green Belt, outline the arguments for and against establishing one about the nearest large town. It would be valuable to read Professor Richard Munton's book *London's Green Belt: Containment in Practice* (London, George Allen and Unwin, 1983). Are there any pressures at the moment from 'free market' forces?

6. The above reasons have been set out in relation to urbanward migration in Third World countries. But the move of New Commonwealth peoples to Britain is part of the same process. The two main sources have been the West Indies and Pakistan. Why did these people migrate to Britain in the years following 1945? What were the natures of the source areas and the target areas in Britain? Are the reasons given above adequate and have the processes been the same?

CONCLUSION

This chapter has constituted a broad review of urban and rural populations, the bases of their distinction and some of the characteristics of contemporary world settlement. It is a paradox that the countries most highly urbanised and associated with high economic development are experiencing a loss of urban population, a counterurbanisation. But as a consequence, rural settlement itself is being transformed and brought into the orbit of the *metropoles*. In contrast, those countries with low levels of economic development and relatively low urbanisation are experiencing an unparalleled growth of their city populations to an extent where their ability to cope with growth is brought into question. Many of the issues introduced will need to be taken up again as the consideration of settlement is shifted from the general level of this chapter to more particular and specific issues.

7. The urban proportions in countries have been related in this chapter to two possible major determinants:
   a) The political system and the degree of control which can be exerted by government.
   b) The extent of development or modernisation as it is sometimes called.
   To which of these would you give preference?

2

Rural Settlement: Pattern and Form

INTRODUCTION

The first chapter has demonstrated the great difficulties which arise in making the distinction between urban and rural settlements. Indeed, it was suggested that in the western, developed world, the fundamental difference between urban and rural is disappearing. In spite of these reservations, the distinction must remain the basis for the systematic study of settlement for the only viable option is to adopt a regional approach where all settlements in a defined region are encompassed. But, for that a general systematic basis of appraisal is required. This chapter and the next, therefore, lift out from the totality of the settlement pattern a group called rural in the full awareness that it is an arbitrary procedure.

The various aspects of rural settlement which need to be considered can best be introduced by the consideration of a specific example. Figure 2.1 is a section of a British topographic map of the area in Wiltshire to the east of Swindon. The physical geography is that of the classic scarp and vale character. To the south are the chalk downlands (the Lambourn Downs are further to the east), and to the north is the Vale of the White Horse developed on the Kimmeridge and Gault clays. The well-marked chalk scarp, trending south-west to north-east, marks the boundary between these two contrasted *lithologies*. It is not, however, a simple feature, for a clearly marked Upper Greensand platform, corresponding with a distinct spring line, characterises the scarp foot. Table 2.1 presents the various aspects of rural settlement which the geographer has to consider and these will be discussed in relation to the map.

Table 2.1 *Aspects of rural settlement*

1. Patterning   – typology
                      village, hamlet, farmstead
2. Patterning   – spatial organisation
                      nucleation – dispersal
                      regularity
3. Morphology – settlement form and layout
4. Function   – settlement role
5. Community – social structure and relationships

1. Patterning – typology. Rural settlement is itself made up of a scaled array. At the bottom is the single farmstead and at the top is the large service village. Inspection of Figure 2.1 will reveal an obvious contrast between Ridgeway Farm (252 827) and Bishopstone just to the north. On the other hand, it is much more difficult to categorise Horpit (214 841) which is a much smaller settlement for which one might use the description hamlet. To some extent this is a functional question which will be introduced under *4*.

2. Patterning – spatial organisation. Overriding the hierarchical array of rural settlements is an apparent fundamental contrast between the single farm and any sort of nucleation whatever its size or character. One of the first questions asked, therefore, is the extent to which an area is dominated by the one or the other, that is whether it has a nucleated or dispersed pattern of settlement. Thus, in the example of Figure 2.1, there is most certainly a number of single farms but there is little doubt that the most significant element is the village; it is primarily a nucleated pattern.

But there is a further question to be asked, regardless of whether the pattern is one mainly of villages or isolated farms, and that is the degree of regularity in the spatial organisation. Do the farms, hamlets and villages exhibit any systematic distribution or are they random in distribution? In the example, the physical control of the scarp foot, constituting a spring line, has produced a pattern of some regularity and it could be argued that there is a *linear* and *equidistant* pattern of villages.

3. Morphology – settlement form and layout.

If the scale of analysis is changed then the actual layout of the individual elements becomes an item of geographical interest. It is most clearly manifest in village plan. There is little evidence of any regularity in the form of the villages shown in Figure 2.1. Bishopstone and Hinton Parva, to the east, have individual houses huddled together along a series of roads. On the other hand, it is immediately apparent that in those to the west, such as Wanborough and Liddington, extension has taken place along the main roads to produce distinctive

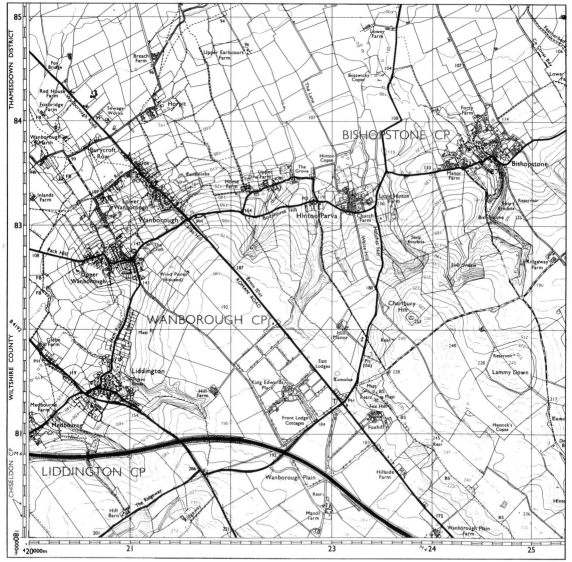

Figure 2.1 *Settlement in an area of Wiltshire to the east of Swindon, 1:25 000 (map reduced)* © *Ordnance Survey*

linear sections: consider Ham Road in Lidding-ton. But individual farms, as well as villages, have their layouts defined by the arrangement of the composing buildings. These, too, can be analysed and contrasted. *Morphology* is significant at all scale levels.

4. *Function – settlement role.* In Chapter 1, where an attempt was made to contrast the functions of towns and villages, it was apparent that villages are much more than aggregates of farmsteads and the cottages of those employed in agriculture. They are also rural service centres. Other functions were also noted. Villages can be primarily residential and commuting settlements for large cities. Even the function of the individual farm can vary. *Hobby farming*, or even tax-loss farming, have brought into the countryside city business men whose main aim is not to run the farm as an economic unit on which to base a living. Not all farms are simply family farms.

5. *Community – social structure and relationships.* The final relevant aspect of rural settlement study is the nature and structure of social relationships within it. Figure 2.1 shows a major estate centred on King Edwards Place (225 814) and this raises questions as to the relationship between such an estate and the nearby villages. The map is in some ways a lifeless thing representing the physical, visible aspects of a complex system of activities and relationships. The geographer might well refrain from entering into a field which is that of the sociologist but it has to be borne in mind that the farms are, at least in part, a product of the economic system, the way the land is worked, and of the social system, how people relate to each other.

This chapter and the next will be taken up by a consideration of these five aspects of rural settlement. In this chapter the emphasis will be on pattern and form (aspects 1 to 3 in Table 2.1), whilst Chapter 3 will concentrate on function and community (aspects 4 and 5 in Table 2.1).

ASSIGNMENT

1. Given Figure 2.1 and the aspects of rural settlement to be studied, consider what types of data and information you would require to undertake a consideration of these aspects. To what extent are the data available?

PATTERNS OF SETTLEMENT – TYPOLOGY AND SPATIAL ORGANISATION

Before proceeding on the discussion of pattern, two general points need to be made.

a) Rural settlement is inextricably bound up with the method of farming, the way the land is worked and the resultant field patterns. This is a very large topic, briefly considered here, which should never be forgotten.

b) The first two elements in Table 2.1 are both aspects of patterning and have been called *typology* and *spatial organisation*. Their separation derives in many ways from earlier studies when they were seen as distinct, the one concerned with whether settlement was in the form of villages, hamlets or farms, the other with the spatial arrangement and especially the degree of regularity in distribution. Modern analyses, as will become apparent, tend to negate such a fundamental distinction and, therefore, the two aspects will be discussed together.

The division of rural settlement into two fundamentally contrasted types, agglomerated or nucleated and dispersed, is derived from the work of the late nineteenth century German scholar Meitzen, and especially his book, *Siedelung und Agrarwesen der Westgermanen und Ostgermanen, der Kelten, Romer, Finnen und Slaven.* Reviewing settlement patterns in Europe, he argued that there were the two fundamentally different types to which he gave the names *dorf* or the village and *einzelhof* or

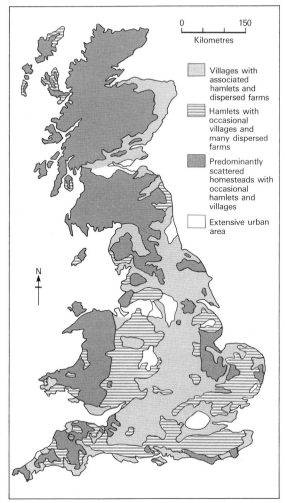

Figure 2.2 *Rural settlement in Britain (after Thorpe)*

Legend:
- Villages with associated hamlets and dispersed farms
- Hamlets with occasional villages and many dispersed farms
- Predominantly scattered homesteads with occasional hamlets and villages
- Extensive urban area

0   150
Kilometres

N

and Ireland, those of relict Celtic cultures, were dominated by a scattered habitat of farms and small hamlets.

Early in the twentieth century, geographers expressed doubts about Meitzen's interpretation of the facts, and subsequently about the facts themselves. No simple correlation existed between Germanic lands and village settlement. For example, the north-west of Germany, parts of Denmark and Sweden are characterised by a scattered habitat. More pertinent is Figure 2.2 which is an attempt to generalise the typology of rural settlement in Britain. At first it seems that Meitzen's view is valid for there is a contrast between Cornwall, Wales, Cumbria and Scotland, with predominantly scattered homesteads, and much of England with village settlement. Even in detail, the village settlement of the early and thoroughly Anglicised areas of Wales, the Vale of Glamorgan, the Gower Peninsula and South Pembroke, is set against the very different characteristics of the rest of the country. But it is most certainly not the whole truth as the hamlets, occasional villages and many dispersed farms of East Anglia demonstrate.

But there was an alternative explanation, especially attractive to geographers who were greatly concerned with the relationship between human kind and the environment which was lived in. The main determinant, which took in the anomalies of Meitzen's interpretation, was the physical condition and the type of farming which was associated with it. Where water supply was limited, and especially where it was associated with springs and wells, as in Figure 2.1, and where farming was concerned with arable cultivation, then agglomeration ensued. Where there was no water supply problem and where farming was essentially pastoral, the single farm was the main settlement form. The explanation thus offered was partly a physical one based on the relation of climate and farming type, and partly also an economic and organisational one. A farmer cultivating arable crops, which do not need a high frequency of attention, does not incur significantly greater costs with distance from his farmhouse. But a

the single farmstead. Meitzen's interpretation of this typology (and note that it is a typology which is now under review) was a cultural one. The village was identified as an essential part of the Germanic tradition, and the lands occupied by and colonised by that tradition were dominated by agglomerated settlements. The dispersion of settlement into single, isolated farms was viewed as part of the Celtic cultural inheritance. Thus, applying these notions to Britain, the south and east, the lands occupied by Saxon or Dane, that is by Germanic peoples, were those of village settlement; the lands of the west and north, Wales, Scotland

Figure 2.3 *Farms near Bow Street, Aberystwyth. These two farms, Ruel Uchaf and Ruel Isaf, are characteristic of a settlement pattern of single or dispersed farms with a network of small, hedged fields. The adjectives Uchaf and Isaf (upper and lower) suggest that they were at one time part of a single holding which has subsequently been split*

dairy farmer will since the animals need constant attention, for example the milking of cows twice daily, and the time and effort taken moving to peripheral land will be so much the greater. It follows that arable cultivation is more economically associated with agglomeration than pastoral farming. Certainly these arguments are equal, if not better, explicands of Figure 2.2.

Whatever the reasons, cultural, physical or economic, the discussion of Meitzen's views seemed to accept the basic principle, that rural settlement could be divided into the two distinct groups with distinct causal associations. But it became evident that such was not the case, and so the factual basis itself came under scrutiny. It has already been demonstrated that Figure 2.1 shows a mixture of settlement types – village, hamlet and separate farm. It could be argued that, although they bear no relationship to the broad continental sweep of Meitzen's argument, locally they show some accord with the explanation according to physical conditions; the scarp foot is a zone of villages, the clay vale of single farms. But the separation, even at the micro-scale, is not complete. Because of these difficulties, the great French geographer, Albert Demangeon, in his report in 1928 on *La Geographie de l'Habitat Rurale*, proposed four types of dispersion. These were:

i *Primary dispersion* of ancient origin. This was an acknowledgement of Meitzen's Celtic grouping.
ii *Intercalated dispersion.* This is where there is a mixture of villages and single farms, with the farms intercalated or set between.
iii *Secondary dispersal.* In this case, due to economic and social change, an originally agglomerated settlement has been broken up and dispersed leaving a pattern of single farms.
iv *Recent primary dispersion.* This was especially associated with the more recent colonisation of less favoured terrain or the occupation of new territories.

Demangeon's attempted classification indicates that two new factors have entered into the discussion.

a) There is no longer an absolute differentiation between agglomeration and dispersion. Type ii in particular showed an acceptance of a situation of admixture, whilst remnants of nucleation could remain in Type iii. There would seem, therefore, to be no absolute distinction but a continuous scale between total nucleation and total dispersion. Once that is accepted, then by implication an attempt can be made to take measurements to place areas on that scale.

b) In order to explain secondary dispersal, and, indeed, intercalated dispersion, unspecified social and economic changes have been introduced. It is suggested that typology and spatial organisation, the two having now become part of the one argument, are the product of historical evolution. Thus, by a variety of different paths, the same observed pattern can be produced. This is the problem called *equifinality*.

These two factors must be discussed further.

ASSIGNMENTS

2. Examine Figure 2.2 which displays areas of contrasted rural settlement in Britain. There is a long-standing and conventional division of the country into a Highland Zone, north of a line connecting the mouth of the River Exe to the Wash, and a Lowland Zone to the south of it. Does that divide bear any relation to the types of rural settlement? Explain your answers.
3. Consider a rural area in the vicinity of your home by a scrutiny of a topographic map (1:50 000 or 1:25 000). How far is it possible to summarise settlement as nucleated or dispersed? How does your area relate to the generalised representation in Figure 2.2?

MEASUREMENTS OF SETTLEMENT DISPERSION

A number of measures of relative dispersion have been proposed. Two will be discussed here, one deriving from Demangeon's work in the early 1930s, the other from the quantitative revolution which transformed geography in the 1960s by the use of statistical techniques.

Demangeon, well aware that there was no absolute distinction between nucleation and dispersion, proposed the formula:

$$K = \frac{EN}{T}$$

where K is the index of dispersion
   E the population of the commune (or parish) minus its chief settlement
   N the number of settlements excluding the chief settlement
   T the total population of the commune (or parish).

Figure 2.4 demonstrates the application of the index as it was applied to the Department of the Somme in 1933. The index of dispersion (K) is given in a form where the highest values (10 to 50) represent the greatest degree of dispersion. That is where in the formula E tends to be a large proportion of T, or, put another way, the population of the chief settlement is small, and where there is a large number of settlements other than the largest, so that E and N are large and T proportionately small giving a larger value to K and reflecting a greater dispersion of the population. The resultant map shows no startling contrasts but Demangeon called attention to the highly concentrated settlement on the limon-covered chalk plateaux. Santerre, which is named on the inset, is one of the classic areas in west Europe of open-field arable agriculture and of large, compact villages. In contrast, he cited the valley floors where bands of more broken settlement, hamlets and separate farms were found. The main area of contrast to be seen on the map was, however, the extreme west where physical conditions were much more varied, especially on the once-wooded plateau of Ponthieu and particularly the Bas Champs, the low plain of marine alluvium about the Somme estuary where colonisation and occupation were much later and where the highest value, indicating the greatest dispersion, was found. It must be recorded, though, that the limon plateau of Vimeu, closely analogous physically to the central plateau areas, showed a relatively dispersed settlement pattern so that the explanation cannot be simply a physical one but must take into account the history of the area and the process of settlement.

Although Demangeon's index was widely quoted and highly regarded in the 1930s, it has never been greatly used. That was largely because it was closely related to the French

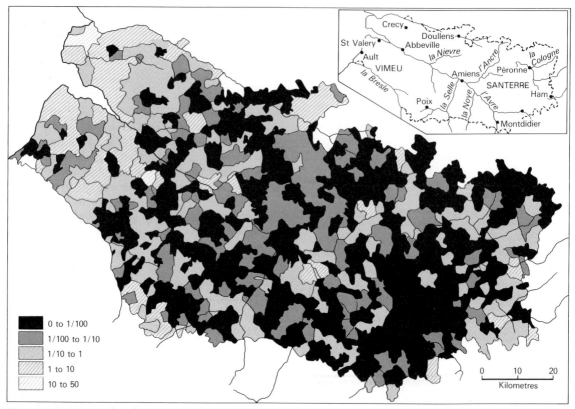

Figure 2.4 *A map of settlement in the Department of the Somme (after Demangeon)*

census. The index cannot be derived from British census data since they do not distinguish the population of the largest settlement in a parish: only the total parish population is given. An estimate can be made from field-work but the index is only of value if mapped for a considerable area and the work involved becomes prohibitive.

The quantitative revolution of the 1960s brought another statistical measure of a distributed pattern into widespread use in geography. This was the nearest neighbour statistic devised for use in plant ecology studies. It takes the form

$$Rn = 2D \sqrt{N/A}$$

where Rn is the description of the pattern

D the mean distance between nearest neighbours

A the area under study in the same units as D

and N the total number of points involved.

It is not a simple measure of dispersion. The statistic Rn can range from 0 to 2.15 where

0 means that the pattern is completely clustered or, for rural settlement purposes, aggregated

1 the members are randomly distributed or, for present purposes, scattered

2.15 the pattern is regularly distributed, introducing a further concept but one already noted.

G. J. Lewis has produced maps using this technique for areas in the Welsh borderland and Figure 2.5 reproduces one of these. The area mapped covers the valley of the river Severn in Mid-Wales from the English border to within some twelve direct miles from its source. The valley floor narrows westward, and to north and south the land rises to altitudes of about 455 metres, though these are lower east of Newtown. The highest degree of agglomeration is, as expected, associated with the towns of Welshpool, Montgomery, Newtown and, further up valley, Llanidloes. But the remaining distribution is surprising for the higher degree of agglomeration appears to be in the west and on the higher land. According to Meitzen's principles, it should be along the lower valley land where the Anglo-Norman occupation was more rapid and effective, and where farming is likely to have a greater arable element. Lewis suggests that the pattern reflects the impact of *depopulation* with the isolated, economically marginal farms having been abandoned leaving farms clustered in hamlets in the lower valley areas. Possibly secondary dispersal had reduced the degree of nucleation in the east. These are very tentative explanations but the implication is clear. Measurement is the only more accurate description and is only of value in that it precipitates the need to search for the operative processes in order to derive acceptable explanation. It is necessary, therefore, to turn to such enquiry.

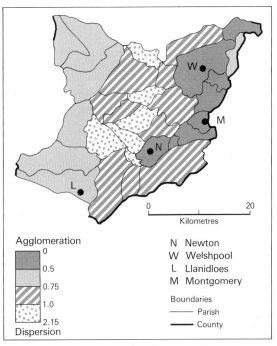

Figure 2.5 *The spacing of settlement in Eastern Montgomeryshire (after G. J. Lewis)*

ASSIGNMENT

4. Examine Figure 2.4. Isolate the largest continuous areas of nucleated and dispersed settlement. To what areas named in the small inset map do they correspond? Are there any contrasts in physical geography between the two areas?

EXPLANATIONS OF AGGLOMERATION AND DISPERSION

The most direct way of approaching the explanation or interpretation of agglomeration/dispersion is to take a specific example from a study by the late Professor Harry Thorpe. Figures 2.6a, b, c and d show the township of Osterstillinge in the south-west of the Danish island of Zealand (Sjaelland) at four dates, 1769, 1865, 1893 and 1949. At the earliest date the entire population was agglomerated in the village of Osterstillinge itself. There were some

17 farms flanking a very distinctive, rectangular green. An earlier land register of 1682 recorded 19 farms so that two seem to have disappeared in the intervening century, one of them being number 12, which does not appear on the map, and the other would have been numbered 18. On the green itself there appear the huts of those cottagers or squatters who did not have land owning rights within the community. It was noted earlier that field system and village or settlement form are closely allied. Figure 2.6a is a classic representation of the traditional and widely distributed three-field system. The three great fields are named, and the strips held by one farmstead, called Pilehave, are identified. This is the direct equivalent of the open-field nucleated villages of England and the type on which Meitzen based his Germanic relationship of the agglomerated village.

By 1805 (Figure 2.6b) quite dramatic changes had taken place. In 1786 the Danish government had introduced urgent land reforms in order to shift the country away from the restrictions of a medieval system and to one where

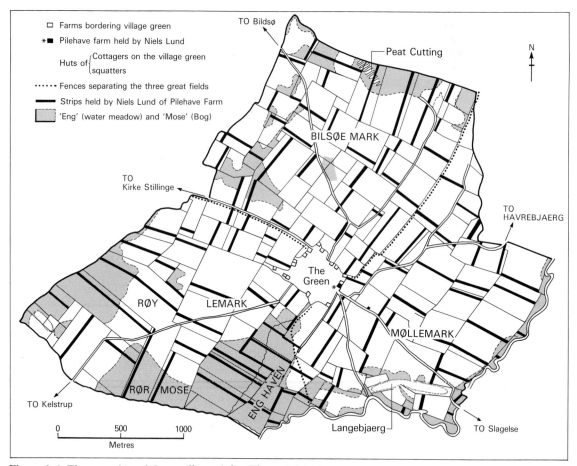

Figure 2.6 *The township of Osterstillinge (after Thorpe) (a) 1769*

freemen could secure a title to consolidated farms and work them economically and effectively. This was achieved by enclosure, by reorganising the lands held in common in the open fields into farms. Legislation was also passed to prevent both merging or amalgamation, that is the buying up of several farms to make larger holdings, and subdivision, the breaking up of farms into smaller units. The map of 1805 shows how all this was accomplished at Osterstillinge. The procedure adopted had been to divide the lands into sectors rather like the slices of a cake so that there was no need to move the farmsteads. The land now held by Pilehave farm (number 2 on the map) conformed to that system. But two other steps introduced strong tendencies to the

break up of the old village. In the first place, a number of peripheral farms had been established (numbers 11, 12, 13 and 14 on Figure 2.6b), and, secondly, the previously landless cottagers had been allocated small holdings by the break up of another peripheral plot (number 15) to the west. The only strips remaining were the shares in the watermeadow and bogland in the south. This latter procedure was in contrast to that usually adopted in England where the dispossessed rural population which had no rights in the redistribution were forced off the land and contributed to the new urban proletariat being built by the industrial revolution.

The consequences for the settlement pattern in Osterstillinge were realised by 1893 when not

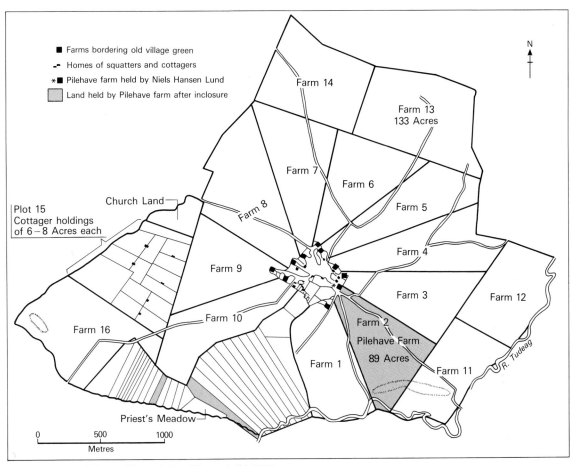

Legend:
- ■ Farms bordering old village green
- ◄ Homes of squatters and cottagers
- *■ Pilehave farm held by Niels Hansen Lund
- ▨ Land held by Pilehave farm after inclosure

Farm 14

Farm 13
133 Acres

Farm 7

Farm 6

Church Land

Farm 8

Farm 5

Plot 15
Cottager holdings
of 6-8 Acres each

Farm 4

Farm 9

Farm 3

Farm 12

Farm 10

Farm 16

Farm 2
Pilehave Farm
89 Acres

Farm 1

Farm 11

R. Tudeag

Priest's Meadow

0   500   1000
Metres

N

The township of Osterstillinge (after Thorpe) (b) 1805

only was there a peripheral ring of farms and the array of smallholders in the west, but to improve convenience and efficiency some of the large farmsteads had themselves been shifted out of the village to new locations more accessible to the land to be farmed; note Kildegaard to the east on Figure 2.6c which was Farm 4 on Figure 2.6b. This now produces a pattern of the old nucleus still identifiable but greatly modified and with a considerable scatter of single farms. Of the 50 dwellings identifiable on Figure 2.6c, some two-thirds are outside the village. This is what Demangeon would have called intercalated dispersion, or even secondary dispersal.

The 1949 map shows that the situation had not greatly changed during the first half of this century. More intensive use of the land, for these changes were accompanied by an agricultural revolution, had increased the number of holdings and the village had become, at least in part, a service centre with garage and shop, and there was also a commuting and retirement element present. The old rectangular green had been completely lost in the process. In many similar cases, of course, the whole village disappeared with enclosure as happened so often in England giving the large number of deserted or *lost villages*. But the main point to stress is not the change in form, since morphology will be dealt with later in this chapter, but the absolute meaninglessness of measurements of dispersion/agglomeration in themselves and of any significance in some

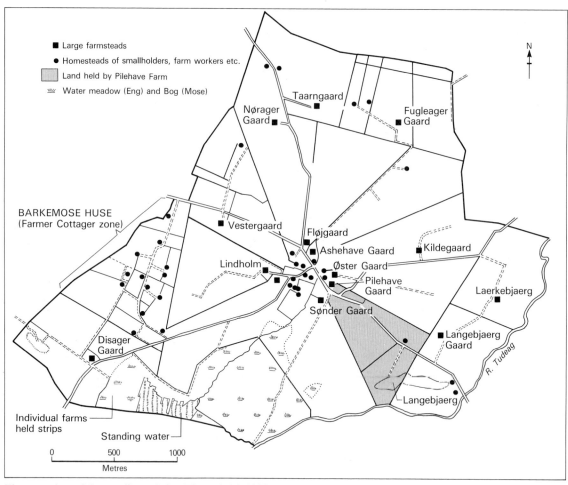

The township of Osterstillinge (after Thorpe) (c) 1893

absolute contrast between agglomerated and dispersed patterns of rural settlement. The actual patterns on the map are the products of long periods of historical evolution and, though statistical measures may be useful indicators of situations at points in time, it is only through meticulously tracing the process of development that any understanding of the patterns will be gained.

This conclusion is markedly reinforced by more recent studies of the dispersal of single farms which Meitzen identified as characteristic of Celtic areas of western Europe and Demangeon subsequently called primary dispersion of ancient origin. Even by 1939 Professor Estyn Evans was offering an alternative explanation

to this view of a primary dispersion. Early Irish settlement, he maintained, was not scattered but loosely nucleated and related to what is called the *rundale* or *run-rig* or *infield-outfield* system. This was one where there was an inner area cultivated in common, the infield, which was surrounded by a more extensive outer area used mainly as grazing land. Farms were grouped about the *infield* and it was only with the later break up of the system, somewhat as in Osterstillinge, that a dispersed pattern was produced.

Similarly, in Wales it has been demonstrated by Glanville Jones that the key concept was the estate, *Maenol* or *Maenor*, belonging to the petty king or ruler with his court (*Llys*) consti-

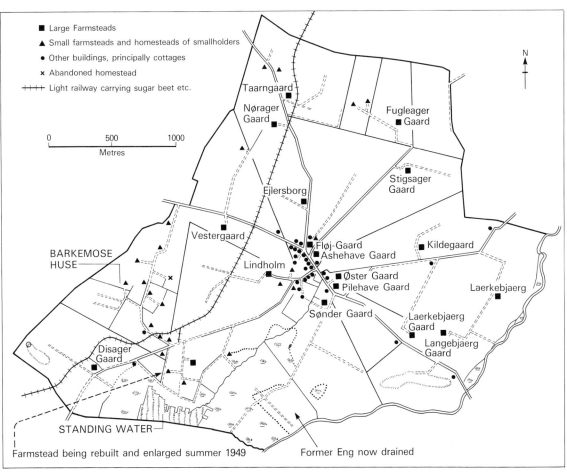

■ Large Farmsteads
▲ Small farmsteads and homesteads of smallholders
● Other buildings, principally cottages
✗ Abandoned homestead
++++ Light railway carrying sugar beet etc.

Taarngaard

Nørager
Gaard

Fugleager
Gaard

0   500   1000
Metres

Stigsager
Gaard

Ejlersborg

Vestergaard

BARKEMOSE
HUSE

Fløj-Gaard
Ashehave Gaard

Kildegaard

Lindholm

Øster Gaard
Pilehave Gaard

Laerkebjaerg

Sønder Gaard

Laerkebjaerg
Gaard

Disager
Gaard

Langebjaerg
Gaard

STANDING WATER
Farmstead being rebuilt and enlarged summer 1949

Former Eng now drained

The township of Osterstillinge (after Thorpe) (d) 1949

tuting the administrative focus and the *Llan* (a very common Welsh place name) being the religious focus. These, with a series of settlements of bond and free men, made up the township (*tref*). This produced a basic settlement pattern of small hamlets since, in areas of limited natural resources, size was inevitably constrained. It was the dissolution of that system after the Norman conquest and the much later process of *encroachment* or *squatting* on the *wasteland*, that is the marginal upland areas, which produced the dispersed pattern that is now observed. But dispersion was neither primary nor ancient.

Analyses of land holding and settlement in these Celtic areas are extremely complex. Yet the above summary clearly reinforces the earlier conclusion. The grand simplicity of Meitzen's nineteenth century schema has disappeared. So, too, has a direct relationship with the physical environment. Both culture and nature played a part but the unravelling of the causes of patterns of rural settlement is a long and difficult task.

In seeking to examine the causes of agglomeration and dispersion, one aspect of pattern, the degree of regularity in dispersal, has been obscured. As has been demonstrated, most patterns of single farms are the product of long evolutionary processes where the results are very uneven scatters of farmsteads across the landscape. But patterns of a quite regular geometry can be found. Three examples ranging widely in time and location can be cited. The first is the Roman pattern of *centuriation*, a process of land subdivision after conquest where the simplest survey procedures divided the land into regular, standard units which were assigned to individual owners. The *ager centuriatus* included, as its name suggests, a hundred arable lots. Inevitably the settle-

ments associated with working these fields reflected the regularity in their distribution. In the nineteenth century the development of the American west was also undertaken on the basis of a great national grid laid down as the basis for all land allocation west of the Ohio. This was established by the Land Ordinance of

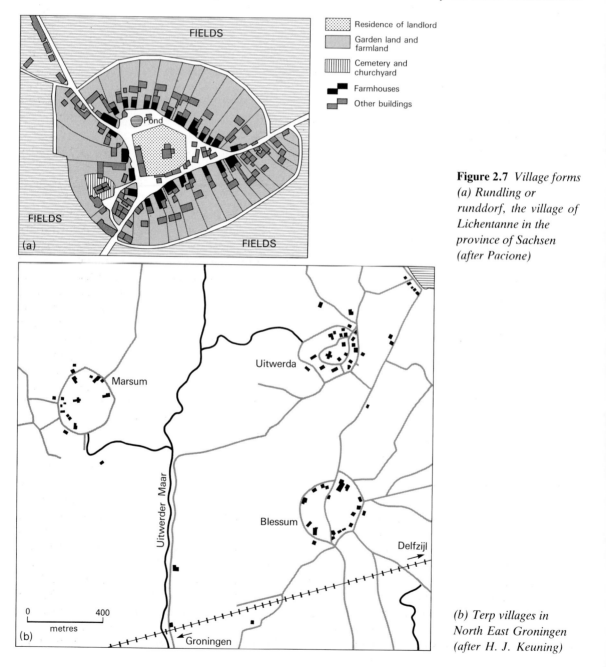

Figure 2.7 *Village forms (a) Rundling or runddorf, the village of Lichentanne in the province of Sachsen (after Pacione)*

(b) Terp villages in North East Groningen (after H. J. Keuning)

30

the Continental Congress in 1785 and became effective in 1802, when all the lands came into the hands of the Federal government. Six mile squares, or townships, were laid out as the basis for land sales and in turn engendered a regular pattern of settlement. Finally, the Dutch reclamation of the polders and the establishment of farms to work the new land has also produced regularity in distribution. There is a common element in all the examples: control, subdivision and allocation by a central authority. Maximum regularity is always associated with the formal allocation of land. Perhaps this is the major case where cultural forces completely dominate, ignoring natural conditions and laying down on the landscape an arbitrary geometry of settlement.

ASSIGNMENT

5. Consider the maps of Osterstillinge (Figure 2.6) and:
   i Can you derive a nearest neighbour statistic for each date?
   ii Given the task of establishing consolidated farms from the 1769 situation, was there any other way of proceeding?

MORPHOLOGY: SETTLEMENT FORM

The problems central to the study of rural settlement form can be introduced by considering two examples.

1. Figure 2.6 shows the village of Osterstillinge at four different times. From the map it is manifest that form changes with time. Initially it was an agglomerated village with a dominant green – hence the name widely used for the type, the *green village*. That situation also gave it a distinct rectangular form, that is a degree of regularity. But the impact of changing economic and social conditions greatly modified its morphology, so that by 1949 its shape had been altered. It had lost its green and its rectangularity. What then should be the basis of its present description and how should its morphology be characterised? Should one use its original nature or its present shape? This is made all the more difficult when later stages do not change the shape but add to it, as at Wanborough in Figure 2.1, so that a composite form is produced.

2. Figure 2.7 shows two villages. One is a good example of the type called a *rundling* or *runddorf*, the other of a type called a *terp* village. They are very similar in shape, especially on a modern map. But the rundling is associated with Slav settlement in what was eastern Germany, for the type was concentrated on the old border between Germanic and Slav cultures. The interpretation of its shape is the needs of defence. Often there was only one entrance which was easily blocked off, whilst an outer wooded fence and the farmsteads themselves made up two circular defensive lines protecting the central green or open space. The terpen were founded in the Netherlands, especially in those coastal lowlands which were liable to inundation before the great modern sea defences were constructed. They were built upon artificial circular mounds and the relaxation of the need for flood protection in modern times has left, in many cases, neat circular settlements. Two similar forms, therefore, characterise two very different areas and cultures. Perhaps it could be maintained that protection has produced similarities, but what these examples do reveal is that similar forms can have very different origins.

Much of the early study of rural settlement was carried out by German geographers; the name of Meitzen has already been introduced. The consequence is that much of the early terminology, which is still used although less frequently, was German, and a series of village types can be identified based on those studies.

The most primitive form, regionally related to the northern plains, was the *eschdorf* or *drubbel*, where a small irregular settlement was related to communal cultivation of the land. The *esche* were raised islands of cultivation, virtual infields, within the common pasture. They were hedged and their fertility maintained by manuring. Figure 2.8 is an example from a modern topographic map. These esche were cultivated from a loose, unformed cluster of farmsteads. There were two possible modes of development, the one a gradual dispersion of those without property rights reclaiming patches of heathland. Reverting for a moment to pattern, such a development produces a settlement pattern of small hamlets and single farms. The other, especially on the richer lands, was the gradual extension of the arable land, the creation of three rather than one field and the intensification of the village into a much larger but still irregular agglomeration. Form again becomes the main issue. This is certainly a possible, though no more than that, interpretation of the *haufendorf*, the large, compact irregular village traditionally associated with

the three-field system. A classic example is, of course, Osterstillinge which has already been considered in some detail. The villages at the foot of the downs in Figure 2.1 would be placed in the same category.

The other main types which occur in the German literature were the product of the clash of German and Slav in the process of the colonisation of lands in eastern Europe. The rundling, the main contribution, has already been introduced (Figure 2.7a). The two main German types were the *angerdorf* and the *strassendorf* (Figure 2.9a). They are somewhat similar in being linear or street villages, the literal translation of strassendorf, but different in detail. The strassendorf was the simpler form made up of two parallel lines of farmsteads along a road with the farm land compacted and running back from the farmsteads. The angerdorf consisted of two lines of

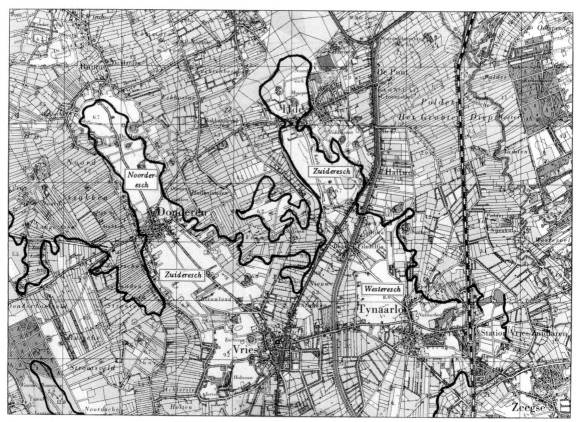

Figure 2.8 *Village form: an eschdorf*

farmsteads about an elongated central open space or green and the farm lands were cultivated in common on the three-field system.

Colonisation also took settlement into areas which had been physically difficult, the woodlands and the marshlands. This movement gave rise to the forest village, the *waldhufendorf* and the marsh or fen village, the *marschhufendorf*. Both were linear in form but, whereas the forest village was often a loose line of farmsteads following a valley floor, the marschhufendorf was much more closely controlled by elements of the drainage system and at times was a very severe line related to a dyke or embankment (Figure 2.9b). In both cases farms were compacted and extended from the central road or waterway out to the limits

of cultivation or improvement.

Finally, there is the *schachbrettdorf* or estate village. Landholders wishing to develop their estates often established settlers for very much the reasons given above in the colonisation process. To do this they established formally planned rectangular settlements. But colonisation was not the only reason. The owners of large estates sometimes found that established villages interrupted their views or inhibited the extension of their immediate parkland. The solution was to shift the whole village and set it down further away in a planned or organised form. A well known example is Harewood which was designed by John Carr of York and built in 1760 and laid out as part of the approach to the Great Gateway of the park to

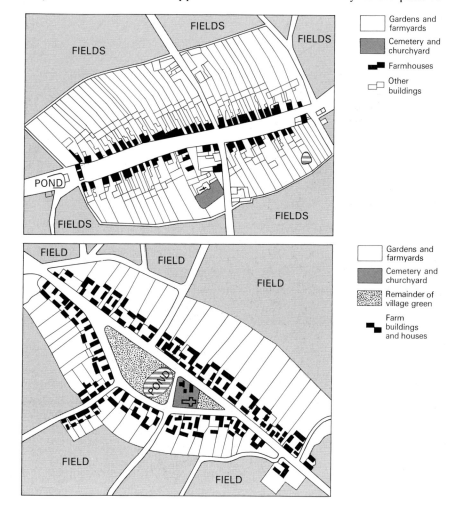

Figure 2.9 *Village forms: (a) (top) Strassendorf: Eicha in the East German province of Sachsen (after Pacione) (b) (bottom) Angerdorf*

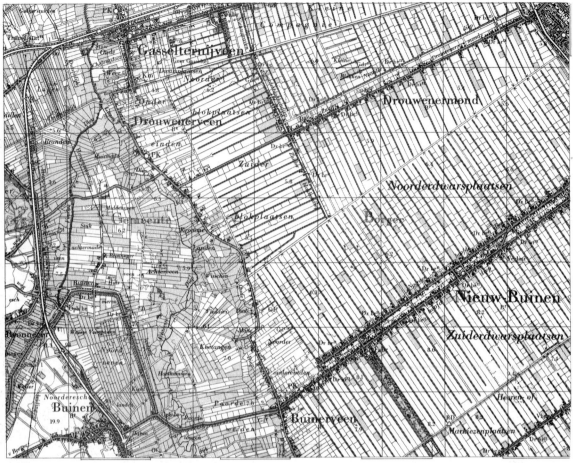

Village forms: (b) Marschufendorf

Harewood House. The estate village thus becomes a type widely recognised across Europe.

The names which have been introduced are still used – perhaps strassendorf has become the most ubiquitous for any linear village – but as elements in a universal classificatory system they have largely been abandoned.

MORPHOLOGY: DEFINING VILLAGE FORM

The main contributor to the contemporary analysis of village form in Britain has been Dr B. K. Roberts, especially in his books *Rural Settlement: An Historical Perspective* (1982) and *The Making of the English Village* (1987).

Roberts begins by adopting a *threshold of dispersion*, that is the maximum distance between two buildings which still permits them to be considered part of the nucleation. The figure used is 150 metres. This sort of distance measure is one which frequently appears as a basis for distinguishing separate farmsteads, that is those which form part of a dispersed pattern, from those which make up part of a nucleation. It is inevitably an arbitrary measure and thus not entirely satisfactory. Remember in the last chapter that similar problems arose in deciding which houses belong to an urban settlement. Thus France defines as urban that population living in communes containing an agglomeration of more than 2000 inhabitants living in contiguous houses or with not more than 200 metres between houses. That seeks to

Figure 2.10 *The village of Coombe Martin in Devon. This is a street village form brought about by the physical characteristics of the site. The settlement has spread along the incised valley or Coombe. Note the tendency for the individual plots of land to run back from the main thoroughfare, a feature which is well nigh universal in such conditions*

meet the same purpose of defining a nucleation by including only these constituent buildings which are within a defined distance from each other. It marks a measured break point between nucleation and dispersal.

After settling this definitional problem, Roberts bases his classification (Figure 2.11) on three characteristics of village form: shape, regularity and the presence/absence of a green.

Composite forms can also occur.

1. There are two basic shapes in which the farmsteads or houses can be arranged; they can either be set out in rows giving a linear pattern or they can be arranged in any other manner which produces an agglomerated form. The use of the word agglomerated is perhaps a little unfortunate since it is also used as the counter of dispersed.

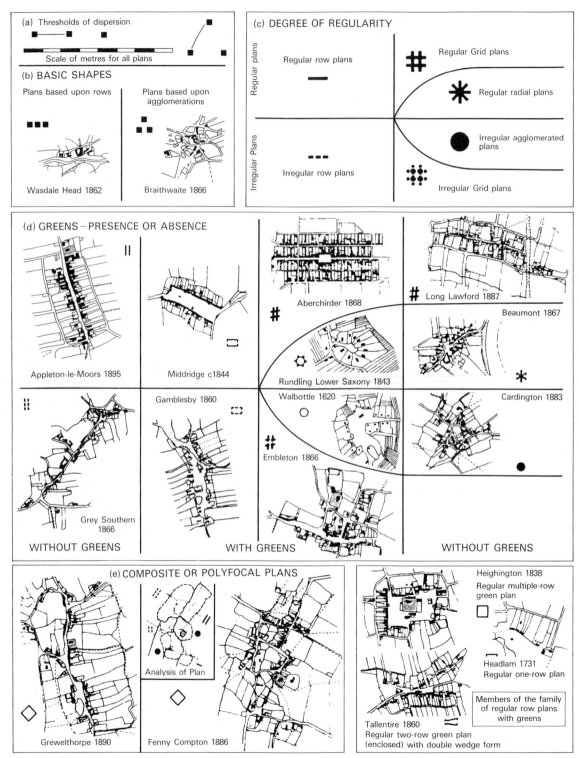

Figure 2.11 *Village form: principles of classification by B. K. Roberts*

2. The degree of regularity divides row plans simply into regular or irregular linear forms (Figure 2.11c) illustrated by Appleton-le-Moors and Grey Southern respectively in Figure 2.11d. The agglomerated plans are somewhat more complex and are divided into grid and radial plans in the first instance, each then being subdivided into regular and irregular. But an irregular, radial plan does not make much sense and it is replaced by a more generalised category of irregular, agglomerated plans (Figure 2.11c).

3. Finally, the presence or absence of a green is added to the above groupings. Thus, Walbottle (Figure 2.11d) is classified as an irregular agglomerated plan with an integral green.

4. It is accepted that more than one of the above characteristics can collect over time so that composite or polyfocal plans occur (Figure 2.11e), as well as a multiple row type where more than two rows of buildings are present.

Roberts makes no mention of the older terminology in his classificatory scheme, but there are obvious linkages which can be set out.

Haufendorf	Irregular, agglomerated, without green
Rundling	Regular, agglomerated, radial plan, with integral green
Strassendorf	Regular, row plan, without green
Angerdorf	Irregular, row plan, with green
Waldhufendorf	Irregular, row plan, without green
Marschhufendorf	Either regular or irregular, row plan, without green
Schachbrettdorf	Regular row or grid plan, with or without green

In all these cases there can be no sharp boundaries between the various categories. The division between what is regular and irregular is very much a subjective one, and it is not always easy to determine whether the widening of a road or verge constitutes a green or not. All classificatory systems, however derived, do no more than draw lines across chaos and are but the first step in the systemisation of knowledge, not a very sophisticated but an essential one. The older German terminology still has some advantage in that there is an implied relationship to a cultural, social and economic context absent in the system set out in Figure 2.11 which relies more completely and exclusively on geometrical notions of shape and regularity.

In Figure 2.11 each of the types identified is accompanied by a symbol so that a map of rural settlement forms can be prepared. An example is given in Figure 2.12 which should be compared with Figure 2.2. In Figure 2.12 not only have the various types been mapped but the size of the symbol is related to the physical size of the settlement. Note also the representation of deserted villages. The purpose of such a map is, of course, to generate questions rather than to resolve issues. There is a clear contrast in Figure 2.12 between the north and west of Warwickshire and the south and east, both in the form and density of village settlement, which establishes a problem and invites a solution. Brian Roberts suggests that it reflects an ancient division between two types of country. In the south and east the land was well developed and became dominated by nucleated villages operating a three-field system. But to the north and west was the Forest of Arden which at the end of the eleventh century was still a considerable woodland together with heathland. Later colonisation gave a much more dispersed pattern and hence the emergence of the division.

ASSIGNMENT

---

6. Can you apply the classificatory system outlined by Roberts to the rural settlements in your home area? Can you make any progress towards preparing a map to show the distribution of the types you have identified (see Figure 2.12)?

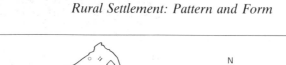

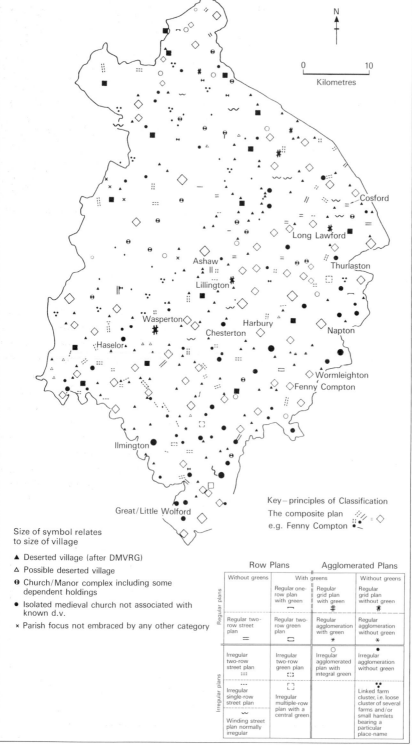

Size of symbol relates
to size of village

▲ Deserted village (after DMVRG)

△ Possible deserted village

ϴ Church/Manor complex including some
dependent holdings

● Isolated medieval church not associated with
known d.v.

× Parish focus not embraced by any other category

Key – principles of Classification
The composite plan
e.g. Fenny Compton

	Row Plans		Agglomerated Plans
Regular plans — Without greens	With greens		Without greens
	Regular one-row plan with green	Regular grid plan with green	Regular grid plan without green
Regular two-row street plan	Regular two-row green plan	Regular agglomeration with green	Regular agglomeration without green
Irregular plans — Irregular two-row street plan	Irregular two-row green plan	Irregular agglomerated plan with integral green	Irregular agglomeration without green
Irregular single-row street plan	Irregular multiple-row plan with a central green		Linked farm cluster, i.e. loose cluster of several farms and/or small hamlets bearing a particular place-name
Winding street plan normally irregular			

Figure 2.12
Warwickshire: the morphology of rural clusters (after B. K. Roberts)

MORPHOLOGY: THE FARM

There is one further aspect of morphology which is rightfully part of settlement study and that is the form of the individual farm. Comparatively little work has been undertaken by geographers on this topic and it is noted here as a proper field of study rather than developed as a theme. The most accessible work is *House Form and Culture* by Amos Rapoport which was published in 1969. The most widely recognised contrast in house form is between the elongated or *long house* and other forms. In the long house all the functions to be performed are set alongside each other. Thus living space for the family and that for the animals is interconnected as is storage space or barns, so that there is one long structure. In other forms these various functions are separated and housed in different buildings usually around a courtyard (Figure 2.13). The arrangement of buildings itself varies as in the French and Italian examples in Figure 2.13. But the usual variation depends on the extent to which the yard is fully enclosed, with an L-shape and a U-shape being stages toward that complete surrounding of the central open space. Most modern farms have grown over a considerable period of time and hence do consist of somewhat unplanned assemblages of the necessary buildings such as cowsheds and barns (Figure 2.14).

In the book referred to above, Rapoport uses the title *House Form and Culture* in order to

Figure 2.14 *This is an example of the form discernible in the farm itself. Note the large and impressive farmhouse and the way in which the farm buildings have grown to form an enclosed square yard. Within the yard further buildings have been located.*

stress that the form of the house can be seen not only as a response to environmental influences, such as climate, and to the economic conditions for most effective exploitation, but also to cultural traits. This can be illustrated by considering a well known and widely occurring form, the inward facing, courtyard dominated house which has characterised the Mediterranean countries, the Near East and the southern states of the USA. Four examples from very different sources in both time and space are illustrated in Figure 2.15. But three different explanations for this form can be offered. The

Figure 2.13

Diagrammatic plans of typical French and Italian farms with yards (after Rapoport)

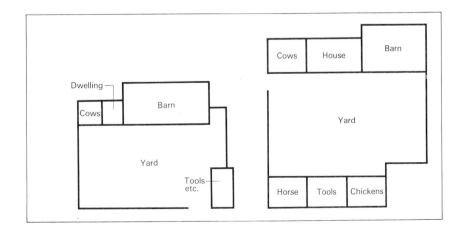

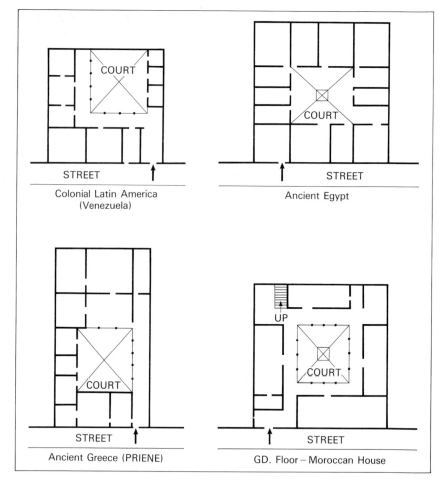

Figure 2.15 *Four courtyard houses (after Rapoport)*

first is an environmental one. In these hot climates, especially before modern air-conditioning, the central courtyard offered a maximum of outdoor living but with adequate shade. The modern westerner copies the style in part when he sets up his barbecue on the patio; note the origins of the words used. The second explanation is primarily a cultural one. These sorts of houses occur where society is strictly hierarchical and where women are secluded, that is they are not allowed to appear in public. The only effective way life can be carried on under such constraints is by the house presenting a big blank wall to the street, usually with few windows and small doors, and by providing an open central space for access to the open air and for general living. There is, however, a third possible interpretation for

associated with these societies was the institution of slavery. That necessitated means of confinement and control which could be most effectively organised where access to the outside world was minimised.

In the above example a whole range of influences needs to be called upon. The explanation of the long house, which is characteristic of western Britain, also has different interpretations. It, too, can be ascribed to climatic influences and the need for immediate access to animals and equipment in the wild wet nights of the west without leaving the protection of the farm buildings. Peate, however, in his book *The Welsh House*, which carried the sub-title *A Study in Folk Culture*, derived it from the organisation of Iron Age communities.

Thus a whole range of influences needs to be

called upon in the explanation of the form, and also the distribution of, farm houses.

CONCLUSION

A conclusion by its nature should not open up new fields for discussion but it is evident that this chapter has concentrated exclusively on rural settlement in the developed west. No attempt has been made to include the vast array of different settlement forms which are found in the continents of Africa and Asia. This is a response partly to the proper procedure of starting from the known, and partly to the problem of attempting to consider an immense range within a brief chapter. But as one looks outward to this wider horizon then at least the same array of controls come to the fore. Way of life, in its broadest sense, perhaps comes first: for the settlements of settled arable cultivators, pastoral nomads or hunters and fishers will necessarily be differently organised. Closely associated is social structure, for the way the group is structured will make an impact on the way it is spatially organised. It is often the convention to demonstrate this by contrasting a polygamous society where each wife will have a hut visited in turn by the male household head, and a monogamous society where one-family structures will normally be characteristic. But within England, the relation of manor house to church and to village (recall the example of Harewood) is nothing more than the spatial expression of social structure. Finally, what can best be called general environmental influences play their part as in the courtyard house. It is difficult to disentangle habitat, economy and society.

It is perhaps unfortunate to leave this chapter without clear and unequivocal conclusions but it is in the nature of the topic that they are unlikely. At least it can be said that the study of rural settlement pattern and form introduces that intricate relationship between cultural inheritance, economic system, social structure and physical environment which is at the heart of geography.

Rural Settlement: Function and Community

INTRODUCTION – FUNCTION AND COMMUNITY

In the last chapter the major physical elements of rural settlement were examined. This chapter looks at the way in which those physical elements actually work or function; it attempts to give some dynamic life to the static forms. There are two aspects of that dynamic which can be identified. The first is the general role which the settlement performs, and the second the relationships which arise between the inhabitants or the way in which a settlement constitutes that nebulous notion, a community. Like so many other characteristics of rural settlement, these are not two separate and discrete concepts but are closely interlinked. In addition, there are two related but identifiable sides to the function of a rural settlement. The first relates to its role in the way in which the land is farmed, the second to its role as a provider of services. The way in which all these interact can be shown in the first instance by referring to the dispersed pattern of settlement, for function and community are often and mistakenly considered to be significant in relation to agglomerated forms only.

Professor T. Jones Hughes carried out a well known study of the social geography of the area about Aberdaron near the western tip of the Llŷn peninsula in North Wales and he recorded that one of the primary characteristics of the settlement pattern in Llŷn is its discontinuity; in other words, it is a classic area of single farmsteads. But although isolated, these farms form a community by the close cooperation which occurs between them, especially over the working of the land. Professor Hughes demonstrates how for certain activities, where

additional labour is needed, cooperation is essential and well developed. It is illustrated in Figure 3.1. No money payments are involved; it is essentially a system based on reciprocity. It is a complex and informal system involving physical help especially at harvest time but it can also include the common purchase of equipment. A parallel study, carried out at the same time and published in the same book, was 'Chapel and Community in Glan-Llŷn, Merioneth' by Trefor M. Owen (Davies, E. and

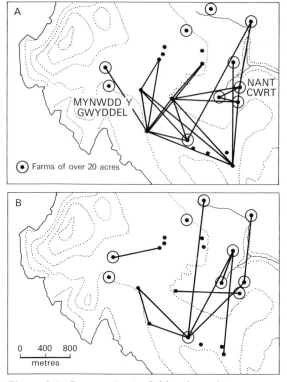

Figure 3.1 *Cooperation in field task work in an area near Aberdaron, North Wales (after T. Jones Hughes) A Sheep shearing and root crops; B Hay and corn harvest*

Rees, A. D. (eds.), *Welsh Rural Communities*, 1960). In his historical appraisal of the study area, that about Bala Lake, Owen notes the former significance of the domestic stocking knitting industry in the late eighteenth and early nineteenth century and goes on to reveal that during that time the *noson weu* or knitting night when neighbours assembled on one another's hearths was an important institution. But that was not the only type of meeting held in the farmhouses. There was also the *noswaith ganu* or singing night, usually held in the barn. And, of course, religious meetings were also held initially at farmhouses before chapels were built.

There are some significant conclusions to be drawn from this brief glimpse of Welsh rural communities. The first is that the working of the land, the prime function of the farm, is closely bound up with reciprocal relationships and hence with the neighbourhood or community. And although the content is historical, it is not only farming that is part of the system. Gatherings for entertainment take place at the individual farms, meetings in barns for singing and story-telling, a format which was significant enough to be now used by Welsh television to present programmes of light entertainment. In this case, the single farm is functioning – and note the word – as the equivalent of a village hall or an urban theatre. But the gathering is also an expression of the strong bonds of neighbourhood and community. So, two critical points can be noted. The first is that the expression *isolated farms* is one relating to physical distance only. An area of dispersed settlement can be characterised by quite intensive community bonds which are discernible by

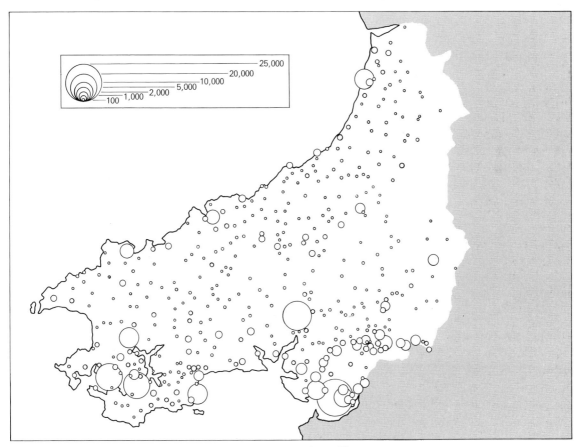

Figure 3.2 *The settlement pattern of Dyfed (Dyfed County Council)*

43

inquiry into the way of living of the people but which remain invisible on the conventional map. The second is that function is significant to the single farm though it is often ignored, and that function and community are closely bound together.

THE VILLAGE AS SERVICE CENTRE

With these notions in mind, it is appropriate to move to consider the function of the village as a provider of services. It is conventional to relate such a study to central place theory which is concerned with looking at the way bundles of functions become associated in service centres. However, central place theory is mainly associated with urban centres and will be dealt with in the next chapter (Chapter 4).

At this point all one needs to do is note the two basic controls of threshold and range. Threshold is the minimum population needed to sustain a service economically, and range is the maximum distance over which it can be provided. Now these will mean that nucleated rural service centres will themselves vary in what they provide. The smallest hamlet may well have only one general store, perhaps combined with a post office, and maybe a public house as well. At the other end of the scale, the line between a large village and a small town is not easy to define and the largest villages, therefore, merge imperceptibly into the lowest levels of the urban hierarchy. Remaining with Welsh examples, the Settlement Pattern chapter in the *Interim Survey Statement* of the Dyfed county structure plan can be used in illustration.

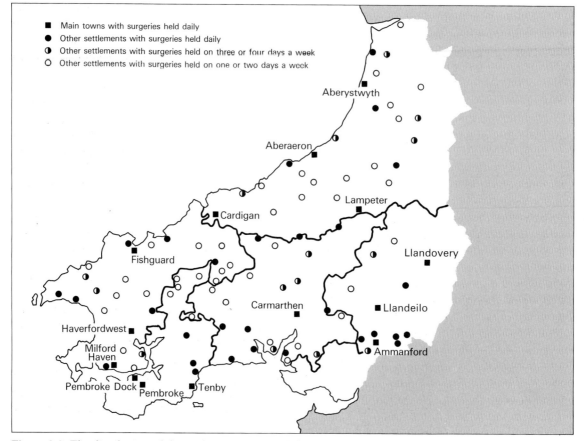

Figure 3.3 *The distribution of doctors' surgeries in Dyfed (Dyfed County Council)*

The plan identifies 421 settlements in Dyfed which are shown in Figure 3.2. Also the distribution of one service, the doctors' surgeries, is shown (Figure 3.3). The settlements are tabulated by size in Table 3.1. Of these, the 407 smaller settlements are selected for detailed review. No specific population break is given although it approximates to an urban-rural division at about 2500. Again, of the 407 selected, 284 or 70 per cent have what is called an estimated population of below 250. It is necessary to estimate as indicated earlier that it is not possible to derive settlement populations from the published census. An analysis of the services and the facilities which are present in these small settlements is then carried out. The material presented in written form can be summarised as a table (Table 3.2). In addition to those shown in the table, two other criteria are used. The first is the relative availability of a commuter service which is broken into two contrasting sets: those villages with a regular, daily commuter service by rail or road to adjacent towns; those where the services fall short of that, being daily but unrelated to standard journey to work times, weekly on market days and school and summer services only. The second criterion is the presence of a secondary school, but it is noted that, because of the long distances which would have to be travelled, that is the problem of range, secondary schools are located in abnormally small settlements, two with populations below 700. The classification in the Structure Plan is a little self indulgent, especially with two groups having only one settlement in them. They can be collapsed into a more economic system with four groups as indicated in the last column in Table 3.2. It is not always easy to generalise from these specific cases. Thus, in Group 6, the distinguishing doctor's surgery is of marginal significance for, of the 12 villages in the category, only one has a population of over 250. These are no more than arbitrarily selected points where on one day a week a surgery can be held reasonably accessible to a widely dispersed population.

The range of functions used in the scheme,

Table 3.1 *Dyfed settlements by population size 1971*

Population size	Number
Less than 100	196
100– 250	88
250– 500	56
500– 1 000	36
1 000– 1 500	13
1 500– 2 000	7
2 000– 3 000	13
3 000– 5 000	3
5 000–10 000	4
10 000–20 000	4
over 20 000	1

Source: Dyfed County Structure Plan. *Interim Survey Statement.*

although selective and limited, nevertheless covers the main types. These can be set out as:

1. Commercial. The prime example is the shop. In the above scheme the post office and the banks are used. The post office, with its role as a distributor of benefits under social security, could be regarded as a public social function but more and more the emphasis is on commercial viability.

2. Social: public. Doctors' surgeries are part of the health system and can be considered as public social functions, as can the schools.

3. Social: private. These are such things as the presence of a branch of the Women's Institute or the Young Farmers' Club. The physical expression is the Village Hall where most social activities are located.

4. Public utilities. These are not always included but the presence of water supply (now well nigh universal) and sewage system (which is not) are examples.

5. Administration. Most administrative functions have moved to the larger settlements.

6. Agricultural services. The provision of the sorts of materials, fertilisers and pesticides, for example, needed by the farmer.

The most important omission from the criteria used by Dyfed is that of the provision of specialised agricultural services which are often a significant element in the functional role of the village.

Table 3.2 *Settlement groups in Dyfed*

Group	Services/facilities present	No. of settlements	Suggested regrouping
1	All of four basic services i.e. post office, primary school, mains sewage disposal, public transport, *plus* secondary school, bank, doctor's surgery, commuter service.	9	Combine 1 and 2 since the secondary school is a special feature. See text.
2	All of the four basic services *plus* bank, surgery, commuter service.	28	
3	All of the four basic services *plus* surgery, commuter service.	25	Combine 3, 4 and 5, villages with two additional services. And Groups 4 and 5 have only one representative.
4	All of the four basic services *plus* bank, commuter service.	1	
5	All of the four basic services *plus* bank, surgery.	1	
6	All of the four basic services *plus* surgery.	12	Combine 6, 7 and 8. The surgery has a special role (see text) and being on a commuter service affects character rather than function.
7	All of the four basic services *plus* commuter service.	57	
8	Four basic services only.	18	
9	Fewer than the four basic services.	256	Retain as a separate group.

It would be possible to compare this Dyfed scheme of classification with others but there would be little purpose and it might be quite misleading. It is mistaken to believe that some universal categories will emerge common to the whole of Britain. Each region, dependent upon the nature of its territory, the character of its agriculture and the historical growth of its settlement pattern, will offer not something very greatly different but what might be called variations on the basic theme. That theme is illustrated by the Dyfed example and is the basic function of the village and hamlet, the provision of the lowest and most ubiquitous services immediately demanded by the rural population.

ASSIGNMENT

1. Make a survey of the rural settlements within a convenient area. It will have to be limited in size in relation to the time available. Attempt to identify all the functions or services which are present. Would you make a selection to draw up an acceptable system of classification and, if so, what would they be? Derive a classification for the area.

THE VIABILITY OF RURAL SERVICES

It is in this situation that the major contemporary problem concerning the function of rural settlement has arisen. It is not only of interest to the academic student and the practical planner, but also raises strong feelings in rural areas. This problem, or it could well be called a crisis, has arisen from a squeeze on the lowest orders or sizes of settlements. It is derived from two sources. The first of these is rural depopulation, which is widely known as a predominant trend during this century. It is also true that rural repopulation or counter-urbanisation has recently been a major feature but, even so, losses especially in more remote areas have continued. As a measure, the population of Cardiganshire, now the District of Ceredigion in Dyfed, was 73 441 in 1871 but 54 882 in 1971. It had increased to 57 459 in 1981. These population losses mean that there are fewer people to support the standard services such as those used in the ranking procedures in Table 3.2: post office, school, doctor's surgery, and public transport. In more formal terms, the numbers have fallen below the minimum threshold required. The last term, of course, epitomises the controversy. A minimum demand or threshold can be interpreted either in commercial or in social terms. Thus, for example, the post office can be judged as to whether it makes a viable living for the person who runs it, or whether it is a necessity for the people of the area and, therefore, should be subsidised. The case for subsidy rests on its function as a social service, particularly in the provision of the basic benefits of the welfare state. Closure of a post office means that the elderly, who often are disadvantaged financially and disabled physically, will be faced with a longer, more expensive, and less convenient journey. And that will be at a time when another service, public transport, also faces cut-backs as the same dilemma arises; is it a purely commercial undertaking or partly a social service?

The second squeeze on the smallest settlements comes from the growing move towards larger and more economic outlets for both goods and services. The supermarket, even on a modest scale, can sell goods more cheaply than the village shop since the quantity sold enables profit margins on individual items to be reduced. It is certainly cheaper for the post office to have one larger branch providing all the services for an extended area than to have to maintain a multiplicity of tiny sub-offices providing partial services. Thus as populations fall and with them demand, so the contemporary view as to the economies of scale, and government demands that services be commercially

viable, all come together to undermine the very existence of the smallest centres.

Before proceeding to examine the consequences for the rural settlement pattern in general, it is appropriate to provide a specific example of the process just outlined and it is proper that it should come from the same area that has been used in illustration of ranking of settlements, the county of Dyfed. Figure 3.4 covers an area to the north of the town of Lampeter. It is derived from a Welsh Education Office publication called *Ysgol y Dderi: an Area School in Dyfed*. Prior to the mid-1970s there were five separate, small primary schools serving the area and the homes of the pupils attending their catchment areas in 1974 are shown. These have been replaced by one school serving the whole area, called Ysgol y Dderi and located just south of the largest village in the area, Llangybi. The study describes each of the five schools which were closed in the reorganisation. An extract from one, Cellan County Primary opened in 1900, is sufficient to set out the problem.

'Depopulation has reduced the size of the community. There are fewer, though larger, farms, and several vacated farm-houses have been taken over as holiday houses. There has been no housing development in the village and the occupants of the existing six houses are settled; their children, like most of the young people, have left the district. The number of children eligible for admission has, therefore, fallen steadily. In the period 1930–40 there were over 50 children enrolled in an all-age school; there are now only 15 children of primary school age on roll.'

The new school was designed for 100 pupils aged 5 to 11 and for 20 under the age of 5. This in turn meant a teaching staff of six with additional part-time and peripatetic help. This provides the opportunity for greater specialisation amongst the teachers, as well as in the equipping of the school. But further, it was apparent that community facilities were barely present in the area so that the school was built to include a hall, meeting room, snack counter,

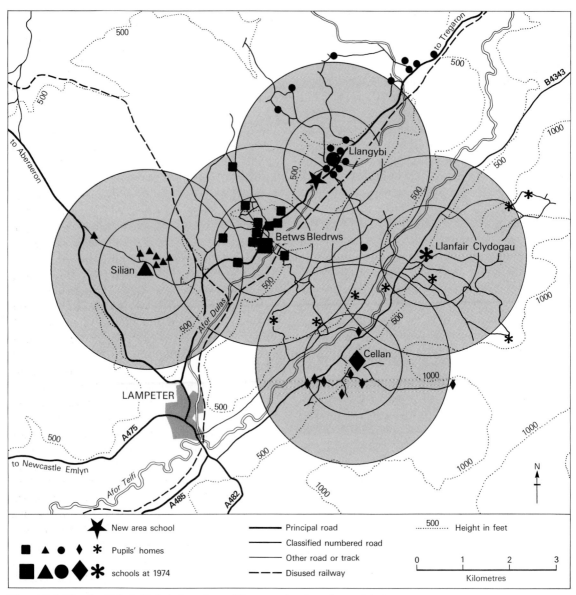

Figure 3.4 *Ysgol y Dderi, Dyfed. Location of former schools and people's homes*

light crafts area and a reading and display area. All these were to be funded from local sources. Again the boundary between a function for an area and the preservation of community support is overlapped.

The study by the Welsh Education Office is directed towards stressing the advantages of the area approach. A newer, more specialised facility with a wider range of services was obviously greatly desirable. There were losses, however, in the greater distance which very young children had to travel daily and also the loss of a very local meeting place. In many areas proposals to close such small schools have been met with the strongest opposition for those reasons.

RURAL SETTLEMENT PATTERNS AND PLANNING

The specific case of school reorganisation in part of Dyfed can be generalised by reference to a diagram constructed by Gilg to demonstrate a theoretical rationalisation of the settlement pattern (Figure 3.5). The map on the left shows an existing pattern with the services scattered over the area with little spatial logic and, presumably, the consequences of an extended period of development. The map on the right sets out a possible pattern after rationalisation, that is the introduction of what can be called spatial logic. Services have been shifted to the largest, and enlarged, settlement. As a corollary, they have been closed in the smallest. Note how the closure of four primary schools bears a close resemblance to the actual process traced in Dyfed. The increase of public services is also matched by commercial reorientation. The number of shops is decreased from 13 to 12, and 8 of them are allocated to the largest settlement. Paul Cloke, in reviewing policies which carry out the procedures which have been illustrated, relates them to four theoretical bases. The first is that of a hierarchical settlement pattern which will be reviewed in the next chapter. The second is *service thresholds* which is, in effect, no different from the first except in so far as it applies to single functions, such as primary schools, rather than to the whole array of functions found in villages. The third is economies of scale and the fourth the notion of *growth centres*. The discussion to date has taken in the first three. The final one, the growth centre, is based on the application of the others in the belief, epitomised in Figure 3.5, that the creation of one larger centre will be a stimulus to development; it will attract other functions, thus setting it off on an upward spiral of growth which will, in turn, be to the benefit of the surrounding countryside. All these theoretical principles and practical procedures lead to the concept of the *key village*, that is of the selection of certain settlements and the concentration of growth in them, sometimes exclusively within them.

Policies directed towards the differential promotion of growth are certainly not new. One of the most controversial schemes was that introduced by County Durham in its 1951 Development Plan which resulted in such descriptions as Durham's murdered villages. It must be emphasised that the context was a little different from the rural situation being discussed here in that the majority of the villages were not traditional rural settlements but small agglomerations which had grown up about nineteenth century coal mines; they were mining villages. But the principle is the same. The Development Plan established four categories of village. Category A was made up of those where population growth was expected and where investment should be concentrated.

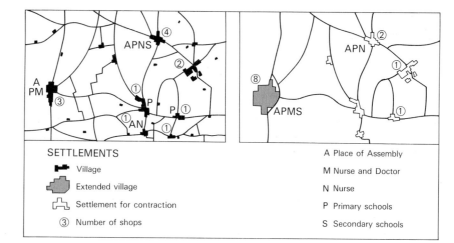

Figure 3.5 *A theoretical rationalisation of the settlement pattern (after Gilg)*

SETTLEMENTS

- Village
- Extended village
- Settlement for contraction
- ③ Number of shops

A Place of Assembly
M Nurse and Doctor
N Nurse
P Primary schools
S Secondary schools

They numbered 70. There were 143 in Category B where the populations were likely to remain stable and sufficient investment to maintain that stability should be guaranteed. Category C villages, of which there were 30, were envisaged as losing population, and investment was to be adjusted to lower levels. Finally there were the 114 Category D settlements where a considerable loss of population was expected. The plan advocated no further investment of capital and that 'when the existing houses become uninhabitable they should be replaced elsewhere'. In a way such a policy was more drastic than concentrating services, for the acceptance of housing decline and replacement elsewhere meant the total writing off of these settlements. As might be expected, the outcry was considerable. Prophecies can be self fulfilling and the identification of villages in the category D would lead to a fall in what demand for housing there was and an even more rapid cycle of decline. The classification was later modified by amendment in 1964 although the basic outline remained.

Paul Cloke and David Shaw have carried out a survey of rural settlement policies adopted in county structure plans (*Town Planning Review* 54(3), 1983, 338–354). They identified three broad policy types and within them six sorts of strategy.

1. Place specific policy. As its name indicates, such a policy involves the identification of specific places where growth, in the form of employment, housing and services, should be concentrated. In that general sense all the strategies under this heading are key settlement strategies, but there are differences of degree between them.

a) Market town strategy. This is most certainly a key settlement approach, but one which limits growth to the larger, urban settlements only.

b) Key village strategy. This is a standard key village promotion with a presumption against development other than in named villages.

c) A tiered (but not key) settlement strategy. Rather than naming key settlements, a

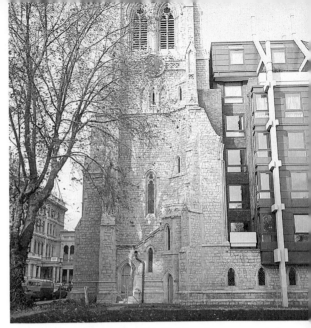

Figure 3.6 *A closed church which has been converted into flats in London. This demonstrates the adaptation of former religious buildings for modern day purposes*

tiered (or hierarchical) array of named settlements is identified, to receive varying degrees of growth and development.

2. Restraining policy. Such a policy is based on restricting and constraining development.

d) Severe restraint strategy. This is a complete blanket strategy of restriction on any growth.

e) Hierarchical restraint strategy. A limited amount of growth is sanctioned, but within a selected array of settlements and against a general background of constraint.

3. Area approach policy. This moves away both from any limitation on development and from its limitation to selected places so that

f) Area based strategy favours dispersal of development according to the opportunities that arise.

Figure 3.7 is the map produced by Cloke and Shaw in 1983 showing the various strategies adopted by the counties of England and Wales. Concentration in market towns was operative in only two counties, Cornwall and Hereford and Worcester. Thus in Herefordshire resources and growth would be concentrated at Bromyard and Kington which would provide services for extensive rural areas. Some sixteen counties

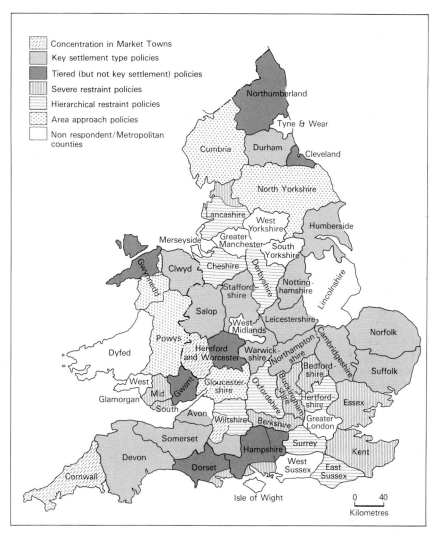

Figure 3.7 *Six rural settlement policy categories in county structure plans in England and Wales (after Cloke and Shaw)*

have adopted a key settlement strategy (although only four actually used the description). Amongst them are Norfolk, Suffolk and Cambridgeshire in the east, Devon, Somerset and Avon in the west and Durham and Humberside in the north. Fewer counties illustrate the tiering principle, amongst them Dorset, Hampshire, Cleveland, Northumberland and Gwent. To some extent this has been due to governmental modification of the county structure plans where settlements were named but were deleted by the Secretary of State. Severe restraint strategies, as might be expected, characterise the areas about London, whilst hierarchical restraint is also characteristic

of counties with problems of pressure on village settlements from urban centres, such as Oxfordshire and Cheshire. Finally, area strategy generally is found in the less densely populated areas of the north and west such as Powys in Mid Wales, and Cumbria and North Yorkshire.

It is difficult to propose any significant patterning of these types, other than that constraint is associated with areas of metropolitan fringes and area policies with the less developed, thinly peopled periphery. But there are many exceptions to that general interpretation for policy and strategy depend, too, on the views of local planners and politicians.

ASSIGNMENTS
---

2. Survey local newspapers for cases of the closure or diminution of services in rural areas – post offices, small hospitals, schools and bus services are the most likely, but do not forget the reorganisation of churches and chapels which is related to the same principles. Review local reaction.
3. Try to consult a copy of the Structure Plan for your county; there should be one in the county library. What is the rural settlement policy proposed and the argument developed in support of it? Do you agree?

THE FUNCTIONS OF RURAL SETTLEMENTS – A SUMMARY

The attempt made so far to restrict consideration to agricultural villages, if that description means anything, is untenable. Already the brief reference to County Durham has meant that mining villages have been introduced. The reference to restraining policies at the margins of the larger cities brings the metropolitan village into consideration. This is the name given to those one-time primarily agricultural villages on the fringes of cities which have become invaded by commuting populations. Those populations are highly selected in that they are the more wealthy section and usually those in mid-career. Their location in the villages sets up new demands: supermarkets, restaurants, antique shops, garden centres, for example. The result is the transformation of the settlement into a highly specialised aspect of the intra-urban hierarchy (see Chapter 4).

Into the same category of specialisation must come holiday villages and those settlements predominantly made up of holiday or second homes. It is worth noting that, at least for a brief period during the summer, holiday villages have a population well in excess of many agricultural villages and they generate the particular array of functional equipment to meet the demands of the holiday-makers.

Holiday villages are, therefore, of a specific functional character. More controversial are second or holiday homes, for external purchase and limited use depletes resident population and lowers the demand for all-the-year-round services. Thus, the demand generated for primary school places would effectively be zero. In turn, the functional status of the village is diminished and its role in relation to the permanent inhabitants undermined. It is, however, not always easy to determine whether decline has led to the buying of houses as second homes or whether the growth of second homes has led to decline.

At this point, a brief summary of the material introduced in relation to the functions of rural settlements is apposite. Three related roles can be ascribed to villages:

1. They are the agglomerated residences of farmers and farm workers. Although the farm is the unit from which the land is worked, the village too has a role in this respect.
2. They are service centres providing an array of those services in most immediate demand, that is with the lowest threshold populations and the smallest ranges. Characteristic are general shop, post office, primary school.
3. They also have specialised roles such as holiday villages or metropolitan villages which give rise to different and specialised arrays of services or functions.

   It is also appropriate to add
4. Adequate infrastructures. These are not functions in the normal meaning of the term, but the possibilities of growth are always constrained by the adequacy of the provision of such services as a sewage system or adequate public transport.

Setting aside the specialised roles, the nature of the agricultural enterprise, especially its intensity, and the effective demand which can be concentrated at a centre, together with the adequacy of infrastructures, will produce villages of different orders or sizes ranging from those which are near-towns to tiny hamlets. Indeed, at the very lowest levels, functions such as the primary school or the place of worship can themselves, like the single farm, be isolated in the countryside. That array was demonstrated by an example from Dyfed but it was maintained that, given the immense variety of physical and social conditions, it would be dangerous to propose some universal system which would be applicable to the whole of Britain.

These arrays of settlement have in recent times been subject to considerable pressures, from rural depopulation and falling demand on the one hand, and the demand for larger units benefiting from the economies of scale on the other. This has meant that the smaller settlements have lost functions and the larger settlements have acquired additional or larger scale functions. Translated into planning policy terms this has generated the concept of the key village.

THE RURAL COMMUNITY

It has been evident that in examining the functions of rural settlements it has been impossible to avoid the use of the word community. A good example to illustrate this relationship is the summary by Blowers of reactions to the proposed elimination of schedule D villages in Durham. 'Opponents of the Plan contend that many of the threatened settlements are not merely an assemblage of buildings occupied by people but contain closely knit communities bound together by ties of kinship, class and common origins. Shared hardship in the past and the prospect of eventual extinction have reinforced their community self-consciousness.' The village, therefore, is something more than a service centre, it constitutes a community. Moreover, that concept need not be tied to the village for an area of single farms, too, can constitute a community as was also suggested earlier in this chapter (page 43). The word community is very widely and persistently used, but it is extraordinarily difficult to define. Generally, it is taken to imply that a group of people, usually though not necessarily associated in geographical location, has a feeling of

common interest, purpose and identity. It is also generally assumed that it is something to be valued. One of the standard objections to innovation in rural areas is that it undermines community feeling, just as pit closures are claimed to destroy not settlements as such but communities.

Against this background there has developed an extensive area of academic enquiry reaching back into the last century. It has been mainly the concern of sociologists, but geographers have become involved in so far as there is a congruence between the community and a specific geographical area or environmental context, that is the community is seen as having a clear spatial dimension and where propinquity in space is a fundamental feature. Much of the work has sought to lay stress on the high significance of community feeling in rural areas as against its lower levels of importance in cities. The argument is a lengthy and complex one, but can be briefly summarised.

The city is, by definition, a large settlement; size as has been seen is the major criterion of contrast with the village. The city also has a dense and necessarily heterogeneous or mixed population. Numbers and diversity result in very weak bonds or links between city dwellers who have not lived together for any length of time and cannot know each other at any depth, if at all. The result is that relations are transitory, impersonal, superficial and *segmented*. The last word requires some explanation. In the city everyone has a specialised job, and workplace bears no immediate relation to job. So the city dweller meets a lot of people but all carrying out different or segmented roles. This is why relationships are impersonal. The checkout person in a large supermarket is not someone the shopper knows in any other way. That person might as well be a machine, and probably sometime in the future will be. All this contrasts with the rural community. It is small in size so, in popular terms, everyone knows everyone else. In a stable context, families have known each other for generations and have built up an interdependence over a long time; and it is time which creates communities. Relations, bad or good, are personal, and people are met in a variety of different roles. The village shopkeeper might also be the churchwarden, and everyone knows the shopkeeper. His shop is a place to meet and discuss local affairs, a social centre, not a machine the success of which is measured by sales per square foot of selling space.

Again, in the city, the lack of close personal ties fosters both competition and mutual exploitation. Status, or place in society, is not given or ascribed, it is won, and success is marked by appropriate symbols, popularly interpreted as 'keeping up with the Joneses'. Social relations are often a means to an end; one has to get to know the right people. In contrast, in rural communities people's status is ascribed; one is known by one's family background. Thus, in rural Wales, a boy or girl is often called locally not by a surname, but rather by the farm from which he or she comes which places them in the proper and understood context. Again, in more popular terms, in a truly rural area, people will want to know who you are: what your family background is; in a city they want to know what you do: your occupation sets you in context. And so the contrasts continue. In a rural community, one has a feeling of belonging, and the pressures to conform, to follow traditional modes of behaviour, are social pressures. In a city, there develops a feeling of isolation, again in popular terms of being lost in the lonely crowd, and the pressures to conform are formal and legal.

These comparisons could be greatly extended. The critical conclusion is that there emerges a view of rural communities as demonstrating these qualities of integration, common interest and purpose which characterise the ideal. The questions that arise, therefore, are: is that true? or, was it ever true? Can the truth be established by any form of measurement? And what is the role of spatial or geographical elements?

These ideas which suggest contrasts between the characteristics of rural and urban communities have been widely criticised and generally rejected by sociologists. An element in that rejection is the unwillingness to accept the significance of locational control and that group relationship can be defined by geographical space. One sociologist has coined an alternative term – *local social system* – which retains the locality element without the implications which the word community carries with it. There is also in the rejection an element of political philosophy not easy to explain but it is necessary to consider it briefly. It is based on the conviction of Marxian academics that social attitudes and relations are created at a fundamental level by the socio-economic bases of capitalist society. The control of the environment, that is whether it is urban or rural, is superficial and of little account. Moreover, the characteristics ascribed to the rural village can also be found in the city in the closely knit (a phrase so often employed) communities which make it up. A city is a constellation of such communities, especially when they have highly distinguishing characteristics such as skin colour or language. Put more simply, TV soap operas are often based on such communities. If Ambridge is an archetypal rural community, then Coronation Street and the Eastenders are equally demonstrative of what has been termed the urban village. Nevertheless, in spite of all these reservations, the types of concept which have been set out in the previous paragraphs are constantly reiterated, largely because they do seem to correspond to what is the ordinary person's perception of town-country differences, to the stereotypes that are carried by most people. They are certainly deeply entrenched in literature and folk lore.

A more relevant criticism is that the differences, and the character of rural communities which is part of them, were once true but belong to the past when the lack of communications and isolation gave the countryside an inward directed character, as contrasted with the outward directed nature of the city. By definition the city had extensive relations not only with other parts of the national territory but with the international world as well. And the bigger the city the more extensive the relations. Now, however, rural settlements no longer exist in isolation. Both in direct physical terms through easier travel and in indirect non-physical terms through the reach of the media, newspapers, radio and television, not even the most remote settlement is far removed from national and international influences. Consider the last sentence and note the two expressions 'most remote' and 'far removed' for they imply that geographical or euclidian distance (most remote) has become, in recent times, less and less significant (not far removed). At a trivial level (although considering the finance involved it is far from trivial) fashions in clothes are still generated in the big cities; the leaders in what women wear are based in London, Paris and New York. But the fashions these leaders determine reach the smallest and most distant hamlet in a matter of months, if not weeks. Traditional dress, that is the unchanging style of the old stable rural community, is now reserved for village fêtes or May Day celebrations. All this means a strong converging character of rural and urban areas.

Leading this convergence, whilst at the same time reflecting its duality, is the metropolitan village to which reference has already been made. It is the name given to former rural settlements at the margins of metropolitan areas which have become the target for city employed commuters looking for the peace and quiet of the countryside in which to establish their homes. Because of the costs in both time and money, those who buy or build houses here tend to be the most affluent. However, there will be existing houses and cottages and the local authority will build housing directed towards longer-standing residents. It is likely, therefore, that instead of a single community contrasted groups will develop in the village, often with conflicting views as to its future. This in effect is a new class structure in the village. The consequence of this is to produce a contrasted class structure in these villages. D. Thorns made a study of 11 villages in the vicinity of Nottingham and concluded that for those who worked on the farm, 'The village is the centre of their lives. They are often born within a few miles of where they now live. They are restricted in outlook and their involvement outside the village area. But for the middle classes their sphere of association and contacts is wider than the village community which is seen largely as a dormitory and a place to spend the weekend.' With two-car families common, wives also have much greater mobility and opportunity to use the whole city, not merely a very restricted part of it.

Note how this conclusion relates to the rural-urban contrasts developed earlier for there is still a divergence between those looking primarily inward and seeing their lives as wholly related to the village, and those looking outward and seeing it as a small part of their way of living. If these contrasts still exist then it might be possible to base a classification of villages upon them.

ASSIGNMENT

4. What are your own perceptions of the contrasts between life in the countryside and life in towns? If you form one of a group or class with different backgrounds, develop a discussion as to whether there are contrasts between rural and urban life-styles.

THE VILLAGE COMMUNITY – A CLASSIFICATION

Michael Pacione in his book on *Rural Geography* revives a study of Devon villages made as long ago as 1951 by Mitchell. Two broad sets of opposite factors were used. The first was called *'open-closed'* where 'open' described a tendency towards a state of willing reception of outside influences, including new inhabitants, and where 'closed' denoted a rejection of new ideas and hostility towards newcomers. The second set of factors was *'integration-disintegration'* where 'integration' was seen as the absence of disharmony in the village's institutional life and 'disintegration' the presence of disharmonies creating conflict. Thus in the metropolitan village, clashes between the interests of the long standing agriculturally based residents and the new middle-class commuters would be evidence of disharmony and disintegration.

Combining the criteria gives four types:

1. The open, integrated rural community. This is usually large in size and diverse in occupational structure and in its institutional and organisation framework able to adapt to changing conditions.

2. The closed, integrated rural community. This is characteristic of the most isolated areas with little change in the population. It is 'inward-looking, self-contained and traditional, maintaining firm boundaries against outside influences' (Pacione, p. 157). Within it, the roles of people are well defined and there are observed limits on the range of acceptable social behaviour.

3. The open, disintegrating rural community. This is a situation where there is a rapid rate of change which the community cannot assimilate. There are strong external linkages developed and internal conflict results. This is the situation where greatest disagreement arises between the locals and the newcomers.

4. The closed, disintegrating rural community. This occurs usually where depopulation has undermined the standard village services and engendered a feeling of despair amongst the inhabitants. Under the impact of change the old settled system is breaking apart.

MEASURING COMMUNITY FEELING

The above categories are useful as indicators of the varying character of rural communities. It is not easy to assign settlements to the categories and in Mitchell's original paper it was simply done on a general descriptive basis with population trends being the predominant criterion. It is possible, however, by means of questionnaire survey, to establish the distinction between open-closed and integrated-disintegrated, but in most cases quite complex statistical techniques are involved. One method is called 'the *semantic differential*'. Its basic idea is simple, perhaps the major criticism being that it is too simple. A sample of residents is asked to assess or rate the community against a set of paired bi-polar adjectives, that is descriptions which are the exact opposite of each other, like good-bad. To avoid too stark a contrast and choice this rating is based on a

Figure 3.8 *Grafitti against migrants to North Wales*

scale which usually runs either from 1 to 5 or 1 to 7. For example, to test whether the village is open or closed one could set out the question:

Do you think the village is . . .

1	2	3	4	5
Very friendly	Friendly	Neutral	Unfriendly	Very unfriendly
Very welcoming	Welcoming	Neutral	Unwelcoming	Very unwelcoming
Totally unclannish	Not clannish	Neutral	Clannish	Very clannish

Each respondent is asked to ring or tick what is considered the most appropriate description. These can be numbered 1 to 5 so that a figure can be given for each answer; a total for all the respondents can be found and the mean or average calculated; and also the standard deviation, that is the extent to which answers group about the mean or depart from it. A larger number of paired adjectives can be used and a profile of the village constructed which can then be compared with other villages. It must be stressed that this is a simplification of a complex procedure and there are questions which this brief account has not broached, such as how the sample is derived and how it can be identified as representative or not. Again, the sample should be examined against attributes of its composition, such as age, length of residence, occupation and so on. But as long as one is aware that there are many statistical pitfalls as well as conceptual reservations, the use of the semantic differential can be presented as one way of measuring the qualities and character of village life.

ASSIGNMENT

5. (See note at end of chapter.) Use the semantic differential to assess the character of a small array of rural settlements. If you are working on your own you can simply try out the idea in one settlement, or see if there are differences between two. Difficulties will arise in making it operational but it will give insight into the procedure and character of rural communities.

CONCLUSION

This chapter has been devoted to the consideration of two linked aspects of rural settlement, function and community. In both of these it was evident that urban comparison, the relation of village to town was of considerable relevance. The largest villages were seen to be service centres not greatly different from the smallest towns. The review of rural community necessitated the development of contrasts with the nature of the city. Clearly there is no sharp break as the first chapter demonstrated, and it is appropriate to turn to consider more specifically the urban element of the settlement pattern.

A further note on the semantic differential for Assignment 5.

If you wish to generate a practice exercise you can draw up a test for your school or College.

School/College

pleasant	unpleasant
passive	active
ugly	beautiful
good	bad
weak	strong
deep	shallow
stimulating	dull

As indicated earlier, you will not wish to offer a bald choice between the two extremes so you must work out a range (usually five) of interpretations. Thus you could offer a choice for the first and last adjectives of

1	2	3	4	5
Very pleasant	Pleasant	So-so	Unpleasant	Very unpleasant
Very stimulating	Stimulating	Neither stimulating nor dull	Dull	Very dull

Note that some of the pairs have been reversed so that the good attributes do not always appear on one side and the bad on the other. Make respondents stop and think. They will have to be put back, however, for simplicity in presentation.

If you can persuade a group of students to participate you can compare their responses, but names should be included only if they are willing to be identified. That is a very important matter for you must make it absolutely clear whether individual returns will be made public or not and keep absolutely rigidly to any guarantee of anonymity. It is most informative, however, to make composite profiles by averaging the responses either for your whole sample or for sections of it, by form or age for example.

You can present your results in the form of a diagram on which differences can be displayed. Note that the pairs of adjectives have been re-arranged so that all the favourable responses are on the left and so that those at the top of the list refer to general appearance and quality, those at the bottom more to the intellectual characteristics. The numbers relate to the range of choices offered and are the average for all respondents. Two traces are placed on the diagram. It is clear that Form A finds the school a pleasant environment but not very good in its intellectual quality while Form B finds it not very attractive but a stimulating place to be. It must be stressed, however, that rarely will complete contrasts of this sort appear: they have been exaggerated for exemplification.

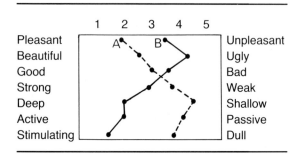

4

Towns: their Sizes and their Distribution

INTRODUCTION

That towns differ in size, and that they are irregularly distributed, is such an obvious fact that it is assumed to be inherent in their nature, of the very order of things. Few people pause to consider that it might be more logical for towns to be equal in size, and in the facilities they have, and that they should form a regular, equidistant pattern. In that way their resources would be equally available to all for they would be equally accessible to all. It is, therefore, a proper starting point for this chapter to ask why such enormous variations in size exist and why the distribution is far from regular.

URBAN FUNCTIONS

The answer to such a question must begin with a consideration of what towns do, that is, what are their functions. For how big they are, as well as where they are, depends upon what they are called on to do. Such a review of urban functions invokes two related but different sets which can be called 'general' and 'special' functions.

1. General functions. There are some functions which all towns, whatever their size or character, perform. These are related to the provision of services both for the town itself and for the surrounding countryside. An example is the provision of retailing facilities: shops, in short. It would be impossible to find a town without shops of some sort and, in addition, the area from which they attract people is likely to extend beyond the limits of the settlement itself. Again, translating that into everyday terms, the town acts as a market place. Because the town is, in this way, a centre

for the surrounding countryside, and because it operates not only in the sphere of retailing but also in the provision of services, such as libraries and hospitals, the specific term market is usually replaced to give the more general expression *central place*. Every town is, to some degree, a central place.

2. Special functions. These are not carried out by all towns. Coal mining or car manufacturing can be taken as examples of activities or functions which characterise some towns, such as the automobile industry at Detroit. But not all towns mine coal or build cars. It is possible, therefore, to isolate a very wide range of activities universally located in towns – there may be mining villages but there are hardly any car manufacturing villages – but not located in every town.

The understanding of variations in town size and distribution must be derived from an examination of both these sorts of functions. They are, of course, related. If a town manufactures cars, the bigger the operation, or the more people it employs, the bigger will be the town and the greater the demand for goods and services. The larger that demand, the bigger the shops for example, the more attractive it will become to the surrounding countryside thus generating more central place activities. Similarly a thriving central place will provide both a pool of employees and a demand that will attract more specialised activities. In this review it is appropriate to consider the general or central place functions first, but the relations indicated above should make it clear that neither set has any *a priori* significance in the origin of towns which can come into being either for special purposes or as central places.

General functions – central place theory

The construction of central place theory is associated with the name of Walther Christaller who published his book *Die Zentralen Orte in Suddeutschland* (*Central Places in Southern Germany*) in 1933. This exposition will be based on his arguments but will not directly follow them since a good deal of modification has taken place since that date. The starting point is that these general or central place functions are physically identifiable in the town by what can be called establishments. Thus, retailing as a function is made tangible by shops in the town, the provision of health services by a hospital. To the shop and hospital the general description establishment is given. There are two controls over the existence of any establishment offering a good for sale or a service. These are the threshold population and the range of the good or service which were mentioned in Chapter 3 when the functions of villages were being reviewed, and which can now be elaborated.

1. Threshold population. This is the minimum number of people required to sustain an establishment. For example, before a shop of any sort can make a profit for the owner, it must have an effective turnover, or total of sales, which is based on the demand arising, or in more popular terms on the number of people using the shop. If the number, or demand, falls below a certain level, then the shop cannot be sustained for it will become unprofitable and go out of business. But thresholds will vary greatly. A baker's shop providing fresh bread and cakes daily will sell a low cost product in large quantities meeting a daily and local demand. In contrast, a specialised furrier dealing only in women's fur coats is selling a high cost product with a very infrequent demand. Some women will never buy a fur coat, others only once or twice in a lifetime. In order to survive this low level of demand the shop will need a very large threshold population from which to draw its infrequent purchasers. The consequences are evident; the bakery will be found in the smallest town, the furrier only in the largest.

Before proceeding further it must be stressed

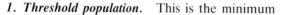

Figure 4.1 *A simple hierarchical array of towns*
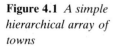

that these establishments are not mutually exclusive in towns but will occur in an additive fashion. Thus, although the small town will have no furrier, the large town will certainly have bakers' shops, and many of them since the threshold is low. But if one discounts the numbers, it is possible to conceive of the threshold population as the critical point at which a type of establishment can survive, or make its entry into a town's retail facilities. So it is now possible to postulate a series of towns at which higher thresholds allow successively more specialised establishments to appear, as in Figure 4.1. In that Figure A could be the baker's shop, whilst B might be a grocer's, C a shop selling electrical goods and D the furrier. Thus town 4 will have all the types of establishments found in towns 1, 2 and 3, plus the additional distinctive one of its own. Also in the Figure, (i) to (iv) are the critical entry points, represented either by populations, i.e. thresholds, or by frequency of need.

By this point an effective argument has been deployed to show why towns *must* be of different sizes. The different functions demand different thresholds and hence different town sizes. But one proviso is needed, that all the places where the functions locate are common. It would not be impossible to envisage all the establishments A to D scattered singly across the countryside and one has to show why that is not so. To do this it is necessary to turn to consider range.

2. The range of a good or service.

A threshold population defines the minimum population required to sustain an establishment which, taking into account the density of population, can be translated into a minimum area, and hence a minimum distance. But there is also a maximum distance or range beyond which it becomes too costly to travel to obtain a good. Reverting to the examples already used, the distance anyone would be willing to travel, under normal circumstances, to buy a loaf of bread is limited, for even at a short distance the cost of travel becomes greater than the cost of purchase. But a fur coat is a relatively rare and expensive item and travel so small a part of the

total cost that one would be willing to travel a far longer distance to buy one. So range, the maximum distance which people will travel for a good, begins to operate. Now it could be argued that people must have bread, but even so the distance or range will become so great that people cannot afford a daily journey in time or money. They could, of course, and do in remote areas, bake their own; but the restrictions of range allow bakeries to be established frequently in space, as they are used frequently in time, and hence they appear in small towns.

But only two extremes have been used in this discussion, the baker where there are daily needs and the furrier where there might be only a once-in-a-lifetime need. Between these are very widely varying circumstances. Thus a grocery shop is frequently used but very often for a weekly purchase of goods. A shop selling electrical equipment, such as refrigerators, vacuum cleaners and toasters, meets needs that arise much less frequently than weekly. For these types of purchase, therefore, the travel distance will vary and range will tend to sort itself out into a set of distances equivalent to the groupings created by threshold populations illustrated in Figure 4.1. Each of the examples there, the baker, the grocer and so on, can be thought of as covering different ranges, or to turn it back into everyday language, people will travel further to them.

It is evident that everyone, in order to save time and money, will wish always to minimise travel costs. Now this can be done by visiting the baker, the grocer and the electrical shop on one and the same occasion and this answers a problem set out above as to why establishments will gather into one place rather than be scattered across the countryside. Their accumulation allows what are called multipurpose trips and by that minimises range.

It is now possible to put the two controls together and maintain that low range, low order goods needing low thresholds will be sold in small towns whilst goods with high ranges and large thresholds will be sold only in large towns. The same will be true of services. Thus, as far as medical services are concerned, a doctor will be found in a small town (even a village, refer back to Chapter 3), a hospital in a town of intermediate size but a specialised eye hospital only in a large city. The same principles of threshold and range apply. And note how both can be still further lowered by offering a service periodically rather than permanently. Again, in Chapter 3 the bank opening on only a certain number of days a week was identified. At the other end of the scale, for very highly specialised medical treatment of a particular illness, people are flown from Britain to New York – both threshold and range have been vastly increased, but the same principle holds. The assumption of all towns being of the same size collapses: towns of different sizes will of necessity occur in order effectively to offer the functions demanded. Moreover, because low order goods and services are in frequent demand, there will be a large number of places offering them and they will be located with small distances between them. High order goods and services, infrequent in demand, will bring into being a small number of large places with great distances between them. Ultimately, at the highest level, there will be only one place – that occupied by London in the United Kingdom. At intermediate levels arrays or bundles of functions will occur.

Two modifications of the generalisations made in the last paragraph must be kept in mind.

1. Not every function at the highest level will be located in the largest city. This is due partly to historical reasons. American Government is located in Washington not New York, Australian in Canberra not Sydney. It is also partly due to many governments' policy of attempting to disperse high order functions in order to offset the overdominance of one city. In Britain, the National Exhibition Centre is in Birmingham, not London.
2. The most highly specialised of functions can at times dictate their own location regardless of settlement size. A very special clinic or hospital, such as Stoke Mandeville, is an example.

Having put the two controls together one can proceed further and from them generate a theoretical distribution pattern. But two assumptions need to be made for without them major distortions would arise. The first is that there is a completely even distribution of population with no variation in spending power; the second that the distribution is generated on a level and uniform plain, what is technically called an *isotropic surface*. The starting point, therefore, reflecting the two assumptions, is an equally spaced and most closely packed pattern of points or settlements, that is the points are arranged so the maximum number occur in a unit area (Figure 4.2). If one of these is now selected as a centre with a range of functions ABCD as on Figure 4.1, then it will dominate the area about it as far as a circle which intersects an equivalent circle from the next adjacent ABCD centre. This is indicated on Figure 4.2 and it will be seen to pass through the six nearest settlements. At that point the highest D level establishment is outranged.

Attention can now be directed to the internal structure of the area served by the ABCD level settlement. It is distinguished by the critical good called D from all the other settlements marked on the diagram and at the next lower level is surrounded by six settlements at the ABC level, as in Figure 4.2. Thus Figure 4.3 is an enlargement of the circle drawn in Figure

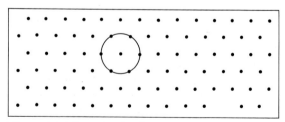

Figure 4.2 *The most closely packed equidistant distribution of points (settlements) and the smallest possible association of settlements. Below the level indicated by the circle each has a separate and independent role*

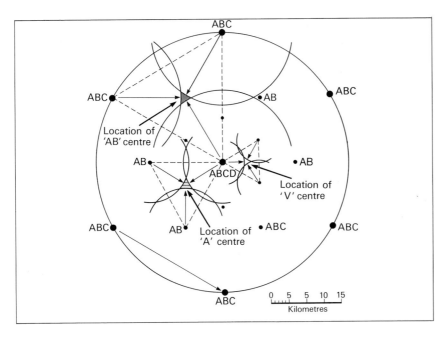

Figure 4.3 *The derivation of the urban hierarchy. In this diagram the usual symbols for the various routes used by Christaller (GKB) have been replaced by descriptions (ABCD, ABC, AB, A) to match Figure 4.1*

4.2. If within this common area the range of good C is examined it will be seen that circles drawn with their centres at the seven settlements (the one ABCD and the six ABC) can be increased until they touch and then overlap. But there will still be an unserved area which is shaded in the north-west quadrant. There, an opportunity arises for a further settlement to develop offering goods A and B. That is, an AB centre will come into being at that point which is least effectively served from the existing ABC centres. These AB centres are marked on the diagram. The process is repeated in relation to the AB centres in the south-west quadrant. The same poorly served area emerges and an A level settlement arises to take advantage of the opportunity. Some, but not all, of these settlements are marked on the diagram. Finally at a still lower level indicated immediately to the east of the ABCD centre, a 'V' or village is located, indicating the link up with the village functions discussed in the last chapter. This offers the lowest order of goods even below the rank of what can be defined as a town, bearing in mind all the problems of definition which have been discussed. It must be noted that, as the range is increased from the ABC centres, a

whole number of different ranges are encompassed so that in reality one is not dealing with a single good C but rather with a number C_1, C_2, C_3 etc. Each level is not characterised by one good or service but by what in the early days of central place studies was called a 'trait complex', or a characterising assemblage of goods and services. Christaller ascribed actual distances of 36 kilometres, 20 kilometres and 11 kilometres to identify the points where unserved areas appeared. These have been approximately preserved on Figure 4.3, but such a mixture of the theoretical and the empirical is not very sensible.

Christaller went on to demonstrate that circles are inappropriate since one cannot exactly fill space with them; there are overlaps as Figure 4.3 shows. He therefore substituted hexagons and produced the system shown in Figure 4.4. This diagram purports to represent the way towns would be distributed if they were only central places, that is they only performed general functions, and if the distribution of population were even. It is now apparent that, even under these highly theoretical conditions, the notion of all towns being of equal size has been abandoned, though a regular hierarchical

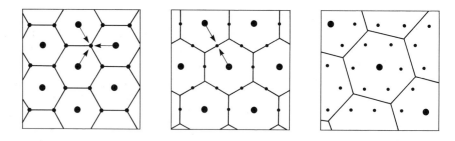

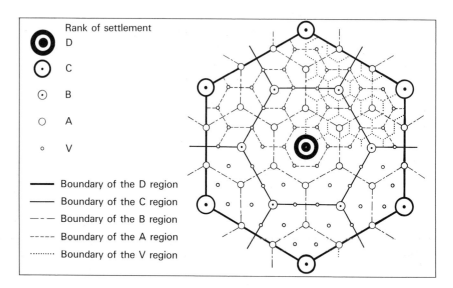

Figure 4.4 *The central place system as set out by Christaller. The smaller diagrams show that different systems can be derived. In K = 3 the number stands for the total settlements which are tributary. Thus in K = 4 there are six settlements shared by two centres, as shown by the arrow, giving a total for each of three plus the settlement itself making four*

structure has been substituted. Regularity of distribution has been preserved, however, although it is simply a product of the assumptions relating to environment (a level plain with no variations) and population distribution.

Two predictions as to the arrangement of towns follow from Christaller's theoretical structures:

1. Towns should demonstrate a distinctively stepped hierarchical order, as in Figures 4.1 and 4.4. Each step should be identified by a distinctive trait complex of functions, that is an assemblage of goods and services or establishments which mark the arrival of a new threshold.
2. For each order, the town should serve a distinctive area which is the range for each good or service. That area should be definable by examining the extent over which the various functions operate.

A good deal of early empirical work was devoted to testing the above predictions or hypotheses as to their validity in the real world.

The basic model which Christaller derived was seen by him to be less than adequate, for it only considered one way in which a hexagonal mesh can be thrown over the regularly distributed settlements. Two more are shown in Figure 4.4. In the first of these each of the smaller settlements is equidistant from three larger settlements (turn back and look at the hatched area in Figure 4.3) so that travel to them is the same and the provision of services at the higher level will be shared by the three larger. Each large settlement, therefore, dominates the equivalent of two whole settlements (6 divided by 3) and all of itself at that level, giving a total of 3. Hence the concept of each larger settlement serving the equivalent of 3 smaller, or K = 3. In the second example each smaller settlement is equidistant from two larger, so that the constant (K) figure will be 6 divided by 2 plus again the whole of itself giving K = 4. In the third example the larger settlement dominates all six smaller giving 6 + 1 so K = 7. Christaller regarded these three as the basic situations and attempted to give names to them. K = 3 he called the market principle, K = 4 he interpreted as a transport principle since the smaller settlements were on direct communication lines between the larger. K = 7 he called the administrative principle since in local government terms it is not possible to divide the allegiance of settlements.

Thus Christaller was aware that more than one type of system could be generated, but it was the contemporary economist August Lösch who maintained that an ever extending series of meshes can be realised. When these are superimposed, the neat regularity of Christaller's scheme disappears and both a clear hierarchical ranking and regularity of distancing are lost. Lösch also rotated the networks about the central point producing what he called city rich sectors, that is with a large number of settlements, and city poor sectors. This even further reduces the regularity of Christaller's basic scheme. Quite rapidly, therefore, even in theoretical terms, the assumed system of equally spaced, equally sized towns is lost, but when special functions are considered even more disruption is introduced.

The special functions of towns

Just as the hierarchy of central places is acknowledged in everyday speech by reference to hamlet, village, town, city, so too the identification of special functions appears in reference to resorts, ports, railway towns and so on, for by using such terms a classificatory system is being employed. The approach to the analysis of special functions has, however, been somewhat different and it lacks the development of a theoretical basis which has characterised central place studies. Indeed, the main thrust has been in the initial problem of how to allocate towns to functional groups. Thus, for example, Oxford is associated across the world with its university and the general

appellation of university town would be widely accepted. But it is also an important car manufacturing centre. So the simple classification, university town, is inadequate and some other system has to be devised where both aspects are included. But that problem has ceased to be a central theme in the study of urban settlements for three reasons. The first is that, over the recent period, deindustrialisation in Britain and the west has seen the significant decline in specialisation amongst towns. For example, one might have classed towns as shipbuilding centres but this means very little at the present with the virtual collapse of the shipbuilding industry. It could well be argued that there is a convergence in towns in relation to the functions they perform; they are getting more alike and the special roles which once gave such diversity are disappearing. The second reason is an operational one. Statistical procedures have become much more sophisticated and in particular what is called *multivariate statistics* enables not one diagnostic criterion representing functional character to be used but a large number of others and categories of towns can be derived on a much broader basis. The final reason is that classification has tended to become an end in itself and has not led directly to significant progress in the analysis of size and distribution.

Whatever the method, however, data on the occupational structure of towns is critical. No-one would contest the classification of Blackpool as a seaside resort. The town claims that the annual turnover derived from tourism is some £250 million and that there are some six million visitors. But these are highly individual figures which would be difficult to obtain and use on a national basis. Nearly all classifications, therefore, use occupational data and one should be able to identify resorts by the high proportions employed in hotels and catering. Two problems arise, however, one related to the data themselves, the other to the method of their use.

The first problem, as far as the United Kingdom is concerned, is that of simply gaining easy access to relevant figures since those published by the Office of Population and Census Surveys have become less useful and those available for 1981 are severely limited. The main difficulties are:

1. The data are only 10 per cent samples with an element of unreliability.
2. They are only available in the County Economic Activity series at District level, and on microfiche. This makes them of very little use for specific urban analysis, especially for smaller towns.
3. There is a special series of volumes of Key Statistics for urban areas where more specific definition of the settlement is used. But again these are only available for towns over 50 000 and the data are generalised to a degree that renders them next to useless.
4. Certain aspects of the Census presentation must be kept in mind.
   a) Data are presented either on an occupational or industrial basis. In the former the type of occupation is used so that all clerical workers, wherever they are employed, are grouped together. In the second the particular industry is the basis so that clerical workers will be divided accordingly.
   b) There are two spatial bases: place of residence, so all those residing in a town are included, or place of work where all those who work in a town are included. With more and more extensive commuting the differences could be very considerable.

The second problem revolves around determining what proportion of employment is critical in deciding whether a town is placed in a particular category. Table 4.1 presents the proportions employed in the various industrial groups for Blackpool and York, two instances where the district boundaries are reasonably related to the actual settlement areas. The proportions for Blackpool demonstrate its resort function. Hotels and catering, together with retailing, account for 28.7 per cent of employment, and the addition of services, such as recreational and cultural, brings the proportion

to over a third. York is not as straightforward. The highest proportions are in food manufacture, retail distribution and railways. These do effectively encapsulate the city as primarily based on manufacturing foodstuffs, mainly confectionery, on the role as market or service centre and as a railway centre. These would

Table 4.1 *Usually resident population in employment industry classes by workplace 1981 Blackpool and York*

	* Percentages	
	York	Blackpool
Production and distribution of electricity, gas and other forms of energy	1.3	1.6
Manufacture of non-metallic mineral products	1.7	–
Mechanical engineering	1.0	1.2
Manufacture of motor vehicles and parts	4.5	2.3
Food, drink and tobacco manufacture	15.7	4.6
Manufacture of paper; printing and publishing	1.6	2.1
Construction	6.1	6.4
Wholesale distribution	2.2	3.4
Retail distribution	11.1	16.2
Hotels and catering	5.5	12.5
Repairs of consumer goods and vehicles	1.7	1.4
Railways	7.5	–
Other inland transport	1.5	3.1
Postal services: telecommunications	3.3	1.9
Banking and finance	1.9	2.6
Insurance	2.0	–
Business services	3.0	3.5
Public administration	5.0	7.6
Sanitary services	–	1.1
Education	5.2	3.9
Medical and health services, veterinary services	6.9	6.8
Other services	2.5	3.0
Recreational and cultural services	1.8	4.2
Personal services	1.3	2.0
Other classes not identified*	5.7	8.6

* All groups with employment below 1 per cent have been omitted.

correspond with common perceptions. The problem arises in converting these selected figures and perceptions into precise and universal statistical measures. The most common method has been in some way to compare the local with the national. From the tabulations in the volume on *Key Statistics in Urban Areas*, Blackpool has 29.9 per cent employed in 'Distribution and Catering' which is the most detailed category presented. The figure for Great Britain is 19.2 per cent. Thus Blackpool's figure is 1.6 times the national one, a measure known as a *Location Quotient*. But Table 4.2 will show a whole range above 100 and the decision as to where to draw the line is quite arbitrary.

Attempts have been made to avoid arbitrariness and especially subjective judgement by employing complex statistical procedures permitting the use of a large number of variables and which group towns where the differences within the group are minimised and between groups maximised. Even these, however, reveal anomalies.

Such investigations as those which have been examined seek to relate size and location to function, but whereas the relationship is manifest any consistency is limited. Thus, Blackpool grew as a town not because of any central place function, although it may have acquired one as a *result* of its growth, but because it became a seaside resort for industrial Lancashire. In an absolutely direct sense its population reflects its popularity. York was a central place, certainly since Roman times, serving and providing for a surrounding territory not only as a commercial and administrative centre but also as a major ecclesiastical centre. It acquired its other roles, as a manufacturer of chocolate and a railway node, later. The core of the problem is that these towns based on, or having in part, specialised functions display an element of individuality; they are not amenable to generalisation in relation to size. The presence of such functions destroys what little of order in size and location central place functions might engender.

It will have become quite apparent that there has been a real difference in the section on general or central place functions and that on special functions. The former represents a theoretical (*deductive*) approach, an attempt from first principles to set up a model which shows how towns of different sizes are distributed. But the latter is a much more empirical (*inductive*) method, that is it attempts to derive conclusions by examining real world examples. The differences reflect the ways in which geographers have worked on these problems.

A point has now been reached when these two aspects of urban functions, the general and the special, have to be brought together and the only way is by examining the consolidated outcome of their conjunction, the urban population.

ASSIGNMENTS

1. Consider the shopping habits of your own family. Do you use different shopping centres? If so, why? Rank them roughly in relation to:
   a) the types of shop present;
   b) the frequency you visit them;
   c) the distance you travel.
   Is there any relationship between (a), (b) and (c)?
2. The simplest way to examine the central place structure of your local area is to ignore the numbers of establishments and concentrate on presence/absence. Select an area away from the complexities of a conurbation or metropolis. Set up an array as below where a cross indicates the presence of a function.

Functions

Settlements	a	b	c	d	e	f	g	h	i	j	k	l	m	n
1		x	x	x	x	x	x		x	x	x	x	x		x
2		x	x	x	x	x	x	x			x	x		x	x	x
3		x	x	x	x	x		x			x	x		x	x	x
4		x	x	x	x	x	x
5		x	x	x	x
n		x	x	x		x

The settlements are arranged in population size order (1 to n) and the functions according to their ubiquity (a to n). The functions could be types of shop, such as a baker or furrier noted in the text, or public service institutions such as secondary schools or hospitals, or they could be named shops such as Marks & Spencer or Woolworth.

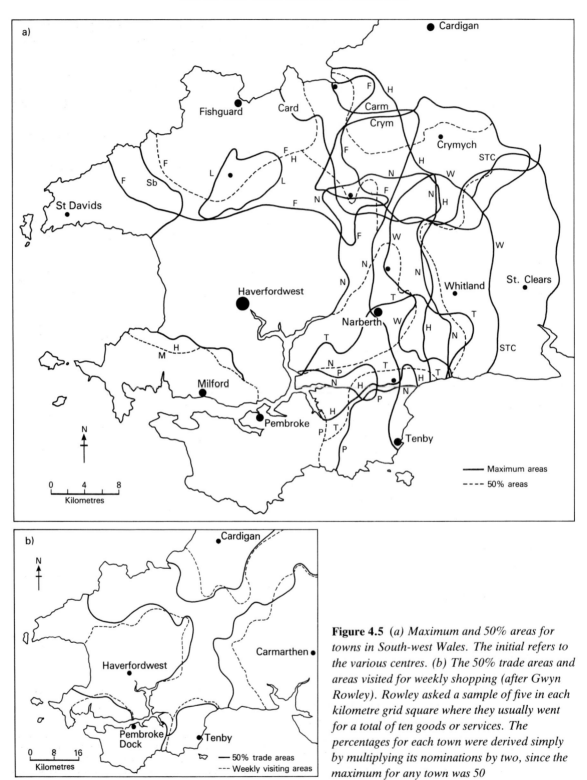

Figure 4.5 (*a*) *Maximum and 50% areas for towns in South-west Wales. The initial refers to the various centres. (b) The 50% trade areas and areas visited for weekly shopping (after Gwyn Rowley). Rowley asked a sample of five in each kilometre grid square where they usually went for a total of ten goods or services. The percentages for each town were derived simply by multiplying its nominations by two, since the maximum for any town was 50*

At this stage there is little point in attempting statistical analyses of the array; it is sufficient to inspect it by eye to see whether distinctive levels occur.

The various areas, or urban spheres of influence, can be established in three ways:

a) You can plot the areas covered by the functions a to n as far as it is possible. The delivery areas of shops, the catchment areas of schools, the extent covered by a regional hospital, and so on.

b) You can ask people in the town centre
   i where they live, and
   ii how frequently they visit the town.
   Maps of distance and of frequency can be drawn.

c) You can question people over a large area asking them where they normally buy, or last bought, goods and used services (a dentist for example). That is, you use all or the appropriate part of the functions a to n employed in the ranking scheme above.

   Construct maps to show the places visited for selected goods and services or the proportion going to each centre. Thus if a, b, c, d, f of the series was bought in Settlement 4, then that is 5 out of 14 or 36 per cent. Draw isopleths such as those shown on Figure 4.5. The usual method in carrying out this survey is to use grid squares from the Ordnance Survey map and question a number of people in each to avoid problems derived from a single aberrant result.

3. a) Select two or more towns where the District boundary is reasonably close to the settlement extent and abstract the employment data from the county census volume on *Economic Activity*. Work out the percentages employed in all those groups registering over 1 per cent and present a reasoned interpretation of your table.

   b) Select one other (i.e. not the Distribution and Catering treated in the text) of the seven employment groups given in the census volume of *Key Statistics for Urban Areas* (Table 4.2) and abstract all towns and cities with proportions above the national average. Develop an interpretation of your list.

4. The four columns in the following table are:
   • A classification of towns which were resorts and spas in 1961.
   • A similar classification in 1971 though the groups were not named.
   • The proportions employed in Distribution and Catering in 1981.
   • Location quotients for Distribution and Catering in 1981.
   Develop an interpretation of these figures.

Table 4.2 *Classification of towns in 1961 and 1971 and employment in Distribution and Catering (Urban Areas) 1981*

Group 1 mainly seaside resorts	Group 1	Census 1981 % employment in Distribution and Catering	Location quotient
		Great Britain 19.2	100
Worthing		24.5	128
Hove	Hove	25.1	131
Hastings	Hastings	24.5	128
Eastbourne	Eastbourne	27.4	143
Torquay	Torquay	33.9	177
Southport	Southport	24.5	128
Harrogate		23.8	124
Brighton		22.3	116
Blackpool	Blackpool	29.9	156
	Bournemouth	29.2	152
	Kensington	24.1	126
	Margate		
	Weston	24.8	129
Group 2 mainly spas, professional and administrative centres	**Group 2**		
Bath	Bath	20.5	107
Cheltenham	Cheltenham	18.7	97
Poole			
Oxford			
Cambridge			
Exeter	Exeter	24.2	127
Maidstone			
Bedford			
Colchester			
Southend	Southend	20.3	106
	Brighton	22.3	116
	Crosby	17.3	90
	Harrogate	23.8	124

Note The areal definitions of the towns are not the same in 1961, 1971 and 1981. No names were given to the 1971 groups.

THE POPULATION SIZES OF TOWNS

At an early stage, the examination of towns by the arrays of functions they possessed, a difficult and time-consuming task, was largely replaced by reverting to the oldest measure of significance, size measured by population. Size is, of course, an indivisible attribute, which was seen as having the virtue of lumping together both central place and specialised functions in one overall figure. It became most widely used in making a direct plot of size against rank in the sort of array set out on page 60 on a functional basis. This takes the form set out in Figure 4.6. If towns are organised hierarchically in distinctive orders, layers or ranks, then the graph line joining the members should take a stepped form. As might be expected, few studies demonstrated such a situation; consider all the complexities derived from the modifications made to Christaller's simple model by the need to take in a whole range of networks, and from those consequent upon the presence of special functions. But the graph did take on a distinctive form, especially when the logarithm of the population was plotted, giving a straight line as in Figure 4.6. This conforms with another interpretation of the relationship, although interpretation may be the wrong word since it is really an observed condition. This is called the *Rank-Size Rule for Cities.* It takes the form

$$R^n S_R = M$$

where R is the Rank of a city in the array, S is the population of city R and n and M are constants. But where R is 1 whatever the value of n, S will equal M so that the constant M is the size of the largest city and the rule simply states that the population of any town or city can be obtained by dividing its rank into the population of the largest city. Why this should be is a more difficult question but it is generally interpreted as some form of balance or equilibrium between forces acting towards centralisation, that is towards the concentration of population in a small number of large towns, and forces acting towards dispersion, that is the tendency towards a large number of small towns. But the validity of the Rank-Size Rule has itself been challenged; and it is not easy to apply. Thus, in Britain, the largest city is London but its population can vary enormously dependent on the boundaries one takes.

From all the material so far surveyed, it is evident that there is a whole variety of controls of size and location. They all remain valid. Threshold and range are highly significant determinants of the functional status of a town. Before a major chain store locates in a town, tests of the threshold, converted to purchasing power, are made. Likewise, in spite of de-industrialisation, special functions are still significant in the maintenance of a city's population. But none of these provides either a simple or complete answer to the basic question: why are the towns of a country of the size they are and where they are? To answer that, all the controls have to be brought into consideration and because much is derived from the past the discussion needs to have a historical dimension. The next section attempts a review

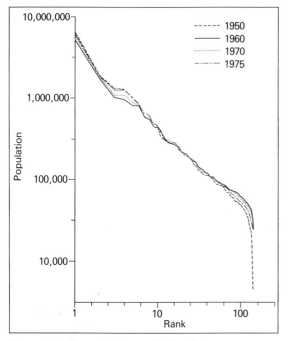

Figure 4.6 *Great Britain: rank size plot 1950–60–70–75 (after Hall and Hay)*

of the urban hierarchy in Britain to exemplify all the problems.

5. The graph below (Figure 4.7) shows a plot of city size against rank for France and Japan. With both axes on a logarithmic scale the rank-size rule would produce in each case a straight line. Why does the French graph take the form it does? What differences does the Japanese graph demonstrate?

THE DEVELOPMENT OF THE URBAN HIERARCHY IN ENGLAND AND WALES

The earliest layer of towns in England was that made up by the Anglo-Saxon burghs, many occupying the sites of former Roman settlements. By 1086 there were some 112 places (including Rhuddlan in Wales) recorded as boroughs. Of these, London was undoubtedly the largest, probably followed by York, Lincoln, and Norwich. In the early Middle Ages, after the Norman Conquest, this system was modified and extended. The growth of

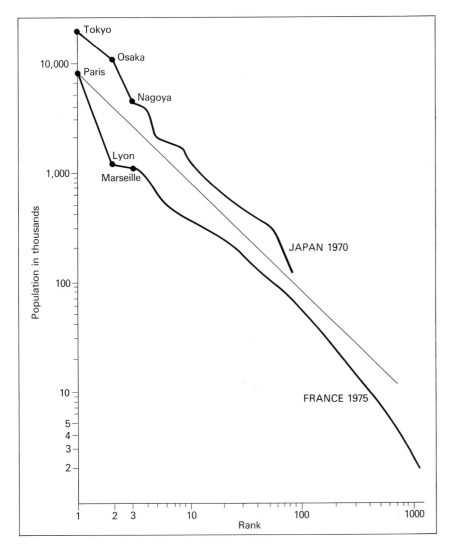

Figure 4.7 *Rank size plots for Japan and France 1975 (after Hall and Hay)*

71

administration, which was based on the shires and executed from the county towns, the growth of commerce and trade, and the plantation of new towns, all served to fill out the system. Although the data are incomplete, and unsatisfactory for a rigorous comparison of ranks, a rough ordering can be established. London was at the top of the hierarchy, followed by York, Norwich, Lincoln, Newcastle-on-Tyne, Bristol and Exeter.

By the early eighteenth century a complex urban system had emerged taking in the whole country and operating in a hierarchical fashion with a complete coverage of the country by the service areas of the larger provincial capitals, within which nested smaller market towns. Again the major centres after London were Norwich, York, Bristol, Newcastle, and Exeter,

a situation which was much as it had been in 1600. It is possible to regard this system as not only long lasting, since it had emerged during the Middle Ages, but also as extremely adaptable for it has survived beneath the massive transformations of the nineteenth century and of the present. It is true that these centres are no longer in the highest rank of British cities, but along with county towns such as Oxford, Northampton, Gloucester, Shrewsbury, Hereford, Canterbury, and Cambridge, they constitute the traditional provincial capitals, free-standing towns serving well-developed rural areas and characterised both by trade and the industry which developed from it. A. McInnes (1980) has published tables of the populations of leading provincial towns in England at two dates, 1670 and 1750. These are reproduced in Table 4.3.

It is apparent that even by 1750 significant changes were taking place with the rise of Manchester and the entry into the list of Birmingham, Liverpool, Leeds and Sheffield. These were the great new industrial centres which were superimposed upon and transformed the earlier system of towns which had emerged from the medieval period. Yet the revolutionary nature of this change should not be over-emphasised. Most of the early centres of industry had benefited from the stimulus of developing trade in the pre-industrial period and the process was one of evolutionary transformation rather than a sudden revolutionary break in the pattern of city growth.

Even so, by the middle of the nineteenth century, a completely new set of dominant towns had emerged occupying the rank immediately below London (Table 4.4). Only Bristol and Manchester are common to this list and that for 1670. Professor Robson in his book *Urban Growth* writes:

> 'Even though the generalised patterns do accord with knowledge of the regional economic growth of England and Wales, the details of the spatial patterns can only be interpreted in terms of the particular factor endowments and historical events which underlay the growth of certain towns and the decay of others . . .'

Table 4.3 *Ranks and sizes of the twenty-five leading provincial towns in England in 1670 and 1750*

a) circa 1670		b circa 1750	
Norwich	21 000	Bristol	50 000
Bristol	18 000	Norwich	36 000
Exeter	12 500	Newcastle-on-Tyne	29 000
Newcastle-on-Tyne	11 800	Birmingham	23 700
York	10 500	Liverpool	22 000
Great Yarmouth	9 500	Manchester	18 000
Colchester	9 500	Exeter	16 000
Worcester	8 500	Plymouth	15 000
Ipswich	7 500	Leeds	13 000
Canterbury	7 500	Chester	13 000
Chester	7 500	Coventry	12 500
Plymouth	7 500	Ipswich	12 100
Oxford	7 500	Sheffield	12 000
Cambridge	7 300	Nottingham	12 000
Shrewsbury	7 100	Hull	11 500
Salisbury	6 700	York	11 400
Coventry	6 500	Worcester	10 300
Hull	6 300	Great Yarmouth	10 000
Bury St. Edmunds	5 500	Sunderland	10 000
Manchester	5 500	Portsmouth	10 000
Nottingham	5 500	Bath	9 000
Leicester	5 500	King's Lynn	9 000
Hereford	5 000	Canterbury	8 600
Tiverton	5 000	Colchester	8 500
Gloucester	4 700	Oxford	8 200

Source: A. McInnes, 1980.

The figures in Table 4.3 are derived chiefly from an analysis of the Hearth Tax returns, the religious census of 1676 and local listings.

Integral to the problem was the fact that the great cities created by industry were not free-standing towns serving the surrounding countryside but agglomerations created by special functions via the exploitation of resources which occurred at particular places, and backed by the new transport media of canals and railways. But by the end of the century the most rapid growth was not taking place in the large cities since population was already moving out to residential suburbs. Through the concentration of population brought about by industrial growth and the dispersal and extension due to suburban development, completely new forms of settlement emerged. As already noted in Chapter 1, these were named conurbations by Patrick Geddes in 1915. 'The neighbouring great towns are rapidly linking up by tramways and streets no less than railways while great open spaces . . . are already all but irrecoverable . . . Some name then for these city regions, these town aggregates, is wanted . . . What of conurbations?' These new industrial conurbations were coalfield based and since the carboniferous rocks were mainly northern and western in distribution, urbanisation was extended to the previously more thinly peopled areas. By the interwar period, therefore, it was possible to consider the urban structure of Britain as dominated by the industrial conurbations and this was tacitly acknowledged in the first post-war census in 1951 by the publication of a volume entitled

Table 4.4 *Largest cities in England and Wales, 1851*

London	2 363 000	(Metropolis Management Act of 1855 area)
Liverpool	375 955	
Manchester, Salford	367 233	
Birmingham	232 841	
Leeds	172 270	
Bristol	137 328	
Sheffield	135 310	
Bradford	103 310	

Source: Harley, 1973.

'*London and Five Other Conurbations*' (South-East Lancashire, West Midlands, West Yorkshire, Merseyside, Tyneside).

Change which had been apparent during the 1930s became much more significant after the war. The basic industrial pattern represented by the heavy and traditional industries, which were in decline, concentrated growth in the southeast. Again the decline in coal as a fuel released the locational hold which the coalfields had exercised, while road transport and the motorways took over from rail. The result has been the emergence of the English *Megalopolis*.

It is now apparent that there are three elements in the English urban pattern which can be identified and interpreted. The first of these is the conventional hierarchy where the provision of services for surrounding hinterlands is still the dominant urban role. The second is the industrial conurbation, the creation of point resources or special functions though no longer generally sustained by them. The third is the emergent megalopolis in southern and central England, a consequence of the supreme dominance of London re-exerted after the interlude of the Industrial Revolution and partly overlapping the industrial conurbations.

The hierarchy of centres

It is still feasible to consider the city system in England and Wales as made up of a series of discrete and identifiable levels. As early as 1944 A. E. Smailes had proposed a hierarchy as in Table 4.5.

This was an arbitrary and empirical division which recognised six orders of towns. Subsequent work and changes over time have altered this scheme in detail and local studies have also made modifications but it still remains indicative of the urban patterning of the country. Even so, each order is made up of a wide range of industrial towns, and there is no suggestion that any relationships at this stage can be linked to the predictions of central place theory as to the number and spacing of centres. It is possible to show, however, how the whole of

Table 4.5 *The urban hierarchy in England and Wales*

The Metropolis	London
Major cities	e.g. Birmingham, Bristol, Cardiff, Liverpool, Manchester, Newcastle-on-Tyne, Hull, Norwich
Cities	e.g. Oxford, Preston, Wolverhampton, Swansea, Gloucester
Major towns	e.g. Bath, Chester, Canterbury, Dover, Shrewsbury, Burton, Halifax
Towns	e.g. Ashford, Bridgwater, Brecon
Sub-towns	A large number of small towns

Source: A. E. Smailes, 1946.

England and Wales is effectively integrated within a system of serving and controlling centres and covered by a complex of interlocking and overlapping urban spheres of influence.

At the highest hierarchical levels, a threefold classification below the level of London can be proposed. This includes a hierarchical array in which those dominant can be called A centres. They are Birmingham, Manchester, Liverpool, Leeds, Newcastle, Nottingham, Bristol, Sheffield, and Cardiff (Figure 4.8). These can be regarded as the *organising metropoles*. Linked to them are the B and C centres in a structure which indicates a series of sub-systems below the level of London, as capital, although London functions at this level also.

If one of these sub-systems is taken, then the lower hierarchical levels can be indicated and the spread of the national hierarchy to the more rural and thinly peopled parts traced. Thus Figure 4.9 indicates that immediately below the A level centre of Cardiff comes the B level centre of Swansea (the numbered lines relate to various areas: 1. Wales: the sphere of Cardiff, 2. the sphere of Swansea, 3. urban spheres of influence at the Aberystwyth level, 4. spheres at the Cardigan level, 5. Ceredigion District Boundary, 6. spheres at the Aberaeron level).

Figure 4.9 reinterprets this relationship in the spatial context of south and west Wales and links with the example given in detail in Figure 4.5. Immediately below Swansea are the three regional market-towns and administrative centres of Aberystwyth, Carmarthen, and Haverfordwest. If Aberystwyth is taken as representative of this level (c), then it can be seen that its hinterland covers the western coastal section of mid-Wales. At a lower d level this splits into a northern area, served by Aberystwyth, and a southern area served by Cardigan. Lampeter can also be considered to have functions at this level. At a lower order again the smallest urban settlements such as Tregaron provide the lowest-order services to immediately surrounding areas. Thus one can conceive of a progression down a firmly nested hierarchy of centres which proceeds: London-Cardiff-Swansea-Aberystwyth-Cardigan-Tregaron, giving a six-fold stratification of centres a to f.

It is interesting to observe that local conditions create modifications. Wales consists of

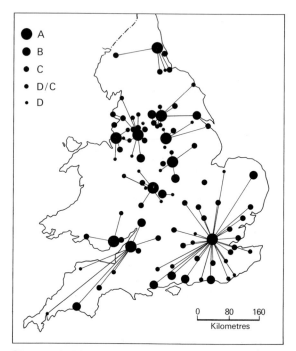

Figure 4.8 *The upper ranks of the urban hierarchy in England and Wales (after Kearsley)*

a thinly peopled upland core with a narrow periphery. The result is that its regional centres have never had the opportunity to grow supported by extensive rural areas intensively developed. In consequence, there is a level missing from the above sequence, but a level which can be identified in the towns along the English border. The interpolation of a town such as Shrewsbury, between Swansea and Aberystwyth, establishes an appropriate grade and a sevenfold system which Christaller envisaged. Here then is a general view of the urban hierarchy in England and Wales interpreted as being made up of discrete levels and effectively covering the whole country in a complex mesh of ranked centres and nested but overlapping tributary areas.

Conurbations and metropolitan counties

Although the name conurbation was coined in 1915, there was no formal recognition of such an entity in Britain until the 1951 census. Even then no objective data were used in defining the boundaries but what was termed in the census volume 'informed local opinion'. That presumably meant consultation with the local authorities concerned. Those identified in England were Greater London, Merseyside, South-East Lancashire, West Yorkshire, West Midlands and Tyneside. Each was based on a central city, London, Liverpool, Manchester, Leeds, Birmingham and Newcastle respectively. There was one conurbation recognised in Scotland, Clydeside with Glasgow its central city. There were no conurbations in Wales and Northern Ireland. It is possible, of course, to move beyond the census and to add what are sometimes called minor conurbations. But in that more general sense every large town, and indeed many small ones, are conurbations, that is what were once separate settlements have coalesced into one. The term is, therefore, best not debased in that way and retained for those major and distinctive agglomerations within the city system.

Even though recognised in the census returns, however, the conurbation had no administrative or governmental role – 'the term

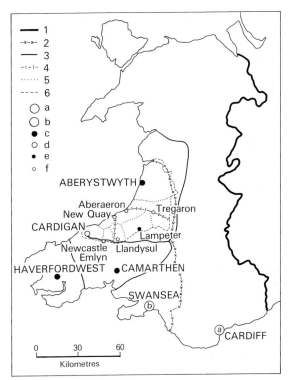

Figure 4.9 *The urban hierarchy in West Wales*

conurbation is a statistical artefact, not a precise legal or political entity' (G. Cameron, *The Future of the British Conurbation*, 1980). Local government was carried on by the county boroughs, boroughs, urban and rural districts which constituted the system until 1974. In that year, however, local government was reformed on a new principle. The old, as the names implied, had divorced urban and rural, the new was to bring them together into new counties and districts. It was logical, therefore, that the large urban territories should also be united under one jurisdiction and so in England the Metropolitan Counties were created and for the first time the conurbations were transformed into single governing authorities. In Scotland regional authorities were created on a different basis. In England the metropolitan counties established were Greater London, Greater Manchester, Merseyside, South Yorkshire, West Midlands, Tyne and Wear and West Yorkshire. Apart from two changes of name, South-East Lancashire to Greater Manchester and Tyneside extended to Tyne and Wear, there was only one addition, South Yorkshire centred on Sheffield. But already disillusion has set in and once again for local government purposes the metropolitan counties, including Greater London, are being broken down into their constituent boroughs. Thus the aim of establishing large urban areas as effective local government units has been abandoned and although data may still be presented according to conurbation or metropolitan county that will be the only purpose they serve.

The real problem for the geographer of settlement in studying these conurbations is that they do not have a lot in common in terms of their detailed internal structure. Generalisations can be made, especially as to the processes which created them, but the resultant structures are greatly diverse and need consideration in regional detail. But any discussion of the national settlement system must take account of these massive agglomerations of population which have occurred largely, though not completely, as the result of the rapid growth of

heavy industry on the coalfields and at the ports in the last century.

ASSIGNMENT

6. Table 4.6 below gives selected data for the British conurbations in 1971. Note that the figures are given in relation to a Great Britain average of 100. Is it possible to define common characteristics of the conurbations from these data? How do you explain the variations from the mean for each index which occur?

Megalopolis England

Beyond the scale of the conurbation lies metropolitan England or what can be called Megalopolis England. This does not imply continuous physical settlement but that the interdependencies and the interlinkages are such that functionally a massive area must be considered as one. The character and anatomy of this feature have been most clearly considered by Peter Hall. He constructs

Table 4.6 *Indices for British conurbations 1971*

	A. 1951–74 pop'n change index, (GB = 100)	B. 1971 % of Pop'n aged 15 to 59/64 (GB = 100)	C. 1971 % of house-holds with 5+ persons (GB = 100)	D. 1971 % of male labour force in s.e.g. 1–4 (GB = 100)	E. 1971 % of male labour force in s.e.g. 10–11 (GB = 100)	F. 1971 % of labour force both parents foreign born (GB = 100)	G. 1971 % of total workers in manuf. (GB = 100)	H. 1971 % of total workers in services (GB = 100)	I. 1971 % of house-holds in public sector rental (GB = 100)	J. 1971 % of house-holds in owner-occupied housing (GB = 100)	K. 1971 % of house-holds lacking basic amenities (GB = 100)	L. 1971 % of house-holds over-crowded (GB = 100)	M. 1971 % of house-holds with no car (GB = 100)
Central Clydeside	84.6	98.7	135.9	81.2	122.0	37.3	111.3	90.6	194.4	51.8	99.4	357.7	136.4
Greater London	77.1	104.7	88.0	120.6	91.2	266.1	78.6	123.6	81.9	83.6	122.2	118.3	109.4
Merseyside	78.4	98.5	131.0	80.6	139.5	49.2	97.7	96.1	109.9	82.6	125.3	116.9	120.8
South East Lancs.	88.1	99.5	99.3	96.4	113.2	108.5	125.8	83.3	97.7	105.6	127.8	93.0	118.1
Tyneside	83.8	100.5	98.6	77.0	116.6	23.7	106.7	97.3	143.1	65.2	117.7	135.2	134.2
West Midlands	94.4	102.2	111.3	85.5	117.1	174.6	155.6	70.9	130.3	93.8	100.0	111.3	104.5
West Yorkshire	92.1	98.8	93.0	89.7	115.1	123.7	130.1	83.9	101.3	108.3	91.1	97.2	122.0
Average index (unweighted)	85.5	100.4	108.2	90.1	116.4	111.9	115.1	92.2	122.7	84.4	111.9	147.1	120.3

Source: G. Cameron, *The Future of the British Conurbations.*

Megalopolis England from two basic functional building blocks. These are:

1. The *Standard Metropolitan Labour Area* (SMLA) which is made up of a core containing administrative areas with a density of 5.0 workers per acre (or 12.3 per hectare) or a single administrative area with over 20 000 workers, and a ring comprising contiguous areas which send over 15 per cent of their resident employed workers to the core. To qualify the total population must be over 70 000.
2. The *Metropolitan Economic Labour Area* (MELA) which is composed of the SMLA plus contiguous administrative areas which send more of their commuting workers to the SMLA core than to any other core.

When the SMLAs are arranged in rank order the break points can be identified by inspection and ranks established as in Table 4.7.

It will be noted that ranks 1 and 2, here defined on SMLA basis, correspond to the conurbations and ranks 2 and 3 to the Grade A cities which were earlier identified on a service basis. Virtually the whole of the country comes within the compass of MELAs and only parts of the south-west and Wales really lie beyond their influence. With these building blocks established, Hall proceeds to envisage Megalopolis England by constructing from

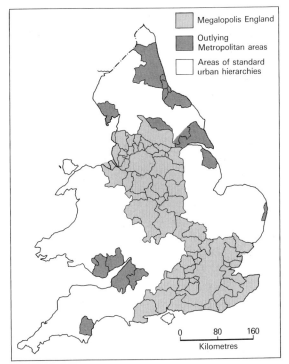

Megalopolis England

Outlying Metropolitan areas

Areas of standard urban hierarchies

0   80   160

Kilometres

Figure 4.10 *The urban structure of England and Wales*

these MELAs a set of contiguous areas which gave the maximum concentration of people in relation to their extent (Figure 4.10). In 1961 Megalopolis England so defined contained 56 per cent of the population of England and Wales living on only 7 per cent of the land and at a density of 6336 per square mile or 2446 per square kilometre. Again it must be stressed that this is not an area dominated by urban building.

'It is a giant urban area only in the sense that here is a large tract of the earth's surface where the great majority of people depend on urban jobs and urban services, and where the impact of these jobs and services, in terms of measurements like commuter zones, service areas and the exchange of goods and information, expands to involve each part of the area in a complex series of interactions with other parts.'

(Peter Hall)

The existence of this large-scale feature has implications for the notion of a city system.

Table 4.7 *Ranking of Standard Metropolitan Labour Areas in England and Wales*

1. London	
2. Birmingham	
Manchester	
Liverpool	
Leeds	
Newcastle-on-Tyne	
Sheffield	
3. Bristol	4. Stoke
Coventry	Leicester
Nottingham	Cardiff
	Hull
	Portsmouth
	Southampton

Source: P. Hall, 1973.

Within it, extensive commuting means that the town-country dichotomy becomes meaningless while ease of movement to service centres means that traditional hierarchies are likely to disappear. Out-of-town shopping centres in so-called rural surroundings and the growth of hypermarkets undermine the notion of conventional urban service centres. Above all, it is characterised by mobility at all scales. Essentially, therefore, a large part of England and Wales must be thought of in terms of this embracing megalopolitan structure which overshadows and integrates the separate pieces of which it is composed.

THE DEVELOPMENT OF THE URBAN SYSTEM: SOME GENERALISATIONS

An attempt can now be made to identify the major stages through which the system has evolved to reach its present condition.

The first stage can be called one of *Separation*, though in the absolute sense of the complete separation and the absence of interaction between towns it cannot be justified. Even the Roman towns of Britain, as elsewhere in the Empire, were formally and hierarchically organised in an administrative system. But at a time when transport was rudimentary, inter-city competition and the rank ordering of centres which follows from it was poorly developed. The structuring of the cities into a hierarchy was probably the consequence of the need for an effective system of government and law enforcement rather than of commercial rivalry.

The second stage can be more clearly seen as one of *Competition and Ordering*. As transport became somewhat easier and especially as administration become more effective, so interaction between centres became more important. With interaction came competition and the sorting of cities into some rank order. These early rankings have already been outlined, but it is not until the period 1600–1750 that they become convincing in terms of the modern implications of the concept of a hierarchy. If the highest ranked towns are considered – London followed by Norwich, York, Bristol, Newcastle, and Exeter – two features stand out. These cities were centres of early industry and above all of commerce. They were sea-ports at a time when sea transport was so much easier and effective. They were the major points of assembly and dispersal both of goods circulating internally via the coastal trade and of overseas imports and exports. By the eighteenth century, with improvements in roads and the growth of a network of stage-coach services and of carriers to market, the whole of England and Wales was served by a hierarchy of free-standing towns, and the city system effectively took in the whole national territory.

The third stage can either simply be called *Conurbation*, or one of *Revolution in Industry and Transport*. The so-called Industrial Revolution and the coming of the railway completely changed the older system. Both exerted a strong concentrating tendency largely based on the exploitation of point resources. To some extent also the railway permitted the major growth of inland centres though the ports still retained a dominant role. The result was the emergence of a number of conurbations owing little to the provision of services for rural hinterlands and superimposed on top and reacting with the older hierarchy. The higher-order towns of the earlier period were replaced by these new massive agglomerations based on the cities of Manchester, Birmingham, Leeds, and Sheffield in England, Glasgow in Scotland, Cardiff in Wales, and Belfast in Northern Ireland.

The next, or fourth stage, can be called one of *Integration*. During this the urban system based on the conurbation was gradually modified. In the period after the First World War, heavy industry and mining were in a state of decline while a more flexible road transport network grew at the expense of the railway. The result was a confirmation of metropolitan dominance and in particular the relative loss of importance by the outlying and marginal conurbations, such as Tyneside or South Wales. This is a period when the country became dominated by the flow of population into what was called the axial belt which extended from London to Manchester and which was identified as an hour-glass shaped feature containing the bulk of urban development. In more local terms this phase corresponded with the beginning of the process of decentralisation and suburban sprawl, some of which was contained in what are called suburban towns. This marks the filling out of territory, within the axial belt in particular, by physical development and the thickening of the complex urban web.

The fifth stage, which brings the process to the present, can be called *Metropolis and Megalopolis*. It is dominated by the rapid growth in private car ownership and motorway construction so that its dominant theme is that of mobility. This vast increase in mobility has produced a number of consequences. Place, as such, begins to lose its significance and people live in a number of what can be called '*realms*'. Thus to a businessman in the city of London, one realm will be the commuter village in which he lives, another the financial world including New York and Tokyo, with which he works. Some of these are aspatial, since contact with the local community or a business contact many thousands of miles away are as easily maintained. In order to meet the demands of the mobile person, and to offset city-centre congestion, out-of-town shopping centres and hypermarkets have developed. These in turn have contributed to the collapse of the established urban hierarchies. The result is a broad regional organisation of a much more complex form than the hierarchical notion of an earlier period. This transformation is certainly not complete even within Megalopolis England, but is still the dominant process and it is accompanied by the decline of the inner city

and the gradual dispersal of population into the outer rings of the metropolitan centres. It is perhaps possible to regard England and Wales as composed of three broad urban areas (Figure 4.10). The first is Megalopolis England, the second the outlying conurbations where modification is proceeding at a slower rate. The third area is made up of those remaining territories where the organisation is still based on ranked towns and nested spheres of influence.

CONCLUSION

This survey of the urban hierarchy in England and Wales has revealed how very far reality is removed from the predictions of theoretical models. The temptation arises, therefore, to dismiss the models as irrelevant. The massive movement of population into the conurbations during the last century and the first part of this, and the more recent dispersal of population and urban functions into the suburbs and beyond, have created patterns which cannot be directly interpreted by models derived to explain the size and distribution of free-standing cities. But that temptation should be resisted for the underlying principles still remain valid. Whatever the actual condition three basic circumstances need to be understood.

1. The operation of threshold and range which provide the limitations for any good or service offered.
2. The range of specialised functions which a town possesses and the controls which operate to locate them.
3. The nature of past growth, for what is present now is only a thin contemporary slice across a process of continuous change.

The Internal Structure of Towns

INTRODUCTION

Anyone who lives in or visits a town, and that means almost everyone in the developed world, is aware that within towns not only are there variations in the uses to which the land is put but that those variations show standard patterns which are similar for all towns. For the types of use a wide variety of every-day terms are employed: shopping centre, industrial estate, high-class residential area are examples. The purpose of this chapter is to introduce a standard terminology for these land-use regions and to develop a systematic analysis of their location. This will lead to an understanding of the internal structure of the town. In this chapter emphasis will be placed on towns of the developed world and a later chapter will consider differences in settlements in the Third, or less developed, World.

There are two approaches which can be adopted in relation to the purpose outlined above.

SIMPLE MODELS OF INTERNAL STRUCTURE: A DEVELOPMENTAL OR HISTORICAL APPROACH

It is self-evident that towns grow outward from a centre or nucleus but as they do so the varied users of land become separated one from the other, hence generating a standard pattern. This was the basic concept behind the best known of all generalisations or models of urban land-use, that proposed by E. W. Burgess as long ago as 1925. There is no doubt that growth was Burgess's main theme; he labelled his diagram, which is reproduced as Figure 5.1, 'The growth of the city'. This model, he argued, 'brings out clearly the main fact of expansion, namely, the tendency of each inner zone to extend its area by the invasion of the next outer zone'. If Figure 5.1 is examined then all the zones there shown were at one time in the early history of the city included within the circumference of the inner zone, the present city centre. But as the city grew those uses which most needed a central location came to monopolise the centre, buying up and replacing or converting buildings previously used for other purposes. Such uses were shops and offices and hence there developed what Burgess called the *Central Business District* (CBD), a term which has become very widely used. As the CBD extended, it displaced other uses, pushing them outward. Beyond the CBD there developed an area of mixed uses, mainly determined by their need to be near to the CBD; such were light industry and warehousing. Moreover, the period of change coincided with the coming of the railway which was able to push in toward the centre but never really penetrated into it.

As a result, railheads and transport depots also coincide with this '*zone in transition*', which was the name Burgess gave it. Outside it was the zone where heavy industry, a creation of the industrial revolution and the nineteenth century, developed. With it working-class housing was closely associated. *Intra-urban transport* (that is transport within the city) was very limited and people needed, for that reason and because of the cost, to live near to their place of work. Still later in date, and further out in location, the middle-class housing estates and, finally, on the periphery, the commuter

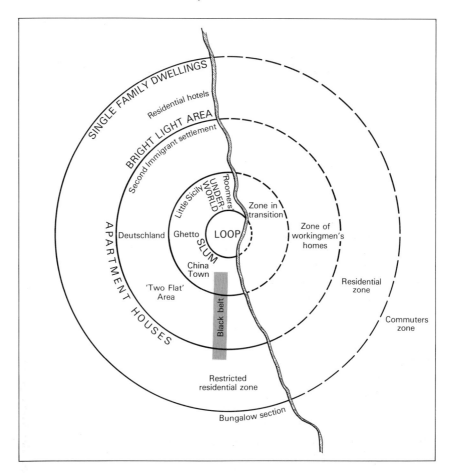

Figure 5.1 *The growth of the city (after E. W. Burgess)*

villes developed, latest in date and furthest in distance.

Two points of critical importance must be added:

a) Burgess was describing a very particular type of settlement at a specific point in time, that is the large industrial city in the mid-1920s.

b) Since it is an historical model, changes will have taken place since the date at which it was devised, and these will need to be considered later in the chapter.

SIMPLE MODELS OF INTERNAL STRUCTURE: AN ECONOMIC APPROACH

This approach can be called ahistorical, that is,

it does not rely on considering development at all but relies on economic processes. There are many apparent similarities to and overlaps with Burgess's model but the derivation is quite different in principle.

The starting point in an economic approach is the assumption that those who want to use urban land will have to bid for it as if in an auction; the highest bidder is successful and obtains the use of the land. The term used for the offer made at this imaginary auction is '*bid rent*'. The amount (the rent) that anyone can bid for land is, of course, determined by the returns or profits that are expected to be made from it. Therefore, the highest bidder will be the retailers, especially the large scale chain and department stores, for they will benefit most from maximum access to the greatest number of people. Office users, such as solicitors or accountants, will also obtain substantial advantage in being accessible to both shoppers and businesses, but they do not rely on casual passers-by so they will value central land a little less than the retailers, and their bid rents will be lower. It can be argued that industrial users, especially those in light industry, will need locations accessible to business offices and transport nodes but their need for real centrality is lower and they will make more modest bids. Residential users have a lot to gain from being 'at the centre of things', near to shops, entertainments and all the facilities of the CBD, but the 'profits' to be made are very much lower, whilst agriculture makes the least intensive, most extensive use of land and will make the lowest bids.

It is possible to put these results of the auction of city land onto a graph of bid rent against distance from the centre (Figure 5.2). The steepness of each graph varies. The retailers' bid rent curve, as it is called, will be the steepest since they need to be right at the heart of the city and the advantage of their location will drop off sharply from '*the peak land value*', that is the point at which bid rent is highest. As the primacy of need for a central

location falls, so the slope of the graph gets less and the bids of other users will be lower at the centre but relatively higher towards the periphery. The result is that the lines cross each other at the point where the bid of the succeeding user becomes greater than the one in toward the centre. This is illustrated in Figure 5.3.

Now line AB is just one of the radii from the centre. The same will be true of all the radii so that each point on AB can be swung around in a circle and a series of concentric zones will be produced closely similar to those in Burgess's model. The end result is the same, although the basis of derivation is greatly different. Even so, the parallels are apparent for the mechanics of the hiving off of uses with growth in Burgess's scheme depends on the same principle of the evaluation of central locations and the willingness to pay for them which underpins the economic approach.

ASSIGNMENT

1. Examine your own or nearest town to see if you can identify concentric zones of land-use.

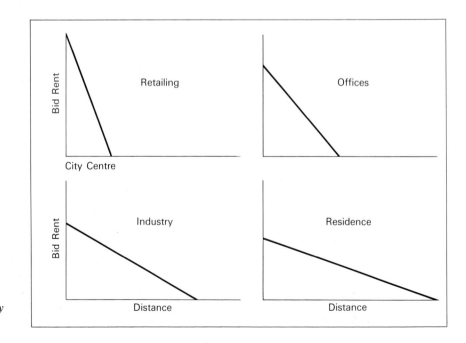

Figure 5.2 *The rents bid by varying uses of urban land in relation to distance from the city centre*

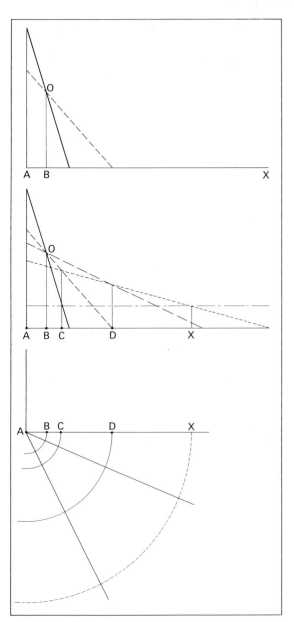

Figure 5.3 *The change of land user in relation to rent bid. A is the town centre and B, C, D, X the uses outlined in Fig. 5.2*

MODIFICATIONS OF THE SIMPLE MODELS

Close examination of Figure 5.2, and the results of your own examination of a sample town, will reveal at least one clear anomaly. If access to the centre is the most prized attribute of residential use, and land is more expensive towards the centre, then according to the diagram and the arguments which have been put forward, those who can pay the most will live at the centre and the poorest will live at the margin. Now that is not totally untrue, as will be found out when Third World cities are considered (Chapter 7), and even in the great cities of the developed world the luxury apartment block is found near city centres; think of London's Mayfair and Belgravia or the recent Barbican developments or New York's Fifth Avenue at Central Park. But, in general terms, it is not so. The poor and deprived live in the inner city, the rich in the marginal commuter villages. At this point, therefore, it is necessary to introduce the notion of a trade-off.

In all the discussion so far, one thing alone has been set up as epitomising what is most desirable, and that is centrality. But there are other things, especially where residences are concerned. These are such things as the quantity of land and environmental quality. If one is bidding for land there is the option of bidding for a greater amount of cheaper land and since people do not want to be crowded they can choose to live further out and have more land; there is a trade off of quantity against distance. Again, the inner city areas are densely occupied and congested, totally built up, and a 'greener, cleaner' more peaceful location might be chosen. Again there is a trade off; a more open, greener environment against a longer, more expensive journey to work. But it is only the better off who have the money to exercise such a choice and generally that choice has been for the outer suburban areas, hence the reversal of the situation expected from the graphs.

It is now apparent that there is a great deal more complexity to city structure than is portrayed by a series of simple concentric zones. Four further aspects have to be considered which make further modifications. These are, (i) building height, (ii) directional contrasts, (iii) planning controls, and (iv) city size.

Figure 5.4 *Cape Town. The CBD and District 6. The limits of the CBD are virtually defined by the high rise blocks which house mainly retail uses on the lowest levels with offices on the upper floors. This is now a universal pattern in all large cities of the world. But on this picture note especially the open area beyond the CBD. This is District 6, an area which was cleared of mixed race occupation under the Group Areas Act which has never been redeveloped, largely because of local opposition to the whole process of enforced segregation*

Building height

It has been assumed in all the comment made to this point that the city has only two dimensions, that it is constituted by a flat, single storied layer of land-uses. That is manifestly not so. The city is composed of buildings varying in height and with the type of use also varying from floor to floor. Two further questions have, therefore, to be answered – why are there great variations in the height of buildings? And, how does use vary with height?

Variations in height. It has already been ob-

served that city land varies in value, that higher bid rents are offered for some locations as against others, and that the highest offers are for city centre land. If a very high bid has had to be made for a location there is one way of off-setting the cost and that is by exploiting the accessibility it offers by increasing the intensity of use. That can be done by accommodating as many users as possible by building high. There is a direct relationship between the height of buildings and land values and hence the well-nigh universal way in which the CBD of a modern city stands out by the height of its buildings (Figure 5.4 Cape Town). Where the land is most valuable, there the highest buildings will occur since the maximum return must be extracted. Hence the famous Manhattan skyline with its skyscrapers. Building height is, of course, also limited by the available technical expertise. It was not until the invention of the hydraulic lift, and especially the electric lift in 1887, and the steel-frame building that skyscrapers could be constructed.

There is another and different type of high building and that is the highrise tower block for residential purposes. The critical control is similar, the need to make the maximum use of a limited resource, the land available. Tower blocks were built in the belief that, through their use, high residential densities could be achieved. The highrise block is no more than a terrace raised on its end. But whereas the terrace provided easy horizontal movement, easy external access both front and back and usually limited garden space, the tower block offers difficult and inconvenient vertical access via lifts, difficult external access, from the upper floors especially, and no family recreational space. As a result, as far as mass housing was concerned, they have been a disastrous failure (see page 104).

Variations in use with height. It has just been pointed out that the tower block is a terrace standing on its end; a central city skyscraper is, in similar terms, a radius out from the centre standing on its end. If one takes the succession of land-uses from the centre outward – shops, offices, industry, residence – it is possible to argue that, with some modification, the same succession occurs upward in the central tall building. The ground floor will be given over to shops, even possibly a shopping precinct in a major development, or a bank. Above will be offices. Industry, of course, is unlikely because of its demand for extensive space, but it is not impossible to find specialised industry using high value materials and intricate manipulation; fine jewellery or haute couture are examples. At the top of the block there may well be flats or apartments leading to the penthouse suite,

equating with the outer city ring of the highest status residences. There might even be a roof garden to parallel the greenery of the outer suburbs! Finally, one of the characteristic uses of land about the centre is car parking and there might well be a basement car park to the block with a parallel downward shift in altitude away from the ground floor.

A critical reading of this chapter must now generate an immediate question. If the most sought after residential location is a penthouse suite, why are exactly similar points in other high-rise towers not equally regarded? The answer lies partly in accessibility; a block at the city centre giving access to all its facilities is very different from one on an estate on the city's periphery. It also lies partly in the very specific environment and standard of building and furnishing of the blocks (see page 104).

Directional contrasts

The ideas developed by Burgess and derived from the analysis of bid rents both assumed that the city was structured into a series of concentric zones. It was soon realised that the factual evidence derived from considering actual cities by no means supported that assumption. The major objection was developed in the 1930s by Homer Hoyt who was the Principal Housing Economist in the USA Federal Housing Administration. As that office implies, he was interested in residential areas rather than the whole range of uses but even so his conclusions had relevance for the whole city structure. Hoyt plotted rental values (especially the high values) for a number of American cities and concluded that the highest values only occupied a part, never the whole, of the outer circumference of the city. Cities did not conform to a simple pattern of zones with residential quality increasing with distance from the centre; rather, they displayed a sectoral pattern, that is, high quality residences were only found in some limited sectors and the city was structured more in the way of wedges. In short, a directional element from the centre was as important as distance.

Hoyt proposed a sectoral model for the city (Figure 5.5) and explained it by arguing that the high-grade residential area had its point of origin near the retail and office centre. Note the agreement with Burgess that all uses were at one time contained in the centre. But as the city grew the high-grade area extended outwards along a radius rather than was successively displaced as a series of rings. Hoyt put forward six reasons:

1. High-grade residential growth tends to proceed from the given point of origin along established lines of travel or toward a specific nucleus of buildings which offer attractions.
2. Such growth develops along the fastest existing transport lines.
3. High-rent areas tend to progress towards high ground free from the risk of floods, and to spread along lake, bay, river, and ocean fronts, where such water fronts are not used for industry.
4. High-rent residential districts tend to grow towards the section of the city which has free, open country beyond the edges.
5. The higher-priced residential neighbourhood tends to grow towards the homes of leaders of the community.
6. Trends of movement of office buildings, banks and stores pull higher-priced residential neighbourhoods in the same general direction.

Hoyt added another possible influence, noting that estate agents, those responsible for selling houses, can bend the direction of extension by their promotion activities. This introduces the third of these modifying factors.

Planning controls and other interventions

So far, the whole of this consideration of internal city structure has been founded on the concept of a completely free market. The very terms used – auction, bid rent – are part of an open, unconstrained process. But again, every reader will know that such a situation is not so. A limited example is sufficient in illustration. The Manhattan skyline of New York does not consist of a simple series of rectangular blocks, for most have wide bases with a sequence of shoulders leading to a thinner capping section. The reason can be traced back to the early days when it was feared that a series of unmodified towers would cast shadows on each other and leave the streets permanently darkened by shadow. Accordingly, in 1916, the city of New York adopted a 'Building Zone Resolution' which set up legal control over the height and arrangement of buildings and imposed a progressive set back of exterior walls above a height determined according to the rule of the 'sky angle'. This produced the leaner summits on much wider bases and the characteristic indented Manhattan skyline. So the most widely known city centre profile, in the country with the freest market economy, is, in reality, the product of planning constraints.

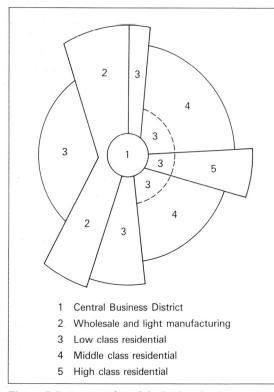

1 Central Business District
2 Wholesale and light manufacturing
3 Low class residential
4 Middle class residential
5 High class residential

Figure 5.5 *A sectoral model of urban land-uses (after Hoyt)*

Apart from the very special example of the Manhattan skyline, intervention by municipal authorities has constantly modified the free operation of the market system. Indeed, New Towns have been planned from the beginning and are totally the product of the planning authority and presumably owe little to the processes which this chapter has been considering.

In most cases in the western democracies, intervention is intermediate in scale between the complete planning of a New Town and the marginal changes brought about by simply limiting conditions of development. The best illustration is in the field of residential development where municipal authorities have been responsible for the extensive provision of housing and, thereby, the creation of quite distinctive residential areas in the so-called council housing estates. Legislation in Britain allowing municipalities to construct housing gets back to the Lodging Houses Act of 1851 but that, as the name implies, referred only to lodging houses and it was the Labouring Classes Dwelling Houses Act of 1866 which allowed the erection of housing. The major piece of legislation was the Housing and Town Planning Act of 1919, usually known as the Addison Act. This imposed the duty on all authorities to survey their areas and to make and carry out plans for the provision of houses. There has been a mass of subsequent legislation, generally related to the financial issues of deriving the capital to build and determining the rent to be charged. But the result has been the contribution of a major section of the housing stock which, until the sale of council houses set out in the Housing Act of 1980, did not enter the market at all. In 1951, 31 per cent of British houses were owner-occupied, 52 per cent rented privately and 17 per cent rented from public authorities, that is were council housing. By 1984 these figures had changed dramatically to 59 per cent owner occupied, only 7 per cent rented privately and 33 per cent rented from local authorities or from an employer. Private rental has virtually disappeared again, largely because of legislation

in the Rent Acts. The critical point is that all this is the consequence of the actions of government and that the character of residential areas has been moulded by those actions, not by the market forces with which most analyses begin.

Comment on this point has been solely concerned with the principle of intervention and its extent. What matters most to the urban geographer is the locational consequence. Because council housing has been a feature since 1919, it is of varying age and character and widely distributed throughout the city. But two predominant locations can be identified.

1. Council estates built soon after the Second World War under an extensive programme for the provision of housing. The houses, usually semi-detached, were of a fairly uniform design conforming to minimum structural standards. In the rush to provide houses, few amenities were built and the estates are somewhat bleak in character. More recent development has followed the same trend. Land was most easily available at the city margins and especially in those sectors of it where private housing had not been located, mainly due to the inverse of the reasons advanced by Hoyt. Municipal housing estates of this type, therefore, are primarily sectoral in distribution and break across any zonal arrangement.

2. The 1960s was the decade of the highrise tower blocks. Such structures were especially used in the process of redevelopment of the obsolete terrace housing of the inner parts of the city. High densities needed to be retained to avoid excessive sprawl at the fringes and they were accomplished by these high blocks.

City size

In his concentric zone model, Burgess assumed reference to large, industrial cities and it follows that variation will result if the size category, vaguely termed large, is itself varied. To some degree this was covered by Burgess's developmental derivation of his model, and by his statement that all the varied uses were contained together in the initial nucleus and only became separated into zones, and segregated from each other, with growth. This clearly implies that the degree to which the various land-uses are separated depends on the amount of growth, or more directly and simply, on the size of the settlement. In the smallest towns uses will remain interspersed and, at most, a two-fold division between a mixed-use centre and a residential surround will be recognisable. At the opposite end of the scale, in the large cities, a much more highly developed separation will take place. In the great metropolis the terms so far used become inappropriate – 'Central Business District' applied to London has no meaning for the central area has itself become a complex of different regions within which very highly specialised users have tended to congregate together. It is possible to begin an analysis of these regions in central London by just writing down the specialised parts which are accepted by common consensus and used in every-day terminology:

1. The West End	Shopping, entertainment, high quality residence
2. Westminster	National Government
3. The City	Finance, business
4. The East End	Industry, low quality residence
	(An area being modified by change in Dockland. But note the use of the term by a TV soap opera as indicative of its special character.)

What has occurred is that with the greatest growth and at the largest scale, the CBD has itself broken down into its specialised components which remain mixed together even in the large town. This parallels the way in which the uses once mixed in the early nucleus or core of a town have become separated with growth; the process has advanced with scale. The most elementary interpretation of the London situation tabulated above would be to

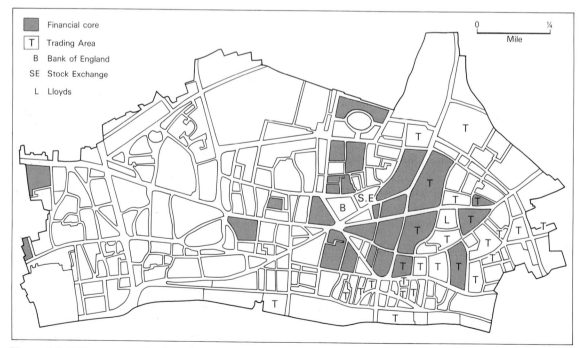

Figure 5.6 *Office areas in the City of London (after Goddard)*

identify four types of use which have, as it were, crystallised out: shopping, administration, finance and industry. But, in a metropolis as large as London, these general use-areas themselves become broken down into still more highly specialised components. Thus one refers to theatreland where entertainment becomes predominant. Figure 5.6 is based on a complex statistical analysis of employment as a surrogate for actual land-use. It indicates just two of the complex of interacting regions, or grouping of activities, which make up the City of London, or just 'The City'. The more central region the author has called the financial core. It is characterised by banks and insurance companies. Note how it groups about the Bank of England and the Stock Exchange. In contrast is the second area shown, the trading region which consists of merchants and dealers concerned with commodities. Its predominantly eastern location reflects its relation to the warehouses and docks which once dominated London's maritime trade. This map was published in 1968. There have been very many changes since then for in such dynamic cities as London change is always acting against the long-standing stability generated by such institutions as the Bank of England. But the Stock Exchange has lost some of its dominance as a physical institution and it will be interesting to see what locational consequences follow.

The question now is in what sequence do uses become segregated as size increases. It is a particularly difficult question to which there is no clear answer, even when given a lengthy historical review. In very general terms, if one takes out shopping as the predominant use then possibly, with the great increase in local government since the 1880s, administrative uses of land have increased considerably and large cities will have distinctive administrative areas, although not always at the city centre. Another trend beginning in the last century was the increase in specialised financial areas characterised by an association of stock exchange, banks and related activities such as insurance. Distinctive and separate administrative and financial areas are those which are most likely to emerge out of the mixed CBD.

It is both possible and useful to set out the analysis which has been undertaken so far in the form of a brief tabulation:

The Simple Model	Developmental or Historical Approach	
The Simple Model	Economic Approach	
		Anomalies in the simple model
Modifications of the Simple Model	i. Building Height	a) Variations in height b) Variations in use with height
	ii. Directional Contrasts	Sectoral model
	iii. Planning Controls and Other Interventions	
	iv. City Size	

Having worked through these varied influences, it is apparent that the simple zonal or sectoral models are good devices for starting to understand the internal structure of the city, but they are little more than that, for in reality one is dealing with a mosaic of areas rather than idealised geometric patterns. Moreover, there is still one further step to take. The models which have been introduced were developed prior to the Second World War in relation to cities as they then were. Considerable changes have taken place since then and these have not been added into the analysis.

ASSIGNMENTS

2. Re-examine your own or nearest town, to see whether high and low quality areas form rings or wedges (sectors) or a combination of both. You now meet a universal research problem in human geography. You have a problem – or hypothesis: the city is structured in a series of zones/sectors.

Now you need the data to work with. So far rents and bid rents have been mentioned but there is no way in which you can collect rental values. You are, therefore, forced to use a substitute – or a *surrogate* as it is called. In Britain at present, and until the community charge is implemented, every property has a rateable value which is used to assess the rates (local taxation) which the owner has to pay. The rateable value is theoretically the amount at which the property could be let given the standard landlord and tenant agreement. So you could plot rateable values – and they have been widely used by geographers. You could also assemble as wide an array as possible of the actual costs of houses from sales and auctions. But both the above are very lengthy and tedious jobs and at this stage it is sufficient for you to use your own judgement and block in on a map which are the most expensive residential areas and which the cheapest. Having done that examine the patterns and make an interpretation in the terms of distance and direction.

3. Return to the patterns for your own town and consider whether all or any of the above reasons apply.
4. If you live in or near to a New Town, examine its land-use pattern and consider whether it has anything in common with the model schemes which have been presented.
5. Locate the main areas of council housing in your own or nearest town and examine its character and distribution in relation to the ideas set out above. Are the council housing areas growing and, if not, why not?

RECENT TRENDS IN URBAN LAND-USE

The predominant trends in the period since the traditional models were suggested have virtually set in reverse those processes on which they were based. Concentration or centralisation, by which all the users of urban land competed for central locations, has been substituted by dispersal by which users have looked to land on the fringes of the city. This has not been so thorough-going or so complete as to invalidate the processes which have been examined to this point, for much of the past is still extant. So much must be evident from local examples. But substantial modification has resulted. Some modification has already been made to account for the strong movement of high quality residential areas to the fringe of the growing city. The peripheral location of some municipal housing estates has also been noted. These form the jumping-off points for the review of recent trends, for it was in response that industry, too, began to relocate. This can be traced back to the 1930s in both the UK and the USA but became much more significant after the Second World War. There were very good reasons for the trend:

1. The residential movements meant that labour supplies, and especially the higher paid skilled labour which could most afford peripheral locations, were now becoming much more easy to assemble at the urban fringe.
2. Modern industrial or manufacturing technology very often requires continuous conveyor belt handling at a single level. It sets up a demand, therefore, for extensive areas of land which are either not available or prohibitively expensive at the centre.
3. The transportation of both raw materials and finished goods has become increasingly difficult in the congested city centre. Moreover, a major switch has taken place from rail to road transport so that the best locations are no longer those with access to railway stations but to the motorway system. New sites on urban ring roads where they intersect motorways provide the best access both to sources and to markets. The rush in the late 1980s to push forward developments where the newly completed M25 around London intersects the other motorways is an admirable example.
4. The inner parts of many UK and western European cities, the traditional location for industry, were greatly damaged during the War and have been comprehensively re-

developed subsequently. This has meant that the old industrial buildings have been demolished and have been substituted by new ones much further out.

5. In the process of redevelopment the industrial estate, often partly financed by public money, has played an important part. Again, for reasons of space demands, such estates are usually developed on the fringes of the city and pull industry with them.

For all these reasons and in a mutually reinforcing way, residence and industry have extended markedly on the urban periphery. These, in turn, have been quickly followed by retailing where internal technological changes marked by the development of the supermarket and the hypermarket have also been influential. Again the reasons for retailing's outward movement can be set out:

1. The peripheral distribution of the most affluent sections of the population meant that the most profitable markets were in the outer areas.
2. The growing extent of car ownership meant that people, and again the most affluent with most money to spend, were more mobile and independent of the city-centre orientated public transport systems.
3. The great volume of traffic at the city centre led to congestion, difficulty of access and, especially, lack of convenient parking facilities. Marginal sites allowed easy access and extensive free parking.
4. The supermarket or hypermarket, planned on a large scale to provide maximum economies derived from size (economies of scale), and on a single level for easy movement with shopping basket or trolley, needed extensive floor areas and hence sites where the costs of land acquisition are low.
5. Easy access by delivery vans is needed by modern shops. Here again an open site near to a motorway provided the best conditions.

The result of these influences has been the creation of large suburban and out-of-town shopping centres and a limitation of retail development at the centre. But it is necessary now to invoke those constraints on free market activities which are consequent upon planning controls. The potential massive shift of retailing from the town centre could do great damage to that part of the settlement; indeed, that has happened in many North American cities to such an extent that one author refers to a former Mayor of Detroit as identifying 'Detroit's sister cities – Nagasaki and Pompeii'! In Britain, town planners have opposed massive out-of-town shopping centres and hence the process has been a much more subdued one, although, of course, suburban shopping centres have grown considerably.

A subsequent mover to the outer city has been office use. It has been generally less developed than retailing but has moved with it for similar reasons. These include:

1. The attraction of new, purpose-built accommodation in a pleasant, green environment.
2. Modern offices with the increasing use of information technology need fewer employees but more floor space and this is very much cheaper at the fringe.
3. Adequate car parking can be easily and cheaply provided without having to resort to specialised multi-storey or basement solutions.
4. One of the traditional reasons for the location of offices in city centres was the need for immediate access to information upon which decisions are made. The revolution in information technology based upon microelectronic systems has met that need in non-central locations.
5. The association both with new industry and with modern retail facilities has encouraged office uses to move to keep in association with compatible users.

These recent changes in land-use location have had a significant impact upon patterns of inequality in the city. These will be dealt with in the next chapter but before moving to that topic some exemplification is needed of the very generalised statements which have been presented in this chapter.

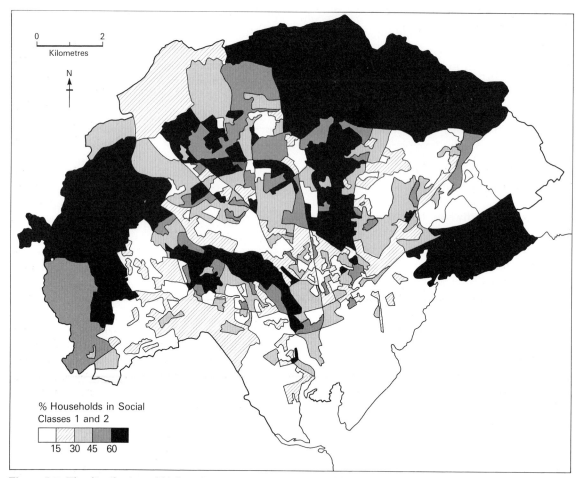

0   2
Kilometres

N

% Households in Social
Classes 1 and 2

15 30 45 60

Figure 5.7 *The distribution of high socio-economic status in Cardiff*

MODELS AND REALITY: SOME EXAMPLES

So far in this chapter the discussion of internal
structure has been largely theoretical and based
on deductive argument. That is, it has been
developed not from looking at a large number
of actual towns but rather from a number of
general assumptions of how city land is vari-
ously valued according to the needs of different
users. From time to time it has been suggested
that you check some of the derived patterns
against reality in towns known to you. It is
important, however, to introduce some exemplification into this chapter in order to make
some pertinent comment on the relation
between models and reality. A problem does
arise in that any example will be particular and
unknown in any detail to most readers of this
chapter. So it must be stressed that the examples which follow are introduced in order to
demonstrate the specific issue of the relation
between generality and the actual city, not to
provide a case study to be adopted. It will be
far more beneficial to use a town well known

to you as your case study regarding it from the point of view of the principles set out in this chapter.

Figure 5.7 presents the distribution of socio-economic status in Cardiff. It is based on census data as to social class so the map is based on hard, factual data and is not a subjective impression by the author.

Examination of the map will show that the distribution of socio-economic status does not accord in any simple or direct fashion with the general models presented at the beginning of this chapter. The first feature that stands out is a zone of low status which rings around the CBD and links with the dock area to the south. But the encirclement is not complete. Note how a line of relatively high social status extends north-westward from the CBD along the southern edge of the flood plain of the river Taff. It is not continuous, for the unshaded areas, representing open, flood plain land, break it up into a discontinuous feature. Although discontinuous, this constitutes a clear sector. There are two other sectors which can be identified. The clearer one with the higher values extends due south-north, whilst the other, somewhat broken and not nearly as easily demonstrated, lies between the two already noted, the one along the Taff and the one extending south to north. There also appears to be an eastern sector. These high-status sectors are separated by lower-status areas also, therefore, predominantly in sectoral form.

Two further elements making up the total pattern can be noted.

At the very heart of the city there is clearly, even if faintly, a higher status area around the CBD, one which is largely made up of purpose-built high-rental flat blocks and some older buildings, either still single family dwellings or converted into flats. They almost make up an innermost zone.

In two areas, one directly to the west, the other to the north east, sectors of low status (they are municipal housing estates) give way quite sharply at or beyond the city boundary to high-status areas. That is, the character of the sector changes so that there is nearly an outer encircling, but discontinuous, zone of high status.

In this interpretation of the map no place names have been used in order to avoid the particularisation of the example chosen. The conclusion from the interpretation must be that whereas the simple models cannot be applied, for all the reasons which have already been put forward as complicating factors, nevertheless the key to understanding is provided by them. The real world example demonstrates an inter-action of zones and sectors which leads to the need to invoke both distance and direction in explanation. It would be possible to provide more detailed support by looking at more local circumstances. One example must suffice. The first sector which was identified, a high-status extension north-west along the river Taff, was a response to the attraction of the open, green land of the flood plain which belonged to the most significant family in Cardiff (the Marquesses of Bute), and which was preserved by that family from being developed. It also led to the Cathedral village of Llandaff. A check back will show how those controls are found in the list set out by Hoyt as responsible for sectoral extension.

Figure 5.8 lifts out the CBD from Figure 5.7 and enlarges it. The sites of the castle, the railway stations and the Arms Park National Stadium (Cardiff) enable the relationship between the two maps to be established. This is a generalised land-use map not indicating the use of each building or of each floor. It shows how the centre is dominated by retailing as would be expected, although not in the form of a circular core or nucleus but as two major streets meeting near the castle. Two other uses are predominant and surround the shopping streets. These are offices and warehousing. Again this reflects in principle, if not in detail, the generalisations which were earlier proposed. There are, of course, a good number of other uses but they are all of a minor order, often no more than one or two special buildings, such as the fire station and telephone exchange; but note the open space to the west made up of Cardiff Arms Park in the south and of the conserved valley land to the north. The largest additional distinctive area lies outside the central area as defined on the map and that is a northern extension which has been marked as Cathays Park. It is not a park in the normal sense but a very extensive administrative and educational area. It includes both buildings of local significance (Cardiff City Hall) and of national character (the National Museum of Wales, the University of Wales Registry). In short, administration has hived off to a very distinctive and clearly separated area.

Financial uses are not identified on this map and it would be difficult to argue that such a distinctive sub-area dominated by them exists in Cardiff. But the section between the Arms Park and the shopping area which is marked as offices is composed primarily of banks and can be put forward with some reservations as constituting a financial area. The implications

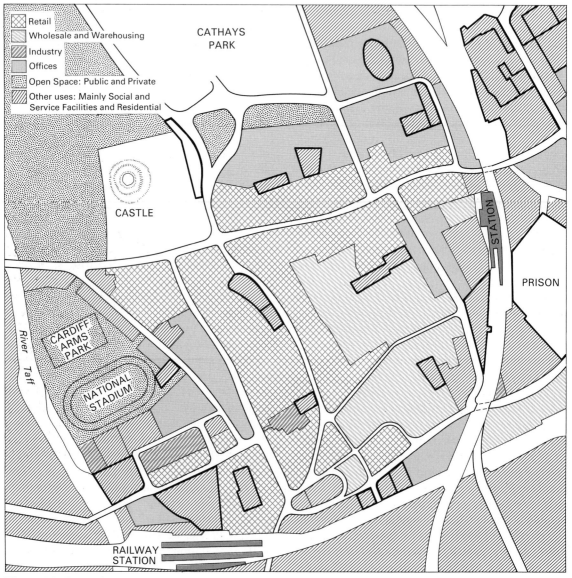

Figure 5.8 *Ground-uses in Central Cardiff*

are that neither in size nor in functional role is the city quite large enough to generate a separate and clearly identifiable financial section. Compare this with the situation in London already described. It is also partly due to the fact that when in the past Cardiff was important in that financial role, especially in the coal trade, the coal exchange and associated financial institutions were located in the dock area well to the south of the present CBD and are now in a state of decline.

Once again, therefore, it can be maintained that although local detail results in a pattern very specific to this city, in general terms the forces which have been put forward as the main controls have been seen to be operative. Moreover, a further element can be added. The map is not one of Cardiff at the immediate present for since then planning processes have wrought change. The central area of warehousing has been considerably reduced and the space has been used in the construction of a new shopping centre, the St. David's Centre, complete with concert hall. In the centre, as well as in the residential areas, planning operates as a modifier, an intervener in the evolution of market force control.

In the brief consideration of Cardiff no mention has been made of an equivalent of the zone of industry and working men's housing which appears on the classic model. Certainly a 'middle city' can be identified but industry in Cardiff grew about the docks south of the city centre where it was largely confined. In order to illustrate the earlier character of such a zone and something of more recent transformation the central part of Birmingham can be briefly studied. Perhaps, of all the cities of Britain, Birmingham best illustrated a distinctive zone of industry which encircled the city centre. The industry itself was characterised by that great variety which was typical of the skilled metallurgical and associated trades. The most well known features were the gun and jewellery quarters. In 1956 some 24 per cent of industrial workers in the West Midlands conurbation were located in central Birmingham, but the firms were generally small in size and many of

the premises were old and inefficient. The industrial establishments were surrounded by and interspersed with terraced housing, also dating back to the nineteenth century, so that in 1946 some 72 per cent were considered unfit for habitation. The zone had been further downgraded by the effect of war-time bombing. Here then was a clear ring of industry and housing according to the classic model which, as has been emphasised, was set out in accordance with conditions in the mid-1920s representing mainly nineteenth century growth.

Birmingham took action earlier than most cities under the regulations of the 1944 Town and Country Planning Act. The basis of the schemes adopted was to clear the whole industrial/residential area and rebuild it, and extensively to remodel the central area itself. Within the housing and industry zone five areas were defined for comprehensive redevelopment. These were Ladywood, Newtown, Nechells Green, Highgate and Leebank, and can be seen on Figure 5.10. These have become

Figure 5.9 *Cardiff: the CBD and Cathays Park. Compare this with the photograph of Cape Town and with Figure 5.8. The distinctive boundary to the central area given by the railway in the foreground is apparent as is also the process of redevelopment in the centre itself. Note especially in the middle ground to the right (east) of the open space, the very distinctive administrative area of Cathays Park*

known as the five 'new towns' of Birmingham. Given the needs and beliefs of the time, high-rise blocks played an important part in these comprehensively redeveloped areas. Along with them went areas specifically given over to industry but inevitably there was a loss both of enterprises and employment.

Part of the replanning of most cities has had to take account of vastly increased traffic flows. Birmingham, like many others, has tried to solve the problem by avoiding the necessity of all traffic proceeding through the centre by establishing a ring road which takes it around. The present central business district of Birmingham is virtually defined by its inner ring road. Within that central area there was also extensive change. One railway station (Snow Hill) was merged with another (New Street) and the whole remodelled with the new Bull Ring shopping centre as a part of it. The process was far more fundamental than in Cardiff for as one author has stated, Victorian Birmingham will finally be reduced to a number of isolated relics, as are the medieval and Georgian periods today, and the central area will be wholly the product of the second half of the present century.

CONCLUSION

Birmingham, like Cardiff, illustrates both that internal city patterns of land-use are universal, the products of the general influences which the models depict, and that they are also individual and particular and the consequence of the impact of intervention and planning. But planning, too, operates on the basis of accepted tenets and works towards standardised systems such as ring roads and pedestrian precincts. It is possible to argue that two widely different sets of forces are in operation. On the one hand there is the absolutely free market uninhibited by control, much as in the models with which the chapter began. At the other extreme there are the completely planned towns often associated with absolutist regimes where market forces are excluded. But even in democratic regimes completely planned towns are built such as the British New Towns. Ultimately convenience becomes the main arbiter and there is a convergence of both extremes so that cities are perhaps not as very greatly different as might at first be expected. And convenience is merely another way of expressing the different spatial demands of land-uses with which the chapter began.

ASSIGNMENT

7. Consider whether the pattern of land-uses in a town completely planned would be different from that in which no planning was involved. How do you explain the differences?

Figure 5.10 *Central Birmingham* © *Ordnance Survey*

6

Inequalities within Cities

INTRODUCTION

The last chapter presented a general interpretation of the reasons why cities show a distinctive arrangement of land-uses within them. Residential use, as one of the land-use types, was seen to be not a homogeneous category but one which could be sub-divided on the basis of socio-economic status and which can further be sub-divided on the basis of racial or ethnic character. Most of the recently published research studies in urban geography in Britain have been concerned with that situation and especially with demonstrating and explaining the gross inequalities which cities reveal. Great contrasts do exist in western countries between the rich and the poor, although in world terms one might wish to insert the adjective 'relatively' at the beginning of the sentence. Those contrasts appear most vividly in the cities. But there is not only an economic basis but also an ethnic or racial one. There is, for example, a high degree of segregation between white and black in the USA, as there is between indigenous and immigrant populations in the United Kingdom. In locational or geographical terms this is expressed as the great gap between the affluent marginal suburbs and the depressed and declining inner city. The problems of the inner city have been made manifest by the series of riots which have characterised them, reaching a peak in the USA in the late 1960s, and in the United Kingdom in the early 1980s when the names of urban districts such as Brixton, Toxteth and Handsworth became widely known to the British public.

There is a further section of the population which is generally associated with poverty and deprivation: the elderly. Now, by no means all the elderly are poor – any more than all the members of ethnic minorities are poor – but there is, nevertheless, a widespread acceptance of a correlation between old age and disadvantage and that, too, must be included as part of this investigation. Against the general background of internal city structure set out in Chapter 5, this chapter seeks to consider the character of and the reasons for locational inequalities in the residential zones of cities.

Figure 6.1 *Inner city dereliction*

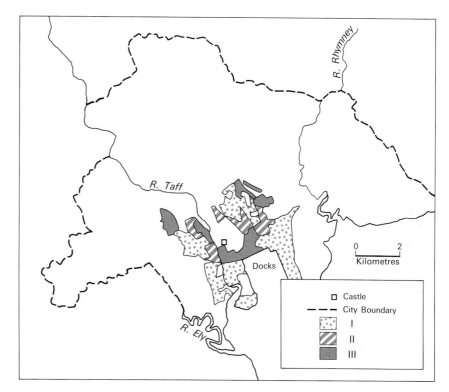

Figure 6.2 *Cardiff. The distribution of deprived groups 1971 (after Davies)*

THE CHARACTERISTICS OF THE INNER CITY

The first and essential step is to review the relevant facts and this can best be done by taking two examples of quite different character. An obvious procedure is to look again more closely at one of the examples used already in Chapter 5. In a study of Cardiff, W. K. D. Davies identified three groups of areas where there was some element of deprivation. These he identified as:

1. Inner city: decay and immigration. This group of areas is principally associated with areas of substandard housing, immigrants and low social status.

2. Inner city: non-family and transient. There the characteristics are very similar to Group *1.*, but with a high proportion of young adults and single people, a transient or a changing population and a good deal of bed-sitting room accommodation. Burgess included this in his zonal scheme using the American description of 'rooming-house' (see Fig. 5.1, page 81).

3. Inner city: ageing status. This had a more mixed character with not only young single but also an elderly population and also some high status. Davies interpreted this as formerly of high status but now with a residual old population and an invading young section of the 'bed-sit' type.

These groups are mapped in Figure 6.2. Some comment has already been made in Chapter 5 (p. 93). There is a distinct collar around the city centre, although it is broken to the north-west, and merges into a dockland area to the south.

In contrast, a study by Jackson and Oulds of Stoke-on-Trent using 1981 data can be reviewed. They identified six types of social areas, three of which demonstrated elements of deprivation.

1. Inner city transitional areas. These are dominated by rooming house, bedsit or subdivided, often rented accommodation. There is a high incidence of young adults and immigrants.

2. Inner city residual areas. These are

99

dominated by older owner-occupied terraced housing with a more stable and an older population with medium to low social status.

3. *Local authority housing areas.* These are distinctive by tenure, but exhibit low social status and other indicators of relative deprivation.

There are clear parallels with Davies's study.

The Inner City Transitional Areas cover Davies's Groups *1.* and *2.*, whilst there are limited parallels between Group *2.* in Stoke and Davies's Group *3.* especially in relation to the older character of the population. Group *3.* in Stoke certainly has parallels in Cardiff although Davies uses the description 'low status' rather than introducing the notion of deprivation.

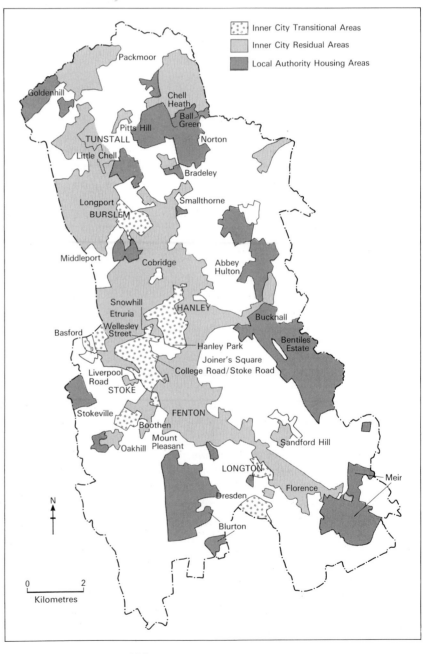

Figure 6.3 *Stoke-on-Trent. The distribution of deprived groups 1981 (after Jackson and Oulds)*

If Figure 6.3, where the three groups in Stoke have been mapped, is now considered, there are both similarities to and differences from the Cardiff map. Stoke was made up of the initially separate six towns – Tunstall, Burslem, Hanley, Stoke, Fenton and Longton – so it is a conurbation in the full sense of the term. The second group – inner city residential areas – form what the authors call a classic urban core of the traditional industrial city – a stable, working class and densely populated inner zone. It has an over representation of the elderly – 'a classic concentration of older age and pensionable people'. It forms nothing remotely approaching either a zone of a sector in shape but due to the growing together of the separate nodes it now constitutes an extended axis running through the heart of the conurbation. Within it Group *1.* – the inner city transitional areas – stand out, distinguished by mobility, high density and population with heads of households born in the New Commonwealth or Pakistan. These are the poorer quality terrace houses occupied by those elements which classically gravitate to the poorest or rented sectors of most modern cities, including the young in bedsits. But it is significant that the old nodes at Burslem, Hanley, Stoke and Longton show through.

The third group at Stoke is made up of council housing estates. These are quite obviously characterised by the tenure which defines them, but also by low socio-economic status, high unemployment and a high proportion of families without cars. Davies identifies a similar group in Cardiff, dividing it into the older and newer estates, but does not find any distinctive disadvantage associated. The location of this group is greatly contrasted with the others for it is peripheral. There are no associations with immigrant or elderly populations, indeed the reverse is the case for the estates are dominated by native born and young families.

Setting aside the peripheral housing estates with their own nature and disadvantages, it is apparent that, in spite of the great contrasts in structure between the two examples, they both show inner areas distinguished by a set of common features.

1. Low socio-economic status, or, to translate it into everyday language, a degree of poverty.
2. A high proportion of immigrants from the New Commonwealth.
3. An elderly population.
4. Single, highly mobile young adults.

In terms of significant deprivation the last group is less important. Those in it are often attending educational establishments and are seeking the cheapest accommodation for purely temporary purposes. The other groups denote the permanent inhabitants of the inner city.

Cardiff and Stoke do not have very large immigrant populations from the New Commonwealth and hence Figure 6.4 has been added to underline the very distinctive way in which the inner city is defined by their presence. Wolverhampton (Fig. 6.4) is a classic example of the formation of an inner ring of immigrant occupation about the city centre. It also provides two modifications which need to be made. In detail it is wrong to aggregate together New Commonwealth and Pakistani immigrants, for there is quite a clear spatial separation between those from the Caribbean and those from India and Pakistan. Secondly, the neat ring is often broken by local circumstances. There are well marked immigrant areas to the east (South Wednesbury) and south-east (Ettingshall). These are predominantly Indian and reflect the urban structure of Wolverhampton where the higher quality residential areas are to the rural west, as against lower quality areas at the eastern boundary where the city merges in to the Black Country.

The association of the elderly with the inner city has attracted less attention from geographers as against the high public profile of ethnic or racial issues. Figure 6.5 is taken from a study of Leicester. It plots what is called a '*factor*' derived from a multivariate analysis, that is an analysis of a whole range of data in the same way as noted in town classification on page 67. Again, the way in which the factor is derived can be ignored. It is described by the

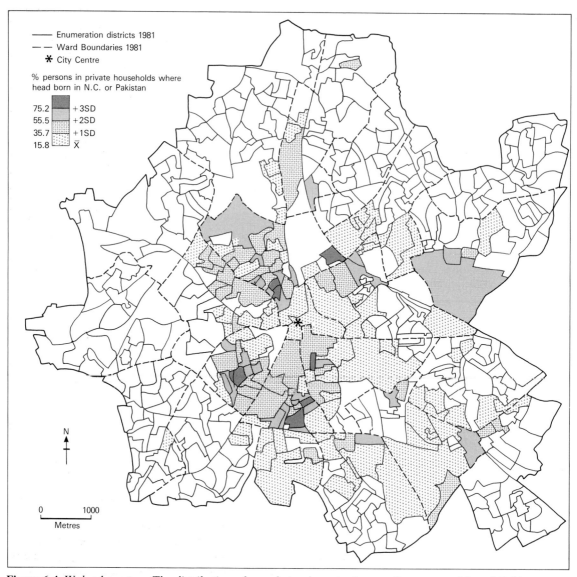

Figure 6.4 *Wolverhampton. The distribution of population born in the new Commonwealth and Pakistan 1981. The shaded areas relate to standard deviations above a mean of 15.8 (after Evans)*

authors as representing 'stage in life cycle' and identifies those in the later stages of that cycle. The actual variables associated are those over 60, those between 45 and 59 and households with pensioners, together with others relating to tenure and density because often the elderly, living as couples or alone, give a low density of occupation. Figure 6.5 demonstrates that same ring around the central areas of Leicester and the association of the aged with the inner

parts of the city.

A brief word of warning is needed here about the interpretation of these maps. All that has been demonstrated is that on an areal basis certain associations have been shown. One cannot, and must not, go any further than that. It would be wrong to assert from the evidence that the indigenous residents are of high social status and immigrants are of low social status; it would be wholly incorrect to assume that

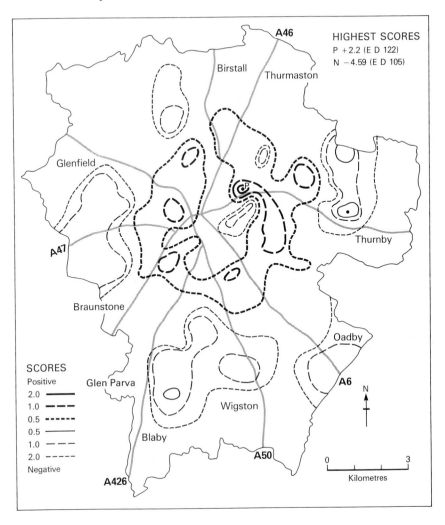

Figure 6.5 *The life cycle factor in Leicester 1961: the distribution of the elderly (after Davies and Lewis). Here yet another method of representation is used. This is the distribution of a factor derived from a large number of variables (see text)*

immigrants are elderly. What one can maintain is that the inner city is characterised by a series of attributes including low social status, poor quality housing and unemployment. Further, a higher than average proportion of immigrants seem to be attracted to the cheapest property to buy or to rent, along with the long standing but entrapped elderly who do not have the resources either to move out or to improve the property they have. Having thus outlined the nature of the inner city one can proceed to ask the question as to why it has come about.

ASSIGNMENT

---

1. Try to obtain data for a city or town you know on:

a) the distribution of those over 60;
b) the distribution of immigrant populations.

Do the patterns conform to those outlined here? If they do not, attempt an explanation.

REASONS FOR THE CHARACTER OF THE INNER CITY

The most direct way in which to provide an answer is to suggest four main reasons. They inevitably overlap but they can all be regarded as partial contributors to the inner city characteristics.

103

1. Ageing and obsolescence. The inner part of the city is by the nature of things the earliest built and the oldest. It is where one would expect to find properties which have become obsolescent, that is, out of date, and in a state of decay. Much of the fabric of these parts of the cities of the western world was constructed in the nineteenth century at a time when growth was rapid, controls on building quality were limited and standards low. The houses, therefore, are both old and poor in quality and lack modern amenities such as hot water and central heating systems and indoor toilets and bathrooms.

As an answer to the question posed, the last paragraph is perfectly correct, but it does little more than raise another question as to why there has been no improvement or replacement. After all, the city centre, the central business district, of most towns has been largely rebuilt in recent times. Certainly one response is that there indeed has been a good deal of rebuilding in these inner areas too, for they constituted the worst parts and were often the first to be dealt with. Slum clearance in Britain goes as far back as 1875 and the Artisans' and Labourers' Dwellings Improvement Act (the Cross Act). But, in the UK, in the rush to solve the critical housing shortage which had arisen as a result of the Second World War, when not only had there been no building but actual physical destruction, the new products turned out to be little better than those being replaced. Comprehensive redevelopment was the favoured policy and that meant clearing everything away regardless of the quality or function of any individual buildings; everything was razed to the ground. In replacement the high-rise tower blocks of the 1960s were constructed. The motive, to retain relatively high densities to prevent sprawl, was admirable but the execution poor. The blocks were built quickly and with few of the facilities which such structures need to make life in them tolerable, let alone attractive. The result has been that they themselves have become part of the inner city problem.

Comprehensive redevelopment had other unfortunate consequences. It took out all those local services, small shops and public houses for example, which were the basis of community life. Above all it removed many small scale industries occupying cheap if somewhat old and inferior premises. Such industries were either forced out of business or to relocate and the newer, more attractive sites were at the periphery. One consequence of clearance was a loss of jobs and the extension of unemployment, especially amongst families who for whatever reason could not move elsewhere.

2. Suburban and peripheral growth. This is a feature already noted but of such significance that a brief repetition is appropriate. As settlements grew due to industrialisation and its consequences, the central areas became less favoured for residence. The inner parts became noisy, polluted and congested, and open space was greatly limited. Fashions, too, changed and the demand arose for houses with all the new conveniences technical progress brought, and especially for larger gardens. To adapt Kipling, house buyers were looking for neater, sweeter houses in a greener, cleaner land (see p. 83). But those who could move to purchase and occupy these new homes were those who not only had the wealth to purchase them but also could meet the cost of the journey to work. Those who could not afford to move remained trapped in the deteriorating inner city. This has been a particular problem in relation to the elderly. Not only can many not afford to move, or cannot face the disturbance of moving, but after children have grown up and left they are faced with houses which are too large (hence the low occupation rate which can be found) and expensive to maintain. Very often lack of care leads to physical deterioration.

But as has been noted (pp. 90–91) residence is not the only land-use to move. Industry has already been seen as disturbed by comprehensive redevelopment. Further, as skilled labour moved away so did industry, following its labour supply. Land at the periphery is cheaper and modern production lines, all on one level, need a lot of it. So industry has also moved to the outer city. Other land-uses have followed. Retailing attracted to its wealthier customers has grouped in suburban shopping centres or massive out-of-town developments. Wholesaling too has moved, for like industry the greater use of road transport has given great advantage to sites where ring roads intersect motorways. Finally, even office uses have been attracted by rural locations with pleasant environments, ample parking space, yet easy accessibility. All these changes not only deprive the inner city of employment, but also of services. It is a strange anomaly that the small shops remaining in the inner city – 'open all hours' – have to charge higher prices to make a profit from a small turnover while suburban supermarkets with large sales can offer goods at lower prices; the poorest have to pay the higher prices.

3. Exploitation. Since it has had so much emphasis in recent geographical literature, it is necessary to introduce a specifically political interpretation. This analysis would be incomplete without it. It is the view of those on the left of the political spectrum that all the characteristics which had been identified are the direct consequences of the exploitative nature of capitalist society. Capital will always be invested where it can find the best return. All sorts of problems arise for the capitalist in trying to regenerate the inner city, amongst them the elementary need to assemble land owned by large numbers of people for development. It is far easier to make profits from the exploitation of new land – what are called greenfield sites – at the city edge. Hence developers and builders avoid the inner city for house building and campaign for the release of land in the green belts which have been established around large cities (see p. 13). This is the issue with which Prince Charles has associated himself.

Under this heading, it is also relevant to introduce the fiscal problems which are endemic to the inner city. The evacuation of these inner sections by so many users – especially industry and commerce – means that the tax base falls. More simply, in British terms, the income which the local authority can derive from the rates paid by large scale enterprises is quite catastrophically cut. This has happened at the very time when the demands for services from the disadvantaged are rapidly increasing. This is the condition behind the conflict between central government trying to cut public expenditure and local government trying to expand services to those it claims are in great need. This can lead to further decline. In order to provide the services, the local authority continues to raise the rates, as long as no limit, or cap (i.e. rate-capping), is enforced by the government. But eventually the rates become so high that they drive out industry and commerce to peripheral areas with lower rates, whilst those seeking locations for enterprises will avoid high-rated inner cities. Unemployment is exacerbated and the authorities in the inner cities become even less able to meet demands. City bankruptcy becomes a distinct possibility.

This is yet a further twist to this issue. Much of the property in the inner city is rented by those living there or using it. But the owners most often live in the suburbs, so there is effectively a draining out of money, or of profits, made in the inner city but not returned there. At a somewhat different level, even the major profits from drug trafficking which afflicts these areas go to the large scale organisers who probably live in the wealthy periphery.

For the reasons which have only been put in outline, socialist interpreters would see inner city problems as the inevitable product of a capitalist system which sees financial viability and profit as the prime movers in making decisions which affect the city.

4. Town and regional planning. The final reason for the decline of these inner parts of cities form another anomaly, for it derives from the beneficient intentions of town and country planning. The problems of housing in Britain after the Second World War have already been mentioned. Part of the reaction was a concerted movement to solve overcrowding in the industrial conurbations by the building of New Towns. People were encouraged to move out to these new settlements which, in theory, were to have balanced populations; the mix of people by age and by social class should have approximated to that of Britain as a whole. But the New Towns attracted especially the younger, more skilled elements, leaving behind the unskilled and the elderly. A corollary of the success of the British New Towns movement has been the decay of the inner city. This was further exacerbated by another form of planning – regional planning – which tried to shift investment from what were seen as thriving metropoles to depressed regions. The greatest response came from entrepreneurs with old premises in congested parts of the cities. A classic example in the public sector is the moving of the Royal Mint from London's East End to Llantrisant in South Wales. Crucial employment was actually encouraged to leave the inner cities by regional policy.

ASSIGNMENT

2. Reasons have been suggested for the decline of the inner parts of cities. Which of them do you think most significant? Are there others which have not been included?

CHARACTERISTICS OF THE INNER CITY: A REVIEW

Two broad aspects of urban inequality have been considered so far. The first was the nature of the inner city and the inequality it epitomised, the second the reasons for such a situation arising. Out of the discussions of those aspects some further points arise which need to be developed. The inner city in one context represents what can be called *entrapment*, that is those least able to cope with the changes taking place in city structure remain caught within its declining parts. But in an entirely different way (although entrapment may eventually also apply) that same inner city offers to immigrants from different cultures an oppor-

tunity to obtain a foothold, what can be called *enlodgement*. What is being abandoned by the upwardly mobile, indigenous or home population can be occupied by the newcomers who succeed to the space in the city; in other words, they find a niche to occupy which is related to their relative poverty and lack of the skills which modern urban living demands. Hence the association of ethnic groups with the inner city which was demonstrated in Figure 6.4.

There is also a further aspect of inequality for these parts of the city too are characterised by disruption and anti-social behaviour. They are inhabited by transient populations, in part adjusting to new environment, and have a high incidence of unemployment. They have thus become associated with visible crime, such as drug peddling and mugging. That association accelerates the spiral of decline.

But the story is by no means one of total and permanent abandonment by the well-off. The facilities of the city still have their attractions and continuous urban extension makes the journey from city edge to city centre long, time-consuming and tedious. There is, therefore, a trend for some of the more affluent to move back and to improve the larger old properties which once formed high quality residential areas. The process is called *gentrification*.

Finally, not all inequality is inner city located. It must be recalled that the marginal council housing estates of Stoke had an element of disadvantage associated with them.

Out of this review of the first part of the chapter, four topics have emerged which need some further consideration. They are:

1. the ethnic area, or the ghetto;
2. multiple deprivation and social disruption;
3. gentrification;
4. inequality and council housing.

The ethnic area or ghetto

The name usually ascribed to areas dominated by a single ethnic group within a host country is the ghetto, but some reservations must be made as to its use. Firstly, it carries overtones of discrimination and of disadvantage. The

Cantonment in which the British lived in Indian cities during the nineteenth century and the early part of this was an exclusive ethnic area. It was technically a ghetto, but the term was and is seldom used other than in a pejorative sense. Secondly, there is no accepted minimum concentration of the ethnically distinct population which would define a ghetto. In the USA black ghettos are usually thought of as having census tracts with some 80 to 90 per cent black. In Britain few enumeration districts in any city reach such proportions and lower percentages have to be adopted. Thus Figure 6.4 uses 55.5 per cent as a limit, a value two standard deviations above the mean, whilst other studies have used lower figures still, in the 30 to 40 per cent range. These percentages do depend on the size of the unit area being employed. At a street level much higher percentages can be attained, but a ghetto must be conceived as a territory, a distinctive area of the city.

With these reservations in mind, one can accept that the ghetto is associated with disadvantage and discrimination, if not necessarily with deprivation. The name itself, originating from a part of the city of Venice, comes from the specific quarter of the city to which Jews were confined in European cities of the Middle Ages. As such it most certainly had a discriminating function, but it also had a beneficient as well as a malign role for the non-native immigrant population. In the isolation of the ghetto, those customs and habits which were greatly different from the host country, even at times offensive, could be followed without provoking upset. After all it is Shylock who says 'I will buy with you, walk with you, and so following, but I will not eat with you, drink with you, nor pray with you.' In other words, the formal relations of business were acceptable, but the culture or way of life was totally different and no compromise was to be made that would modify and eventually eliminate difference. That is the way by which Jewish identity was preserved over the long period of dispersal from the land of Israel. In this way, too, the ghetto provided a haven where newcomers could slowly adapt to a new cultural environ-

ment, including most often a new language which had to be learned.

An admirable demonstration of this last process and its consequences has been provided in a study of Dutch immigration to the American city of Kalamazoo by Jakle and Wheeler. In this case the immigrants were less concerned with retaining their identity than in becoming true Americans. Two of the authors' maps are reproduced as Figures 6.6a and 6.6b. They show the distribution of population with Dutch surnames at two dates. The major Dutch migration into the city occurred in the late nineteenth century and translated a thin and general distribution in the 1870s into one where there were clear concentrations by 1910, remaining as late as 1939 (Figure 6.6a). By that date two distinctive Dutch clusters had appeared, one to the north and the other to the south of the city centre. It is interesting to note that these two clusters were themselves contrasted. To the north were settlers from Frisia, to the south from the province of Zealand, their languages all but incomprehensible to each other. Here were what can be loosely called Dutch ghettos. The second map shows the position in 1965 (Figure 6.6b) by which time complete dispersal had occurred. The Dutch had been completely assimilated and were American in all ways but the names they derived from their immigrant ancestors, and so in a country like the USA, where all are immigrants within historic times, they had become totally unnoticeable.

It is now apparent that the ghetto can play two quite different, even diametrically opposite, roles.

1. It can be the means by which the cultural identity and separateness of an immigrant population can be preserved in an alien environment.
2. It can be the focus from which a culturally different population can be slowly but effectively dispersed into the host nation or into an alien environment and there merged with the indigenous population.

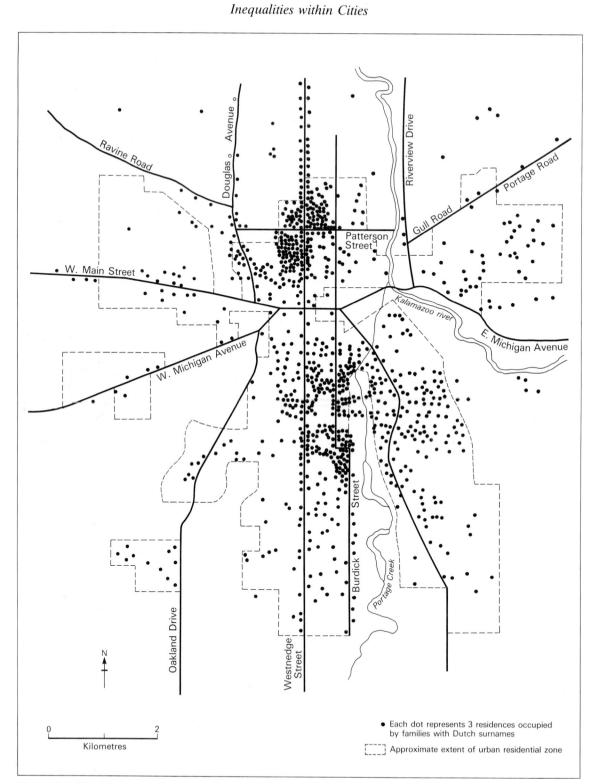

Figure 6.6 *The distribution of population with Dutch names in Kalamazoo, Michigan, USA. (a) in 1910*

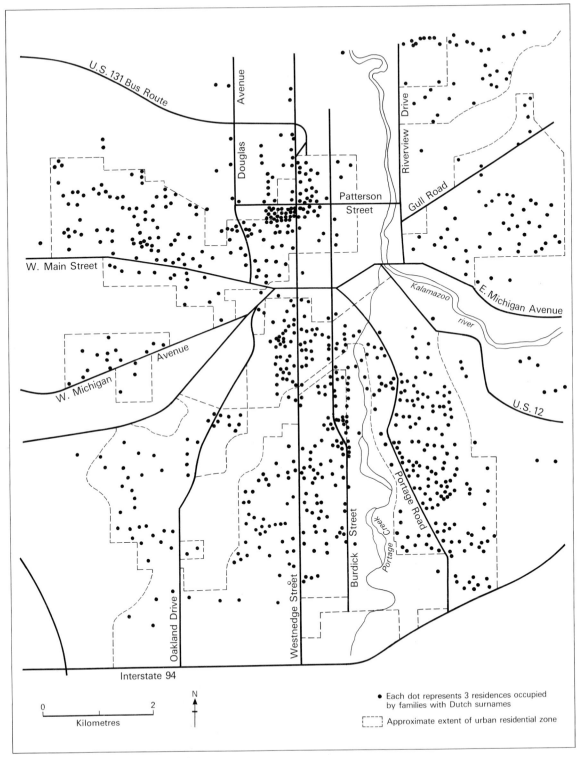

(b) in 1965 (after Jackle and Wheeler)

Presumably it is the second of these roles which the ghetto should play in relation to the black population of the USA and the immigrants from the New Commonwealth into Britain. But a third role must be added for the ghetto.

3. It can be the means by which a culturally or otherwise distinctive population can be prevented from dispersing and merging with the host population by more or less effective segregation, or enforced separate development (apartheid).

Of these three roles 2. and 3. are incompatible, whilst many segregated populations are totally ambivalent over 1. and 2., never quite sure whether the most desirable outcome is complete acceptance and dispersal and merging or a retention of their own way of life.

In the USA it has been maintained that, after the riots of the late 1960s and the Report of the President's National Advisory Commission on Civil Disorder (Kerner Commission) of 1968, progress towards the assimilation of blacks and the elimination of black ghettos was being made. A basis was thought to exist in the Civil Rights legislation and especially in that part of it concerned with Fair Housing which made illegal discriminatory practices in the selling of houses, such as estate agents (realtors in the USA) having two lists of houses for sale, one for whites, one for blacks. This had been one of the main mechanisms by which segregation was maintained. The evidence for this progress is the increasing representation of blacks in suburban populations leading to the assumption that blacks were moving out of the inner city and into the suburban estates. But detailed study has shown this to have little meaning. What has happened is shown in Figure 6.7. The ghetto itself has grown outward and in doing so has crossed the administrative boundary of the city, so that blacks are recorded as suburban whilst still living within the ghetto confines.

In Britain there is some statistical evidence that there has been a decline in the intensity of concentration which marked early settlement of

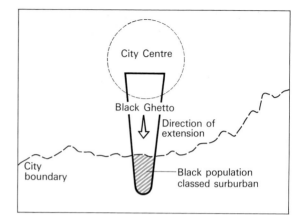

Figure 6.7 *The relation of the growth of black ghettos in the USA to administrative boundaries*

immigrants, but there is no sign of any trend towards dispersal.

The explanation for this seemingly static situation can be threefold.

1. Racial discrimination. There is no legal barrier against immigrants or blacks, rather the reverse, especially in the USA where positive or affirmative action to favour blacks is operative. But there is widespread evidence of discrimination and prejudice.

2. Qualifications and ability. This is a delicate issue but there is little firm evidence of the association of different abilities with ethnicity. The difficulty of gaining the necessary education and training from the disadvantaged basis of the inner city is, however, a much more significant limiting factor.

3. Unwillingness to adapt. Again this is a difficult subject not unrelated to the conflicting desires derived from 1. and 2. on page 107. The host society will expect an element of conformity to its traditions and customs and a refusal to accept that as justifiable can lead to accusations of discrimination. A good example is the education in Britain of young Moslem girls. Should they be brought up in British style so that they can participate fully in British life, or in the way dictated by Islam which will necessarily result in restrictions and limitations? What is the ghetto? Is it a means of retaining cultural traditions or of adaptation to new ways? This does not mean that there is no room for compromise or no possibility of a multi-racial society, but the problems are not to be solved by facile moralising. There are significant difficulties for if the aspirations of those living in segregated areas are not met then there is the possibility of a turning back into the emphasis on difference and the generation of confrontation and conflict which are already apparent in the inner city areas of Britain. But it is a far more complex problem than is covered by the cliché of 'racialism'.

The introduction of the problem of conflict moves the discussion towards situations where the segregation of populations is more absolute, itself an indication of greater stresses. There

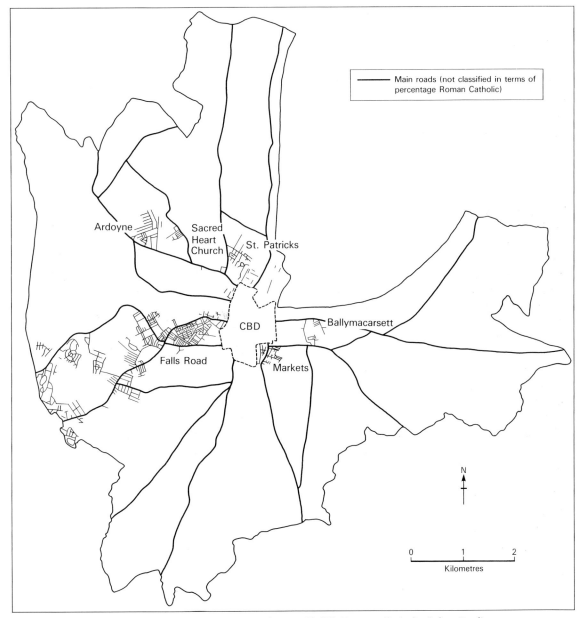

Figure 6.8 *The distribution of streets in Belfast with over 90.5% Roman Catholic (after Boal)*

are two cases, one where the segregation is becoming more emphasised but where it is not institutionalised, that is it is not backed by law. The other, and the most extreme, is where segregation is enforced by legislation.

The most familiar example of the first case must be the segregation of Protestants and Roman Catholics in Belfast and other cities of Northern Ireland. The two most potent symbols of cultural identity, as opposed to racial character where skin colour dominates, are religion and language. In Northern Ireland religion, although the Irish language has a minor role, generates a wide range of cultural and political differences between the Protestant Loyalist and the Roman Catholic Nationalist.

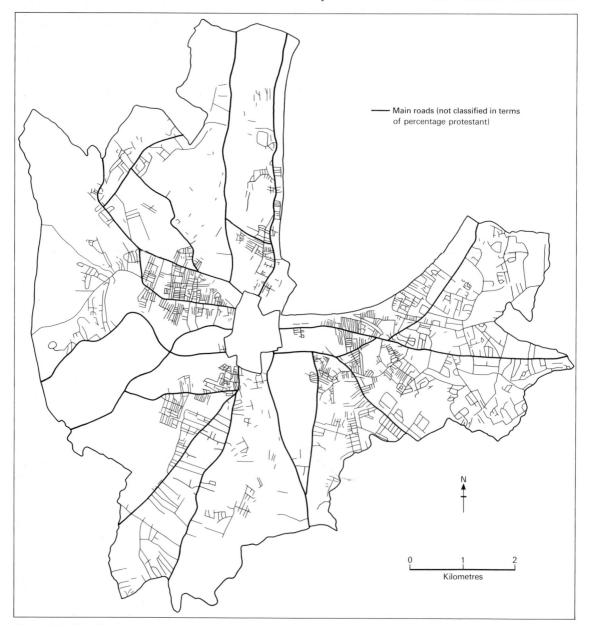

Main roads (not classified in terms of percentage protestant)

N

0   1   2
Kilometres

Figure 6.9 *The distribution of streets in Belfast with under 9.5% Roman Catholic after Boal*

Figure 6.11 *Crossing the border*

However, there is also a strong underlying economic basis in relation to access to jobs, housing and other benefits which is a significant aspect of all the segregation issues in Britain as a whole. This is not the place to trace the origins of the conflict in the past but rather to look at its expression in the contemporary city.

Figures 6.8 and 6.9 show the distribution of streets which were over 90.5 per cent Roman Catholic and under 9.5 per cent Roman Catholic in 1969 whilst Figure 6.10 generalises this, mapping percentages by tracts. These are taken from the work of F. W. Boal who has written extensively on Belfast. The data for Figures 6.8 and 6.9 were derived from information provided by clergy. Interpreting the figures, Boal writes that no less than 99 per cent of those households belonging to such heavily Roman Catholic streets live in just six areas, each of which is what he calls a continuous segment of uninterrupted space consisting entirely of streets in that one category of religious composition. Again, no less than 69 per cent of Protestants live in streets which are 91 per cent or more Protestant. Boal has also studied the divide between the two communities along the Shankhill (Protestant) and Falls (Roman Catholic) Roads and has demonstrated the near absolute character of that divide. Now that boundary has no institutionalised basis whatsoever, but it is certainly recognised by the police and the army. The slogan painted on walls 'You are now entering Free (London) Derry' is indicative of the acceptance of a marked boundary line. Sectarian violence has increased segregation by enforcing the removal of families not belonging to the majority group. This has led to the physical identification of the divide by the erection of steel fences and other barriers between the communities.

This discussion has so far identified and commented on the nature of segregation but not of the fundamental geographical interest, its distribution or patterning. Study of the maps (Figs. 6.8, 6.9, 6.10) will make apparent Boal's conclusion that the distribution of Roman Catholics is not greatly different from that of a standard ethnic minority. Of the six virtually

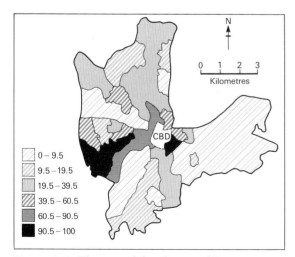

Figure 6.10 *The general distribution of Roman Catholics in Belfast by tracts (after Boal)*

exclusively Roman Catholic areas, four are located as separate pockets adjacent to the city centre with one of them having grown outwards along a sector (the Falls Road) to the city boundary and beyond. The remaining two are the Ardoyne in the north-west and an area to the east of it. This is not greatly dissimilar from the distribution of blacks in the cities of the USA. Note the comparison with Figure 6.7. Undoubtedly the low average social status of the Roman Catholic population, derived from its initial nature as a rural, unskilled urbanward migration, also like the Blacks, has resulted in characteristic inner city locations, but with population growth producing outward extension in the form of a well defined sector.

What is unusual is for a population without distinctive physical characteristics, such as skin colour, to remain segregated over such a long period. Refer back to the changes in the Dutch population in Kalamazoo. The retention of the segregated pattern is the product of the long history of sectarian and political conflict, but its bitterness is probably strongly related to the constrained economic advancement of a minority population.

The second, and more extreme case still, is where one of the predominant concerns of the ghetto, from both inside and outside it, to maintain cultural identity, has been translated into the legal or institutionalised division of the city, or into complete separate development of

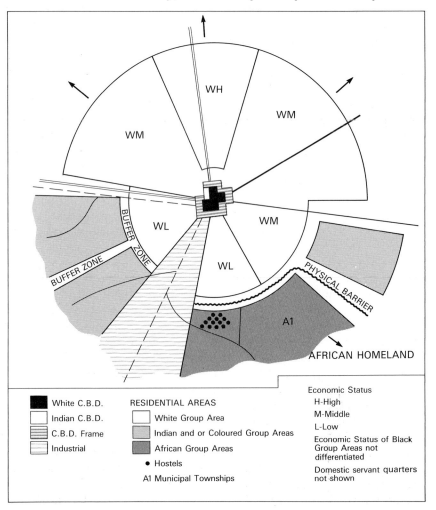

Figure 6.12 *A model of an apartheid city (after Davies)*

		Economic Status
■ White C.B.D.	RESIDENTIAL AREAS	H-High
□ Indian C.B.D.	□ White Group Area	M-Middle
▦ C.B.D. Frame	▨ Indian and or Coloured Group Areas	L-Low
▦ Industrial	▨ African Group Areas	Economic Status of Black Group Areas not differentiated
	• Hostels	Domestic servant quarters not shown
	A1 Municipal Townships	

the communities; what is now widely known from South Africa as apartheid. The South African legislation is complex but is centred on the Group Areas Act initially passed in 1950, although it has been amended in detail since. The central principle of the Act is that in defined areas of the city, land and property can only legally be owned and occupied by people of a specified racial group. In South Africa the main groups are the white, mainly Afrikaner (Dutch) or British by origin; the Coloured produced by interbreeding between the white population and the indigenous Bushmen and Hottentots, now called the Khoi-San; the Black or Bantu; the Indian, mainly brought into the sugar plantations of Natal or attracted as traders during the period of initial gold and diamond exploitation. All these groups are allocated consolidated areas which ideally are separated by marked physical barriers, such as rivers, or by buffer zones of unused or non-residential land. These are designed not only to act as boundaries but to prevent contact and mixing at the margins. Travel of one group through the area of another is also minimised. Taking these principles into account a sectoral form of city is inevitably to be predicated. Figure 6.12 is an idealised diagram or model of an apartheid city prepared by Professor Ron Davies of the University of Cape Town. The Central Business District is the focus although within it blacks could not hold property, the ownership of businesses was reserved for whites only. The Indian trading tradition is, however, acknowledged by a separate Indian CBD, the best known being in Durban. White higher social class areas occupy distinctive sectors although the innermost parts are in lower-class white occupation. The blacks and Coloureds are disposed in sectors clearly separated from those of the whites. There are clearly marked buffer zones formed by physical barriers, industrial zones or communication lines. Until 1986 legislation, it must be remembered that no black was a citizen of the Republic of South Africa (RSA) for they were regarded as belonging to one of the Home-lands, the nominally independent states such as

Bophuthatswana set up within the RSA terri-tory. Blacks were, therefore, regarded as only temporary residents renting temporary accom-modation in the townships. Many of the black workers are indeed migrants from countries outside South Africa and are housed in hostels shown on the diagram. Ideally under the apart-heid system the black areas themselves should be divided according to ethnic origin so that there should be separate sectors for the Xhosa, Zulu or Sotho peoples. To a degree, there has been an attempt to implement such a scheme in the large townships such as Soweto outside Johannesburg. Coloured and Indian popu-lations are also located in distinct sectors but unlike the blacks they have been allowed to own property and hence the division in the diagram between municipally built townships and privately developed areas for the Coloureds.

Figure 6.12 is a highly idealised diagram. It does not include squatter settlements which are made up of illegal immigrants who construct shacks on derelict or unused land. Crossroads outside Cape Town is the best known example. Also, when the Group Areas Act was passed, towns were already segregated in highly local-ised ways. New plans had to be drawn up and approved to conform to the Act but the resultant schemes were quite removed from the ideal. One example can be considered.

The site of Cape Town (Figure 6.13) must surely be one of the best known and most spec-tacular in the world. It is dominated by three elements. Table Mountain is the first with its characteristic flat top and steep sides. The lower slopes are gentler, however, and have provided cultivable land. To the east are the Cape Flats, forming the second element, an area of calcareous sand covered by blown sand. Across this low plain the rivers meander slowly and are blocked by coastal dunes forming extensive lagoons or 'vleis'. The third element is the high ground of the Tygerberg to the north east. Whereas the higher lands have a heavy winter rainfall, they are by far the most preferred locations, even when the purely aesthetic advantages of outlook, especially along the coast of the Cape peninsula, are set aside. The Cape Flats suffer from extensive waterlogging and flooding in the winter whilst in the dry summers the south-easterly winds whip up the sands into unpleasant sand storms.

Prior to the application of the Group Areas Act, Cape Town was most certainly a segregated city but there was a good deal of mixing and a number of mixed areas. This was completley changed, but not until 1960, since the city itself refused to enforce the Act and the reorgan-isation of residential areas was imposed by a Commission. The principles were the obvious ones: that the white population should command the higher ground for reasons of security, dominance and amenity; that there should be well defined buffer zones. It is easiest to set out the group areas shown on Figure 6.14 in a series of comments.

1. The whole of Table Mountain and its lower slopes were allocated to the whites. It is the area with major environmental attractions for it has elevation, outlook and is well drained and flood free. In addition, the white area surrounded the CBD and the in-dustrial zone about Table Bay.
2. The coastal areas (mostly to the west of the area on Figure 6.14) with their spectacular scenery and high quality suburbs were also to be white.
3. The high lands of the Tygerberg were to be white giving access directly to the mainly industrial sector extending east from the city centre.
4. The Cape Flats were largely allocated to the Coloured population, with the Kromboom River together with a suburban railway and

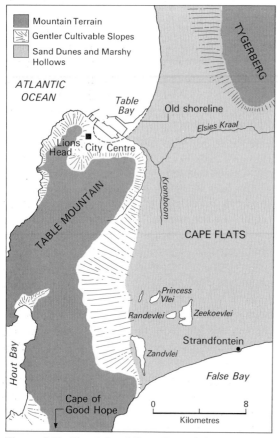

Figure 6.13 *The sight of Cape Town (after Western)*

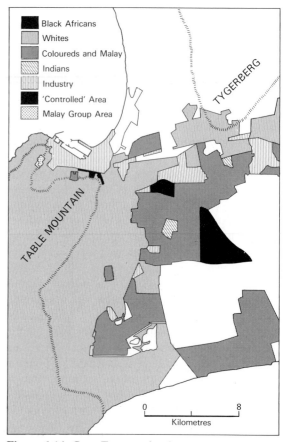

Figure 6.14 *Cape Town under the group areas act 1979 (after Western)*

an industrial zone forming the buffer with the white area to the west. A new settlement of over 250 000 called Mitchell's Plain has been developed on the flats with a major shopping centre.

5. The black population was restricted to the margins, the earlier concentration at Langa being extended to Nyanga and Guguletu on the Flats and to the east.

6. Influx control, the means by which blacks are prevented from migrating to the city, cannot be completely enforced and movement especially from the Transkei has produced squatter settlements. These in general are cleared away but international publicity resulted in Crossroads being left, although internal troubles in 1986 have severely undermined its continued existence. A government sponsored sited at Khayelitsha is intended to replace it.

Within the scheme there is a series of anomalies. A Malay area has been left adjacent to the CBD even though it overlooks it, largely for traditional and tourist reasons. More significantly, Figure 6.14 will show a substantial white extension on to the Cape Flats in the south. This is a response to the attractions of the coastal beaches, one of the classic surfing areas, and the lagoons which constitute a well marked amenity.

This brief survey demonstrates how application in reality deviates from the model though retaining its essentials. It also indicates how the most attractive locations are retained for the controlling group. Here, then, is the ultimate stage of ethnic or cultural segregation where it is enforced by the law or institutionalised. It then becomes not a means of integrating immigrant populations into the community at large but of keeping them permanently separate as was noted on page 110.

Multiple deprivation

This widely used term stresses the fact that the disadvantages of the inner city do not come singly but rather as a range of associated aspects of relative deprivation; hence the use of the word multiple; the adjective 'relative' is also employed since deprivation is always relative to the general condition pertaining in a country or region. The range of associated aspects referred to above are the product of a downward spiral of closely related circumstances. The outlines of that spiral have already been sketched in this chapter. They are represented in diagrammatic form in Figure 6.15. The outflow both of those personally better off, upwardly mobile to use the jargon, and of the major users of urban land such as industry, lowers the tax base or the rates which can be collected as already described. The same movement increases unemployment both absolutely and relatively. In consequence both public and personal financial difficulties are generated for those entrapped (the unskilled and the elderly) and enlodged (immigrants). Public services deteriorate in quality, especially education which is the critical basis for personal improvement. Schools are older buildings usually lacking modern facilities. Housing deteriorates and is characterised both by overcrowding and, paradoxically, by under use by the elderly. Health problems tend to be more severe. There are few recreational facilities available. Because of these conditions people, especially the young, begin to feel that they are being left behind by the mainstream of society, that their interests are being ignored and so they become what is termed alienated, that is turned off from the standard and accepted norms or normal way of life. That, in turn, can lead to anti-social behaviour, such as drug-taking, vandalism, and crime. There is little doubt that in spatial terms recorded crime, especially crimes of violence such as muggings, are closely related to the inner city. The result is that the downward spiral continues. Vandalism and crime drive out business so that unemployment increases, the tax base falls further and the quality of life in the inner city continues to decline even further. Figure 6.16 shows the distribution of murders in Washington DC between 1 January and mid-March 1989. The killings are predominantly of black people; the

117

ratio in 1988 was 97.8 per cent black to 2.2 per cent white. They have been mainly concerned with the distribution and use of illegal drugs. Note the distribution which rings around the monumental core of Washington (see page 169). This is a classic inner city pattern but with a very clear break in the white gentrified (see page 120) area of Georgetown.

It is essential to adopt a critical attitude to the sorts of argument developed above. They are greatly over-simplified and few would accept them in the outline and unqualified form presented here. To counter such sweeping claims it can be argued that crime, such as tax evasion, is related to the affluent periphery, but is much more difficult to map. Again, the children of the well-to-do are also likely to become alienated from the conventions that are termed norms.

It would be very misleading to leave a discussion of inequality and multiple deprivation without a brief indication of the action which has been taken to offset it. In this case the example is Britain. But, as with so many topics in this book, it is wrong to pretend that it is anything but an issue of great complexity. What follows is a brief outline which cannot hope to include all the detail of a large number of government reports and much legislation, itself changing with the political party in power. The three main targets for improvement have been housing and the environment, employment opportunities and personal and social conditions.

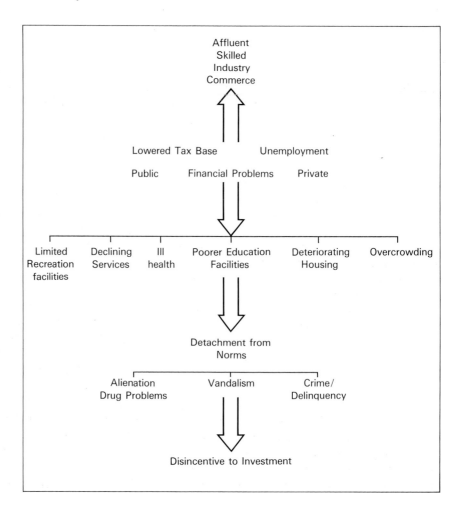

Figure 6.15 *Pattern of decline in the inner city*

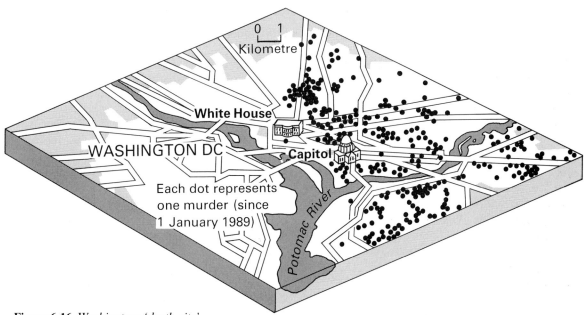

Figure 6.16 *Washington: 'death city'*

1. Housing and the environment. Grants of money have been available for the private renovation of houses since 1949, and various Housing Acts since then have changed the sums available and the detailed conditions. Since 1964 Local Authorities have had powers to undertake more general improvements to tracts of land rather than to individual buildings. After 1969 these were called *General Improvement Areas* (GIAs) and the scope was broadened to include the provision of amenities and the general upgrading of the environment. In 1974 *Housing Action Areas* (HAAs) were introduced for special and more difficult parts where the amount of rented property was high for example, or where significant environmental problems were leading to houses being abandoned. In these Areas the Local Authority had greater powers of compulsion and there was a higher financial provision. There was a third class of area called *Priority Neighbourhoods* which were usually adjacent to the other two and designed to prepare them for improvement.

2. Industry and employment. Employment has been one of the major difficulties of the inner city and its significance as a causal factor has been noted (page 117). In the 1970s the Government of the day had sponsored a massive series of Inner Area Studies and in 1977 a White Paper called '*Policy for the Inner Cities*' was published. Out of the discussions came the general view that the central problem was the one of unemployment derived from the collapsed economic base of the inner city. When the Government moved to legislation, therefore, in the Inner Urban Areas Act of 1978, its main financial provisions were directed to sponsoring partnerships between central and local government and industry, as in the *Inner City Partnership Programmes*, in order to generate jobs. This was to be done by financial incentives to firms as well as the projects directed towards improvement of the environment to make it more attractive to industrialists.

3. Personal and social conditions. The Inner Area Studies generally agreed that personal poverty itself was not specifically a problem of the inner cities for it was as prevalent on peripheral municipal housing estates. Even so, such initiatives as the Urban Programme of 1968 have been designed to offset the special disadvantages of these areas. The general social services are intended to meet major needs and the objectives of the Urban Programme were to provide immediate help with such things as community centres, family advice centres and nursery schools.

It has to be admitted that all the measures

which have been taken have had only partial success as is evidenced by the continuing problems of unrest. The apparent failure of wide-ranging measures is due to the fact that they were in opposition to two very strong forces. The first was the massive stress on suburban growth and the substantial economic forces ranged behind it. The second was that at the time the measures were becoming operative the general problem of economic recession arose and widespread national unemployment. Under such circumstances the claim of the inner cities became only one amongst many others.

Gentrification

The study of inequality within cities has seemingly propounded a view that there is a simple contrast between affluent suburbs and distressed inner city. That is not entirely the case. In Chapter 5, it was noted that in the largest cities the highest quality and most expensive housing remains central. A modest three bedroom house near to London's West End would cost over one million pounds. But apart from these exceptional areas of the world's great cities, there is also an increasing tendency for people of more modest means, though still in the high-income section, to move back into areas near the city centre. This trend for people, usually employed in the professions, to buy and improve older property is called, in the jargon of the social sciences, gentrification. It has been

suggested that the term gentrification should be restricted to newcomers, whilst another jargon term *incumbent upgrading* should be used for improvements by those already resident. This is not unimportant since much of the improvement is carried out by those already resident who get together into associations to develop the areas in which they or their parents lived. Even so, the term gentrification is usually used to cover the whole process. It is difficult to estimate the extent of gentrification. One attempt in the USA argues that some 70 per cent of all cities in the country with a population of over 250 000 'have experienced significant private market housing renovation in deteriorated areas'.

The main reasons for the trend can be summarised as follows.

1. There are still areas of older but good quality houses, in Britain mainly of Victorian or Edwardian age, which can be restored. They offer large rooms and more space than modern houses and a lower purchase cost per square foot of available space. Moreover, grants under the various housing improvement schemes referred to in the last section can be exploited.
2. There is easy access to the still important amenities of the city centre, especially theatres, art galleries and museums.
3. Similarly, the resources of the centre in terms of high quality retailing and res-

Figure 6.17

Georgetown, Washington. This is one of the earliest and best known examples of gentrification. Washington is now primarily a black city and one where rapid deterioration occurs immediately outside the monumental centre. But the demand for accessible housing has led to the gentrification of Georgetown immediately to the west.

taurants are at hand.
4. The journey to work is minimised in cost, but especially in time.
5. These areas provide an alternative to the uniformity of the suburbs and that is especially attractive to special groups such as the artists and the fashionable chic.

It follows from these reasons that particular types of people are usually associated with gentrification. They are generally young, without children, and often with both partners working giving high income. A typical area which has been influenced by gentrification is Islington in London. There is also a tendency for the area of high fashion to change from time to time as one might expect from the types of people involved.

A good example of the shifting location of prestige residence is to be found in New York's Manhattan. The island was, of course, the location of the initial settlement founded at its southern tip. It was laid out in 1653 and protected by a wall from which the present Wall Street, which follows its alignment, takes its name. The present grid dominated by its east-west streets and north-south avenues was established at the beginning of the nineteenth century. But the massive growth of New York led to the abandonment of the family housing by middle and upper income groups. Harlem (Figure 6.18) is a prime example. It was constructed as a mixed middle- and working-class district at the end of the nineteenth century being mainly composed of five and six storey tenements and town houses. During the First World War the white middle-class moved out to the suburbs and was replaced by the growing number of black migrants from the South. By the 1920s Harlem was solidly black. Since then there has been little investment and by the 1960s it was a slum and what Schaffer and Smith, from whose work the foregoing description has been derived, call 'the most notorious symbol of black deprivation in America'. Away from the main axes of business, such as Fifth Avenue, the remainder of Manhattan followed the same pattern of social

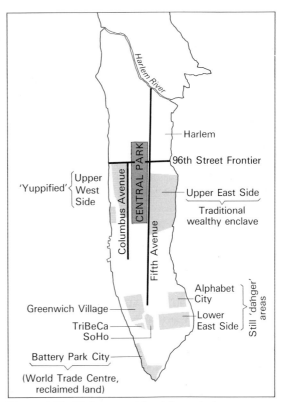

Figure 6.18 *High cost residential area in low Manhattan*

disorganisation and of physical deterioration. The one exception was the Upper East Side, overlooking Fifth Avenue and Central Park (Figure 6.18) which was the traditional area of the very wealthy and has remained a vastly expensive and luxury area of the city.

Increasingly since the late 1960s a process of reclamation has been in process. The upper west side has become the home for upwardly mobile professional people, whilst Greenwich Village took on the very special character of an artistic and literary enclave – the equivalent of Paris's left bank, although popularity and tourism have made their modifying impact. Even so a brownstone in Greenwich Village would cost something like $1.5 million. However, gentrification has spread to other parts. The new development at Battery Park city, near the World Trade Center, is actually being built on reclaimed land. 'SoHo . . . is no longer an eerie no-man's land of warehouses. It is now bustling with chic boutiques, art galleries and $600 000 luxury lofts . . . the area directly south of Soho known as TriBeCa (Triangle below Canal) is now almost as expensive' (*Sunday Times*, 16 November, 1986). Perhaps the most interesting extension is from upper west side towards the north for the borders of development edge into Harlem 'most of which is still a no-go area, though the property developers are eyeing the burnt-out brown stones (houses built of brown stone) hungrily. "Breaking the 96th Street frontier", as the *New York Times* calls it!'

Schaffer and Smith, who have been noted above, have investigated recent change (The Gentrification of Harlem? *Annals of the Association of American Geographers, 1986*) and they confirm that the western side of Harlem is experiencing the beginning of gentrification, although it is limited and sporadic. Even so, it is a development which might provide indications of the future.

Inequality and municipal housing

Areas of municipal housing stand out in standard analyses of cities because of their distinctive tenure. But they are also characterised by populations of low socio-economic status and all the disadvantages that go with it. On some estates these can be sufficiently marked to justify the use of the term deprived. It is necessary to stress this in order to avoid the impression that all city inequalities are inner city located. Figure 6.19 is a map which again uses the city of Cardiff as an example. It shows the areas to which a sample of the population drawn from six contrasted areas of the city stated they would not want to move. The pattern is that partly expected for the ring about the city centre is clearly apparent. But there are also a number of outlying areas. These are municipal housing estates, but not all are adversely regarded. Least attractive to the sample appears to be Ely to the west and Professor David Herbert, who constructed the map, quotes the local newspaper as writing,

'Ely, one of the largest housing estates in Cardiff, does not have a lot going for it. It has poor social facilities for young and old, not enough open space, traffic problems and poor shopping. Among key problems facing the district are truancy, vandalism and delinquency.' That list of drawbacks makes immediate comparison with the inner city itself.

Once an estate gets a bad name, and it is significant that the quotation above came from a local newspaper, then it, too, tends to spiral downwards. Those who have any choice, or can delay a choice, will not go there. The estate becomes a dumping ground for those who are most anti-social in their way of life or unable to cope with the many problems of modern living. That is hardly true of Ely, but Herbert shows how limited are the ambitions and hopes of the people who live there compared with other municipal estates. Thus, whereas in a sample from another estate some 70 per cent hoped their children would go on to higher education, in Ely the figure was as low as 15 per cent. The contrast between council estates has been greatly increased by the 'right to buy' which was part of the 1980 Housing Act. Better-off tenants on the better quality estates have been much more likely to buy their houses thus exacerbating the differences between estates. This brief discussion enables two points to be made, one relative to council estates, the other of more general relevance.

1. Municipal estates are by no means uniform though the bulk of maps imply that they are. Most authorities tend to have one estate to which difficult families are relegated, and it is usually widely known as such.
2. The statement that authorities direct families to locations calls attention to the fact that much of what has appeared in the last two chapters implies that people have a free choice in where they live. That is not so. They are in most cases greatly constrained by all the forces or institutions about them. Can they borrow enough money (i.e. raise a mortgage) to buy the house they want? It is the bank or building society which

decides. These institutions, such as the building society, are usually called *gate keepers* and theirs is an important role. As has been seen under apartheid, the gate-keeper is the state and its legislation, but it is not only in such rigid circumstances that gatekeepers play an important role.

ASSIGNMENTS

3. Why do you think there is such a thing as racial prejudice? Discuss the differences between the ideas represented by (a) culture, (b) ethnicity, (c) race.

4. Apartheid has been widely condemned as 'immoral'. Do you think it is? Is separate development acceptable if the resources available are equitably distributed?

5. One of the main criticisms of policies to help the inner city is that they have been area based, that is, specifically directed towards a geographical area. It is maintained they would have been more effective if aimed at particular people or families. As a geographer can you defend the use of a spatial basis?

6. One of the things an urban geographer should do is to look at the property columns:
   a) in the local press;
   b) in the national press, especially the 'quality' papers where London residences are listed.

   Consult and collect these and after a period of

Figure 6.19 *Cardiff. Residential areas nominated on the basis of low residential attraction (after Herbert)*

some time consider how the data fit into models of cities.

7. The existence and character of contrasts between wealth and poverty in the city, as well as the nature of racial discrimination, are often brought to life in novels. There is a danger that urban geography can seem very abstract and removed from the reality of living in cities. Read the novel *Bonfire of the Vanities* by Tom Wolfe. Identify the various areas of New York referred to and relate them to the social geography of the city.

8. Consider a city you know well. Are there housing estates which have a reputation for being 'tough' and less popular?

CONCLUSION

In this chapter a variety of inequalities has been considered and some of the detail has inevitably led away from the large scale generalisations of the models outlined in Chapter 5. In conclusion, however, it is proper to return again to the scale of those models. The various reviews undertaken have shown that the modern

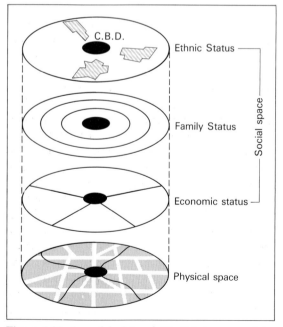

Figure 6.20 *A model of the residential structure of the western city (after Murdie)*

western city can be seen as structured by a number of overlapping elements which together create a mosaic of areas. Three of these stand out as being of the greatest significance:

1. Socio-Economic Status. At its simplest, this is effective through the amount of money a family has to buy or to rent a house. The major divide between private owner-occupied estates and rented municipal accommodation is derived from this circumstance. All the evidence indicates that this element is distributed in the form of sectors.

2. Ethnic Character or Ethnicity. Racial, cultural and ethnic character results in the segregation of different groups within the city. In most cases these groupings are the result of 'natural' factors, that is of uncontrolled interaction. But under apartheid they are made absolute by legal direction. In normal unconstrained circumstances, distinctive ethnic groups are confined to the inner city where they are also influenced by the sectoral nature of socio-economic status.

3. Life Cycle or Age. Age, and the different demands for house space and situation related to it, also is an important element. Young adults, especially in continuing education, are often found in the inner city, but so especially are the aged. The periphery is especially the location of families with young children looking for safe play areas and a greener environment. There is a tendency, therefore, for the life-cycle or age element to be distributed in concentric zones.

It is possible to put all three of these together in relation to the physical space of the city. This is done in Figure 6.20. If the three are collapsed one on top of the other onto the physical space below a neat model will not ensue, but rather a complex mosaic. Even so, the diagram presents the initial bases for comprehension. If into these are added all the anomalies which have been discussed, then the keys to understanding the complex internal arrangement of the city are available.

7

Aspects of Cities in the Third World

INTRODUCTION

Although some references have been made in earlier chapters to other parts of the world, most of the examples have been derived from, and the discussion related to, Britain and the USA, or in more general terms the developed, capitalist west. It is apparent, however, that there are quite substantial differences which occur in the settlement patterns of other areas. This was implicit in Chapter 1 when the urban proportions of national populations were considered and it was found necessary to divide the countries of the world on two bases. The first was the degree of development and the second the nature of the economic system. Now these two are not necessarily separate and independent but for clarity and convenience it is best to consider them apart. This chapter, therefore, will concentrate on the degree of development and Chapter 8 on the nature of other economic systems than those so far assumed.

ASSIGNMENT

---

1. Figure 7.1 on page 126 covers the ESCAP Region (Economic and Social Commission for Asia and Pacific, of the United Nations). It is derived from a Background Report for the Regional Congress in 1982. It shows two features
   a) The share of the 10 largest cities in the whole country
   b) The share of the selected city (or cities) in the 10 cities.
   Refer back to Chapter 1, and as a preliminary for this chapter, make an analysis of these data.

CAPE COAST: AN EXAMPLE OF A CITY IN THE LESS DEVELOPED WORLD

One way to approach the urban settlements of less developed countries is to consider an example and to abstract from it some of the characteristics which are in contrast to the towns of the developed west. Two Dutch geographers have made a detailed study of Cape Coast in Ghana which they called 'Anatomy of an African Town'. Cape Coast has the advantage of being a medium sized town of just over 70 000 when the study was carried out. In the urban hierarchy of Ghana this put it well below the three largest settlements of Accra-Tema (739 000), Kumasi (345 000) and Sekondi-Takoradi (161 000).

The origin of the settlement was as a small fishing port called Oguaa. The present name seems to be a corruption into English of the name given by the Portuguese, Cato Corso. A castle was constructed by the Swedes in 1652 but the British gained control in 1664 and it became the major British fortress along what was then called the Gold Coast. After the establishment of the Protectorate of the Gold Coast in 1850, it was the centre of British administration and remained so until 1877 when the colonial administration was transferred to Accra. This had a major impact in undermining its continued growth, whilst commerce also declined since the major development areas of mineral resources and cocoa production were outside the Cape Coast hinterland and the railway system was based on Sekondi and Accra. The main function it retained was an educational one related to early missionary schools but, that apart, it became primarily a service centre for its own hinterland.

The site of Cape Coast is extremely uneven with dome shaped granite hills dissected by narrow valleys and this has played a significant part in the way the internal structure of the town has developed. The general morphology of Cape Coast is depicted in Figure 7.2. On that map four sub-divisions can be identified.

1. Cape Coast old town. This is made up of the original nucleus about the castle together with coastal extensions both to the east and the west. These are the areas with the highest population density. Figure 7.3 maps dominant house types and it will be seen that the old town is mainly made up of old single houses and compounds. The old single houses are

Figure 7.1

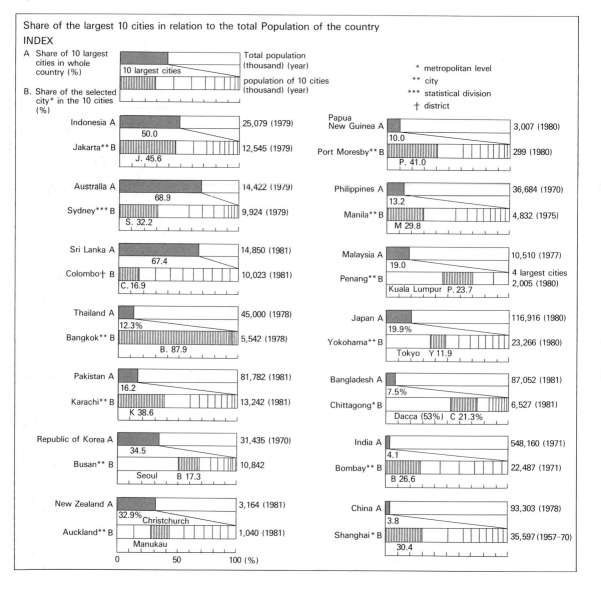

predominantly owned by matrilineal extended families and occupied by several households or nuclear families which are all linked through the female line. Often the house has been irregularly extended to accommodate the growing family grouping. The compound is made up of several dwellings built around a common entrance, with a patrilineal basis to the occupants, that is they are linked through the male line. Both of these form some of the poorest quality housing in the settlement. They are also losing some of their traditional character as the extended family on which they are based begins to break down and change under the impact of development and modernisation.

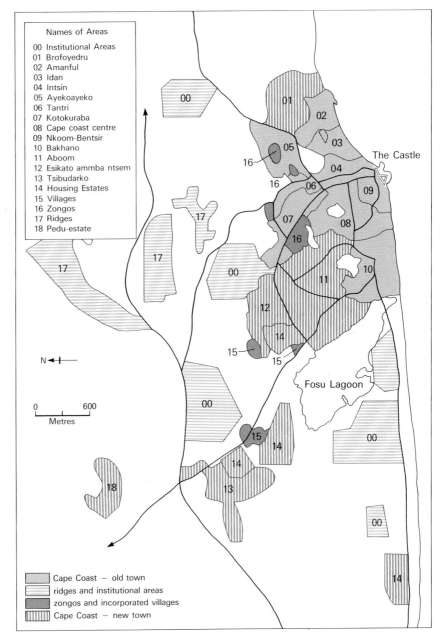

Figure 7.2

Morphological sub-division of Cape Coast (after Hinderink and Sterkenburg)

Names of Areas

00 Institutional Areas
01 Brofoyedru
02 Amanful
03 Idan
04 Intsin
05 Ayekoayeko
06 Tantri
07 Kotokuraba
08 Cape coast centre
09 Nkoom-Bentsir
10 Bakhano
11 Aboom
12 Esikato ammba ntsem
13 Tsibudarko
14 Housing Estates
15 Villages
16 Zongos
17 Ridges
18 Pedu-estate

Cape Coast – old town
ridges and institutional areas
zongos and incorporated villages
Cape Coast – new town

2. Zongos and incorporated villages. The growth of Cape Coast in the nineteenth century attracted a number of Moslem traders and people from the north of the country. They established the first *zongo*, a term which refers to the typical Moslem quarter in the urban centres of Ghana and Nigeria. With further growth others were established and in the present century northerners have settled in surrounding villages subsequently incorporated into Cape Coast. The *zongo* houses are small single-storey buildings of very simple construction from mud brick, sometimes without windows. By now most of the population is locally

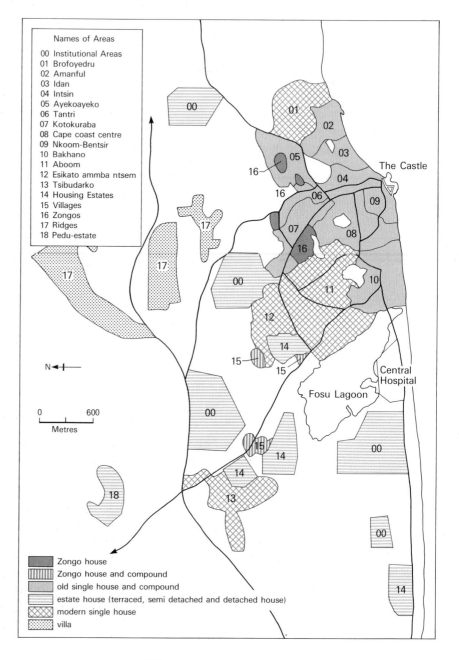

Names of Areas

00 Institutional Areas
01 Brofoyedru
02 Amanful
03 Idan
04 Intsin
05 Ayekoayeko
06 Tantri
07 Kotokuraba
08 Cape coast centre
09 Nkoom-Bentsir
10 Bakhano
11 Aboom
12 Esikato ammba ntsem
13 Tsibudarko
14 Housing Estates
15 Villages
16 Zongos
17 Ridges
18 Pedu-estate

Zongo house
Zongo house and compound
old single house and compound
estate house (terraced, semi detached and detached house)
modern single house
villa

Figure 7.3 *Dominant house types in Cape Coast (after Hinderink and Sterkenburg)*

born. As Figure 7.2, shows, these form a scattered element mainly on the urban fringe.

3. Institutional areas of the ridges.

The old administrative function of Cape Coast as the centre of colonial government led to the construction of administrative buildings and houses, usually the characteristic bungalow, for Europeans. This development took place on the healthier and more attractive ridges between the valley areas. The founding of schools has already been noted and, when other administrative functions were removed, the educational function remained and has been added to by a university campus and also the Central Hospital. The relation between these areas on Figure 7.2 and estate housing and especially villas, the most expensive housing, on Figure 7.3, is indicative of the high social and economic status of these areas. The main occupations are in the professions and in technical and administrative posts.

4. Cape Coast new town.

As the name implies, these are the newer areas within which there are two sub-divisions:

a) Planned estates built by the State Housing Corporation mainly for lower income groups but with an area (Pedu) in the extreme north-west for medium to high incomes.

b) Private speculative building especially of multi-storey property which is let by the room, so is generally of moderate quality.

Into this residential pattern it is now necessary to place other types of land-use. Pre-eminent amongst these is commercial use and especially retailing. There are three types of retailing which can be identified in Cape Coast.

1. Formal fixed-premise retailing.

This is the type familiar in western towns. The department and specialised stores can be identified in Figure 7.4. (Note the different scale, compared with Figs 7.2 and 7.3.) There are two supermarkets. These shops deal primarily in imported manufactured goods.

2. Market trading.

The market is the oldest form of distribution in West Africa. There are three markets (marked in Figure 7.4) but Kotokuraba is by far the largest accounting for some 80 per cent of the market trade. It is located within the commercial core and is walled. The stalls are provided by the Municipality. Although some manufactured goods are sold, the principal commodities are foodstuffs. Traditionally the market traders are mainly women since they were the producers of food crops, and the traders are regulated by market queens or queen-mothers who are elected for each commodity such as cassava, yam and palm oil. However, their present role is more ceremonial than economic, although they settle disputes which arise over selling space.

3. Street sellers and hawkers.

These are at the lowest level and are made up of

a) Street sellers who use non-fixed equipment such as tables by the roadside and who usually occupy the same site.

b) Those with no equipment other than a piece of cloth or plastic on which to set out their wares.

c) Hawkers who take their products to the consumer.

The goods involved are of a great variety but obviously of limited quantity; included are craft products and prepared food.

The physical expression of this activity is the straggling line of Commercial Street and Kotokuraba Street along which most of the shops, the market and the street sellers are distributed. But as Hinderink and Sterkenburg conclude, it is hardly a Central Business District and a more appropriate term would be a roadside shopping belt.

There is no other use which is sufficiently well developed to create a distinctive zone. Fish-smoking comes nearest being concentrated along the beaches to the east and west of the castle. Another feature is that redevelopment of the centre is taking place in the Nkoom-Bentsir area which was once occupied by the agents of trading firms. But decline of the port led to deterioration and new buildings for the Post Office, the commercial Bank of Ghana, a library and other administrative buildings have been erected.

Some conclusions from the study of Cape Coast

It is now possible-to attempt to draw some initial conclusions from this survey of Cape

Coast and the material reviewed in Chapter 1. They can then be used as the basis for extending the examination of urban settlements in the Third World.

1. Colonial impact. Virtually all the major towns of the less developed world have at one time or another been under colonial control from the west. The most immediate impact is to divide the settlement into two parts. The one is what can be called the native quarter which,

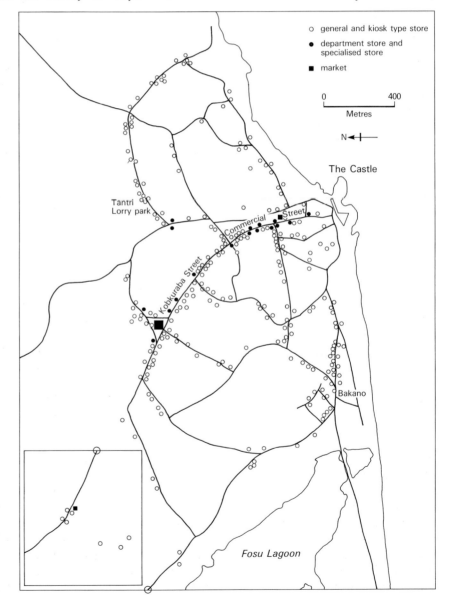

Figure 7.4 *Commercial establishments in Cape Coast (after Hinderink and Sterkenburg)*

having grown without planning, is often a maze of interconnecting alleys and streets. Since development preceded the motor car, these streets are narrow and can be ungraded. The contrast is the other part built by the colonial power to house its administrative buildings and those who worked in them. It is often spacious and sometimes monumental where the desire to impress was greatest. Wide boulevards and single family houses are characteristic.

2. The central area.

There is a parallel tendency, although not a directly related one, for the central area to have a dual character. The growth of retailing has produced modern centres very much in the western style dominated by high rise blocks, department stores and supermarkets. But still extant are the older forms of market and street traders. In some cases these co-exist, but in others the take over by modern forms at the city centre is completed and the street traders are confined to the squatter settlements and lowest quality residential areas.

3. Residential areas: socio-economic status.

There is a marked contrast between elite residential areas, often taken over from the old colonial sections set aside for Europeans, and the poorest parts. These latter are usually the inner city and the squatters at the margin. Although these types can be identified in Cape Coast, it is not a good example for the characteristic contrast between an elite at the centre and peripheral squatter settlements does not appear strongly. The elite have long abandoned the centre and taken over the old colonial areas on the ridges.

4. Residential areas: ethnicity.

The attractions of the city which have already been discussed (Chapter 1) bring in large numbers of people. But the political units, the nation states of the less developed world, represent the divisions imposed by colonial powers; they have not evolved from nuclear areas as in the west. The result is that peoples of very different ethnic origins are drawn to the cities and once there

attempt, or are forced, to preserve their distinctive cultures. A complex mosaic of ethnic groups is, therefore, often found in the larger cities.

5. Other uses.

Cape Coast had few distinctive other uses and indeed traditional craft industries are closely associated with residence, that is place of work and place of living have not been disassociated as in the developed world. But the growth of manufacturing especially will tend to bring that cleavage about and is likely also to appear in the larger settlements.

The remainder of this chapter will take each of these headings in turn in order to elaborate the characteristics which have been abstracted from the example taken and initial discussion in Chapter 1.

COLONIAL IMPACT

As has been noted in *1.* above, most of the larger towns of the Third World at some time experienced a period of occupation and rule by colonial powers, mostly European. At the time of occupation, the existing native cities were found by the colonising powers to be cramped, confined and usually insanitary. Moreover, the Europeans had little desire to live in close contact with the indigenous population, partly for cultural reasons (see p. 107) and partly for reasons of security. The response, therefore, was to build a new European city removed from, but usually adjacent to, the native city – creating the dual character. The British in India created a whole new vocabulary of urban terms such as cantonment (the military area), civil lines (the civilian area), with perhaps the most ubiquitous term of all which is in the widest use, the bungalow.

Professor Janet Abu-Lughod, who has written extensively on Third World urbanisation, cites Rabat-Sale in Morocco as a city which still clearly demonstrates the dichotomy between the native and European city. Rabat (ignoring the adjoining settlement of Sale to the east of the river, the Bou Regreg) was founded in the second half of the twelfth century as a

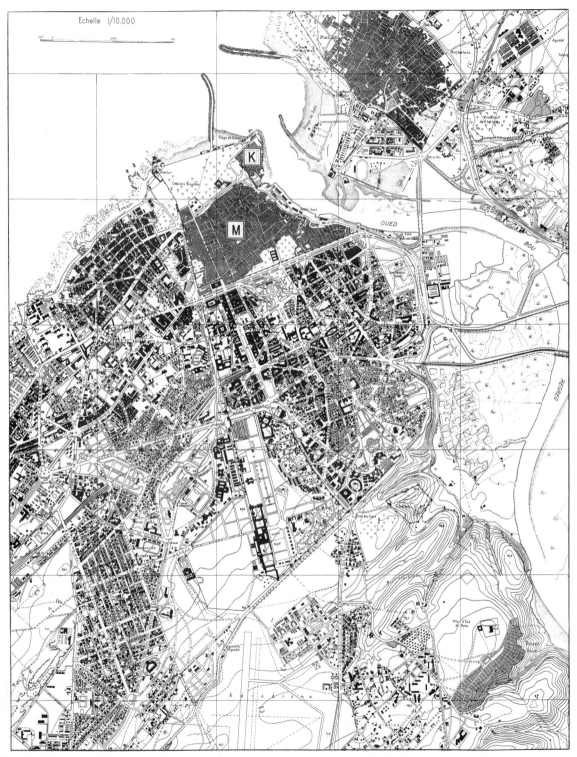

Figure 7.5 *Rabat-Sale. A general morphological map. M marks the location of the walled Medina*

staging post related to the Arab occupation of Spain. It never developed, however, and was effectively abandoned until the early seventeenth century when the Moslems were expelled from Spain and rebuilt the walled city. First they constructed the Kasbas des Oudaias, the defensive castle and stronghold to the north (K on Figure 7.5) and then the Medina (M on Figure 7.5), a characteristic intricate network of narrow streets and alleys. When the French established a Protectorate over Morocco in 1912, Rabat was made the administrative centre. The native Medina was left as it was surrounded by its walls which were not destroyed for they were retained as a symbolic and a legal barrier between the indigenous Moroccan population and the occupying French. A new city was built by the French to the south of the Medina (Figure 7.5) characterised by all the elements of classic town planning, round points or circuses, or *places* to use the French term, connected by broad avenues. All the new buildings of the French protectorate, both administrative and cultural, were located there.

Thus the two completely contrasted elements of urban structure, the Medina and the colonial French city, stand side by side separated by the still extant walls of the early city.

Before leaving this first characteristic of colonial impact two further points, both in qualification, must be made.

1. The contrast between old and new, unplanned and planned sections of towns is not restricted to the less developed world. Indeed many of the features can be identified in European towns in past times. Thus the contrast between the old medieval nucleus of Edinburgh and the new town built after plans approved in 1767 mirrors the dual character of many colonial towns.

2. Not all cities of the less developed world were unplanned, indeed town planning probably began in the east. Some of the most elaborate city planning can be found in Anghor in Cambodia and in the great pre-Columbian cities of Central and South America such as Tenochtitlan in Mexico.

THE CENTRAL AREAS AND RETAILING

The way in which two elements develop in the retailing systems of developing countries was exemplified by the modern supermarkets of Cape Coast on the one hand and the street traders on the other. So, in many cities of the Third World, there exists what is called a dual economy. The first element of this dualism is called the formal economy of the international sphere of manufacturing, trading, business and commerce. It is epitomised by the modern towers of concrete and glass which are found in the centres of all large cities and represent

Figure 7.6 *(a) Kuala Lumpur. This street scene in the city is China Town. It shows a surviving pattern of retailing from street stalls, as well as the modern buildings in the background*

(b) Bangkok. This is a part of the floating market. Where communication is easier by water the same phenomenon develops but the market is carried on from small boats

part of the process of transformation or modernisation. This is especially true of the great cities of Latin America, such as Rio de Janeiro or Caracas where the process has proceeded furthest. But Singapore and Hong Kong are equally good examples. The second element is the informal economy which is most characteristic of the marginal squatter settlements. It is equivalent to what is known in the west as 'the black economy'. It consists of a great multitude of minor activities of repairing and refurbishing, often of material rescued from rubbish dumps, of selling even of the most trivial items such as empty medicine bottles, as well as the provision of immediate personal services such as hair cutting. No records are kept and no taxation is levied and the whole system operates independently of the higher, formal level of the business world. It penetrates, however, as Cape Coast exemplifies, into the same territory through the street traders and especially the hawkers.

It would, of course, be totally wrong to imply that there was nothing between these two extremes. Again, as Cape Coast demonstrated, there is a whole range of situations from tables set up daily, to permanent kiosks and craft-cum-retail stores which represent the transition between the two extremes. Many governments, however, have deliberately set out to upgrade the quality of the central areas of their largest cities by clearing out the small businesses and replacing them by modern shopping complexes and specific craft centres mainly directed at the tourist market. Singapore has undergone massive redevelopment since becoming a republic in 1965 and much of the old small scale trading-shopping provision has been replaced by large modern complexes (see Figure 7.16).

RESIDENTIAL AREAS: SOCIO-ECONOMIC STATUS

It was observed that although Cape Coast demonstrated a strong contrast between high status and low status areas, and also a peripheral location of some of the low status areas, it was by no means typical of urban settlement in developing countries, especially in the lack of large squatter areas. Lusaka, the capital of Zambia, can be considered in order to advance the analysis of residential areas. Figure 7.7 outlines quite simply the basic urban structure. The high income residential areas are central in location and related closely to the commercial core. But they also extend in sectoral fashion to the east-south-east where, critically, they take in the major administrative area (remember Cape Coast), and also to the northeast. The major low income residential areas are quite clearly peripheral, indicated by the ring of concentrated squatter settlements.

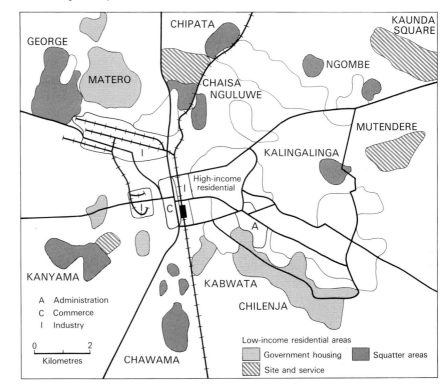

Figure 7.7 *Lusaka: the basic urban structure (after O'Connor). For an explanation of site and service see text page 141*

KAUNDA SQUARE

CHIPATA

GEORGE

NGOMBE

MATERO

CHAISA NGULUWE

MUTENDERE

KALINGALINGA

High-income residential

C

A

KANYAMA

A   Administration
C   Commerce
I   Industry

KABWATA

CHILENJA

0   2

Kilometres   CHAWAMA

Low-income residential areas

Government housing   Squatter areas

Site and service

There is also some low income government housing and what is termed *'site and service'* which will be discussed later in this chapter (p. 141). Lusaka illustrates the most basic structure with those highest in the social scale still resident at or near the centre with the poorest housing not only inner city, as in the west, but much more importantly in a peripheral band. This fundamental feature of cities in less developed countries needs both explanation and development.

The elite and central residence: some explanations

It is clear that the city centre is associated with the highest prestige for that is where the major attractions, and the widest range of facilities, still remain; theatres and night clubs, restaurants and art galleries, concert halls and museums. Even in western cities, and in spite of suburbanisation, the most exclusive and prestigious areas are still found at or near the city centre. Boston's Beacon Hill or Manhattan's Upper East side (p. 121) are admirable examples from the USA. There is, therefore, an inherent attraction in city centre location. But to that a number of other critical considerations are added in developing countries.

The first is the direct problem of mobility. Suburbanisation depends on effective mass transit and where that is inadequate then there is little attraction in moving to the periphery. Moreover, there is every reason to remain within the security of the improved and policed centre rather than to incur the dangers of the less well supervised peripheral locations. Again, those locations are much less likely to have the out-of-town shopping centres and all the other advantages of western suburban living.

The second consideration is that it is critical for an elite in society, especially in new countries where political conditions are not stable, to ensure that its control is maintained and that neither riot nor rebellion can succeed. This implies a secure hold on all those buildings in the city related to government and order. Traditionally in the past they were palace and

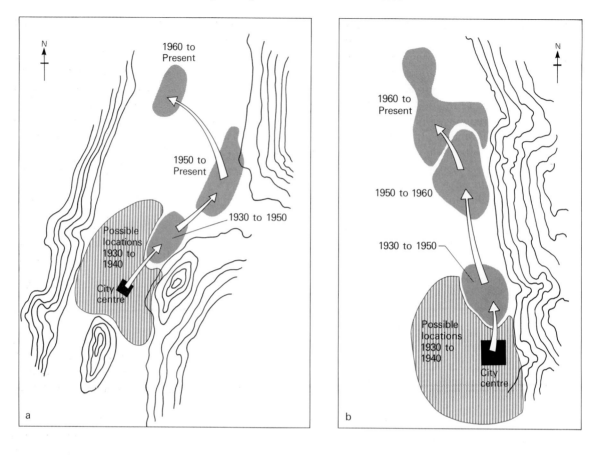

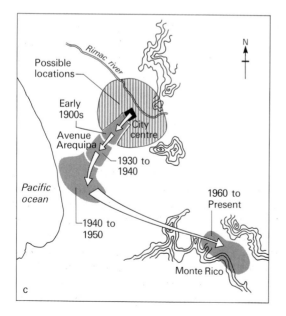

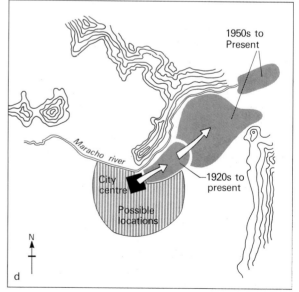

church, possibly also cathedral, and at a lower level guild hall and town hall. At the present, the President's palace is still significant, as is the parliament or centre of government. But even more relevant is the radio and TV station from which misinformation can, literally, be broadcast. As long as authority retains control of the real and symbolic centres of power no revolution can claim success. In 1986, the deposition of President Marcos of the Philippines illustrated the process of the overthrow of a government being achieved by a takeover of the significant buildings in Manila. All this being so, it is vital for the elite to retain their hold by dominance of these central symbols of power and to do that they must live close to them. In times of instability one cannot afford to be out of town. Those in power will certainly have country retreats or estates but they are very different from permanent peripheral residence.

The elite and central residence: some development

In Chapter 1 it was observed that the countries of Latin America did not fit easily into the proposed categories since neither developed nor less developed were appropriate descriptions. Indeed, these examples can be taken as representative of most contemporary changes. The internal structural developments of four large Latin American cities are illustrated diagrammatically in Figure 7.8. In each of the four cities there has been a clear extension of the upper-class or elite areas of residence accompanied by a progressive abandonment of the centre and of the inner city. That extension has been quite unmistakably sectoral, dominated by all the principles set out by Hoyt and noted in Chapter 5. Indeed, the main purpose of the original study was to stress the elongated shapes

Figure 7.8 *The movement of the elite in four Latin American cities (after Amato): elite locations in (a) Quito, Ecuador 1537–1967 (b) Bogota, Colombia, 1538–1964 (c) Lima, Peru, 1535–1967 (d) Santiago, Chile 1541–1967*

of the settlements which ensued. The first movements date in three of the cases (Quito, Bogota and Santiago) to the 1920s and 1930s, appropriately somewhat later than in the western industrialised countries like the USA and United Kingdom. The exception is Lima where the initial movement was, in the first decade of the twentieth century, largely related to earlier industrial growth and transportation development. In the 1920s, the *Avenue Arequipa* exerted a specific attraction since it gave access to the Pacific shore. Large houses were built along it and by the 1950s a continuous front had developed. But by the end of that decade the area had become surrounded by middle-class housing so that in the 1960s the younger sections of the upper-class elite began to move to the uplands of the *Monte Rico*. They were certainly not driven by lack of land although the mountain climate was more attractive. But the main incentive was the search for more exclusive locations with much greater privacy. Indeed, large homes have been built in extensive grounds which are enclosed by high stone walls.

At this point it would seem that, in these Latin American cases, there is a clear parallel with the developed west with the same processes being operative. But that conclusion has to be modified if a broader view of the city structure is taken. It is possible to use a *Measure of Centralisation* which is the average distance from the city centre of each social group. It takes the form

$$Ce = \Sigma \frac{(D.P.)}{N}$$

where Ce is the Measure, D the distance of a sub-unit from the city centre, P the numbers in a social group in that unit and N the total in the social group in the city. D is usually measured to the centre of the sub-unit. Table 7.1 shows the Measure of Centralisation for the major social groups in each of the four South American cities. The figures, which show the average distance of each group from the centre, are in kilometres. The middle socio-economic group (middle class) has been divided into two, the lowest group into three (except in the case of Santiago). These measures seem to be at odds with the implications of the maps for only in Bogota is the upper group clearly at the greatest distance. In Lima, where the move to Monte Rico, illustrated in Figure 7.8c, suggests a marked peripheral development, those lowest in the social order are still, on average, furthest away.

Table 7.1 *Measurement of centralisation for socio-economic groups in four Latin American cities (after Amato)*

Class	Quito	Bogota	Lima	Santiago
Upper 1	3.48	9.69	6.06	6.25
Middle 2	5.69	5.84	6.18	4.14
Middle 3	0.95	9.04	5.08	6.89
Lower 4	2.39	3.01	4.72	–
Lower 5	2.47	6.20	11.96	7.13
Lower 6	3.60	–	6.82	–

Note i. Six socio-economic groups are used, the conventional middle order being divided into two and the lower into three (cf. the five social groups of the British census).

ii. The three divisions of the lower group are amalgamated for Santiago.

The residential locations of the poor

In explanation of this situation it is necessary to refer back to Chapter 1. There one of the characteristics of the less developed world was identified, a massive urbanward migration of population which the employment opportunities available could not absorb. But more significantly in the present context, the housing available is also totally inadequate and the municipalities cannot from their resources meet the enormous demand. The result is that the immigrants simply squat on whatever land is available bringing into being enormous squatter or spontaneous settlements. This, of course, is not unique to South America, but is found widely throughout the Third World as indicated in Chapter 1. Professor Dwyer, who has made a

special study of these settlements, wrote in 1975 about Lima where the great distance from the centre of those lowest in the social scale has been noted, 'In the case of Lima, the capital of Peru . . . a mushrooming of squatter settlements began during the 1950s. The number of urban squatters increased from 120 000 in 1956 to 800 000 in 1970 and today squatters constitute about 40 per cent of the total population. In all, the construction of squatter settlements probably accounted for more than four-fifths of the physical growth of metropolitan Lima during the decade 1960–70.' Professor Dwyer goes on to note that whereas the largest squatter settlements were on the periphery, some of the more recent are over 25 kilometres from the centre; and he continues, 'This pattern of spatial extension will probably remain the city's predominant means for accommodating further population growth for the foreseeable future since it has been estimated that by 1990 there may well be as many as 4.5 million people in Lima's squatter settlements out of a total urban population of 6 million.' Clearly, the distances set out in Table 7.1 are greatly increasing as far as the lowest groups are concerned as the city fails to cope with the housing demand set up by this massive influx.

The locations taken up by these newcomers to the city can be set out in the form of a diagram which also indicates something of the dynamic processes (Figure 7.9). The city centre, with its perceived concentration of job opportunities, is the preferred location and, as in the developed world, the predominant movement of low status immigrants is to the inner city. But that area is incapable of assimilating the numbers. Moreover, at the centre, with growth, commercial and associated uses are extending and rents are rising so that many of the inner city residents are forced out towards the periphery. People in the lowest social groups are displaced outwards just as many of the new immigrants move directly to these squatter settlements at the margin. The term squatter has a specific connotation for it implies that the residents have no legal right to the land on which they build their shacks or shanties. The only land available to them is waste or unwanted land which most often is unused because of environmental problems such as the extremes of flooding or water shortage, or steepness of slope (see Fig. 7.15).

With this model in mind further consideration can be given to Lima (Figure 7.10). The squatter settlements which have been noted above are usually given various names across the world. In French speaking areas they are called *bidonvilles*, in many Spanish speaking countries they are called *barrios*, in Rio de Janeiro they are called *favelas* and in Calcutta they are called *bustees*. In Lima the name used is *barriadas*. The distribution of the barriadas of Lima is shown in Figure 7.10, where it can be seen that both inner city and periphery are

involved. Much of the early development was near the central parts of the city in keeping with the model so that the internal barriadas form a distinctive group dating mainly to the 1940s and the early 1950s. They are in general those showing the densest distribution of population and the worst physical conditions. There is a second inner group to the east and north-east of the centre identified by the names El Agustino and San Cristobal. The earliest phase of peripheral growth took place in relation to the industrial area to the west of the city in the mid-1950s forming the barriada of San Martin de Porres. Subsequently, the major growth has been to the north forming the Carabayllo complex (Comas and Cuevas on Figure 7.10), whilst more recently a southern group has

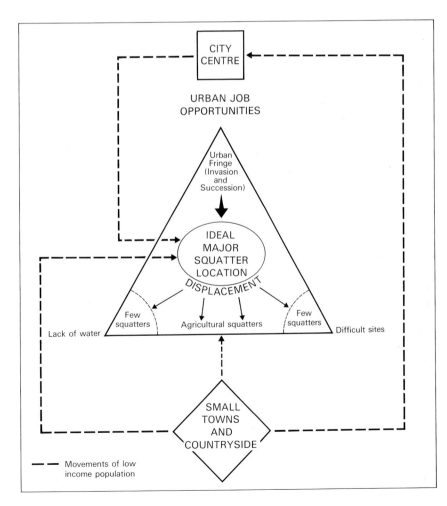

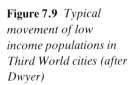

Figure 7.9 *Typical movement of low income populations in Third World cities (after Dwyer)*

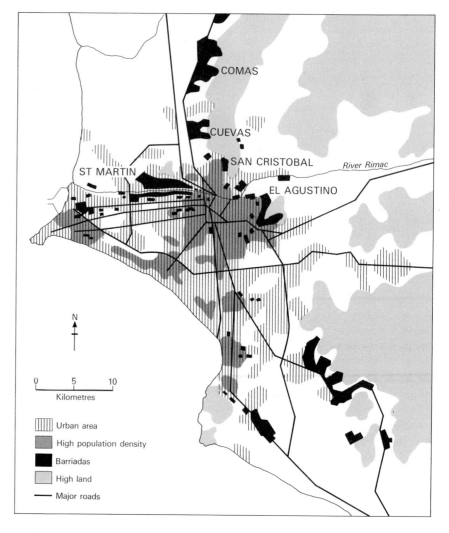

Figure 7.10 *The distribution of squatter settlements or barriadas in Lima (after Deler)*

developed. In these cases characteristic sites were the dry unirrigated valleys breaking the mountain front which were unused and unoccupied. There is manifestly a clear relationship between the model of Figure 7.9 and the actuality of Lima as depicted in Figure 7.10.

Also, reference back to the example of Lusaka will indicate the basic elements of the residential structure of cities of the less developed world. High and middle status areas remain central but extend in sectoral fashion to the margins. In contrast, and located away from the quality sectors, are the areas of public housing representing the totally inadequate attempt by the authorities to solve the problems

of housing. These are again usually in sectoral form. Areas of slums and squatter settlements are found both in inner city and peripheral locations. Lusaka, itself, can be taken as a model. One qualification needs to be made. There is a proper difference between slums and squatter settlements. In the former, however dilapidated the conditions, the resident holds rights by virtue of paying rent; in the squatter settlements no such rights are held.

The upgrading of squatter areas. Extensive studies have been undertaken of squatter settlements largely related to identifying the ways in which conditions can be improved. Since these are, to use another name for them, spontaneous settlements, they come into being without any infrastructure whatsoever. The widely used term infrastructure covers all those underlying services which virtually support urban living such as water supply, sewage treatment and drainage, energy supplies such as gas and electricity and also roads, street lighting and transport. Given the impossible financial task of providing even the lowest quality municipal housing for all, the way forward for Third World cities is seen through what is called sites and services, a phrase introduced earlier in this chapter when commenting on Lusaka on page 134. By this approach, the responsible municipal authority tacitly accepts the rights of squatters to the lands on which they have settled and sets out to provide what has been called above an infrastructure, that is those essential services at the occupied sites so that some form of upgrading can begin; hence the name sites and services. This usually takes the form of the most basic elements of infrastructure, particularly electricity and water supply, with roads and drainage closely associated. Given these environmental improvements, the squatters are encouraged to improve their own homes, replacing board and corrugated tin or galvanised sheets with bricks and mortar and extending the accommodation by adding rooms. In this way a gradual improvement is envisaged.

The aim of government, both local and national, is to transform both the environment and the economy so that both eventually become part of the one unified national system and that the people of the squatter camps no longer live at the margins. Marginality is another word sometimes used to describe the condition of these populations. In many ways that transformation is in accord with the aspirations of the inmigrants themselves. The urban newcomers have been divided, by scholars who have studied them, into three groups. The first group is called the *Bridgeheaders*. The analogy is clear. These are the most recent migrants who are establishing a bridgehead in the city and who are seeking to establish minimal shelter. They are, therefore, most concerned

with rights to the land they have occupied and they are predominantly involved in the informal economy since few jobs are available to urban newcomers with few skills. The second group is called the *Consolidators*. These are usually in process of improving their initial crude dwellings and they are beginning to look to the formal economy to provide jobs and hence greater stability. They become less concerned with property rights, which have possibly been acquired, and are much more concerned with such things as education and the provision of schools to open up opportunities for their children. Finally, there is the third group of *Status Seekers*. They have achieved stability and relative security and begin to look for improved education and health services, and also for financial credit either to improve their housing or indeed to move to better quality accommodation.

There is manifestly an assumed progression in this classification of urban inmigrants whereby infrastructures, housing and employment are gradually improved to a condition where the squatter settlement is transformed into a normal suburb and the population wholly absorbed into the formal economy. Such a progression is, of course, highly idealistic. The tide of inmigrants is such, the financial resources of municipalities so limited and the economic growth of the countries so constrained, that the transformation is seldom achieved in the simple terms set out here. But, nevertheless, it is the envisaged path of progress.

Even when such processes are successful problems can arise. The Tondo squatter area in Manila is one of the largest, covering some 450 acres. It occupies the foreshore, north of the Pasig River (Figure 7.11) and developed as a consequence of a massive inmigration of population after World War Two. This initial phase saw the occupation of land which had been devastated by the War and was, therefore, central in location rather than peripheral. In the early 1960s attempts were made forcibly to remove the squatters but they failed to have any impact and Tondo itself and its condition

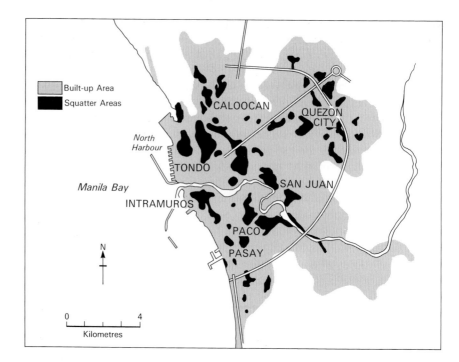

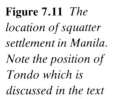

Figure 7.11 *The location of squatter settlement in Manila. Note the position of Tondo which is discussed in the text*

became a significant political issue. As a result, in the late 1970s the World Bank provided finance for its upgrading (Crooke, P. 1983 Popular Housing Supports, in Skinner, R. J. and Rodell, H. J. (eds.) *People, Poverty and Shelter*. Methuen, London). Included were drainage and sewage works and the provision of water supply. Above all, the provision of land titles to those who had built dwellings was ensured, nominally leasehold but with the option to purchase after five years. But all this has brought the area into the formal economy. Property can be sold with ownership rights so that a land market has developed with rising prices for what is a location convenient to the port. This in turn has led to rising rents and the poorest are being squeezed out. The difficulties of those at the bottom of the social scale have been increased by the upgrading process, rather than solved.

RESIDENTIAL AREAS: ETHNICITY

The diverse ethnic or tribal composition of many modern states created out of formal col-onial territories is reflected in the cities which are the common targets of migration. Ethnic diversity is, therefore, characteristic especially of the largest cities which offer the apparently greatest attractions. It is, however, not a simple matter of ethnic difference alone since the distinction between socio-economic and ethnic status is not a very sharp one and the two are often associated. Moreover, within ethnic groups there are also distinctive social gradings as in the caste system amongst Hindus. All these overlie each other creating very complex situations, none more so than in Calcutta which can be cited in illustration.

The internal structure of Calcutta, as so many cities of the less developed world, has been greatly influenced by the presence of the British under the old imperial system. It has also been af-fected by the extensive immigration of a great variety of populations, including refugees at the time of the establishment of the separate states of India and Pakistan in 1947. Two approaches can be made to the urban geography of Calcutta. The first is to identify the poorest area, the equivalent of the spontaneous or squatter settlements, of other countries; the second is to review more directly the varying ethnic elements against that background.

Figure 7.12 charts the predominant land-use patterns in Calcutta and especially emphasises the distribution of the *bustees*. These are the poorest type of tenement house where 'there is but one water tap for every 25 persons and no means of disposing of sewage. Cholera is endemic. Life is often brief and brutal.' Those words were writtten by B. J. Berry in 1977 (*Contemporary Urban Ecology*. Macmillan, New York, p. 156). He also outlined the way in which these poorest residential areas had come into being. 'Around the periphery of the city are found the poorest residents of and migrants to the city . . . the process at work in

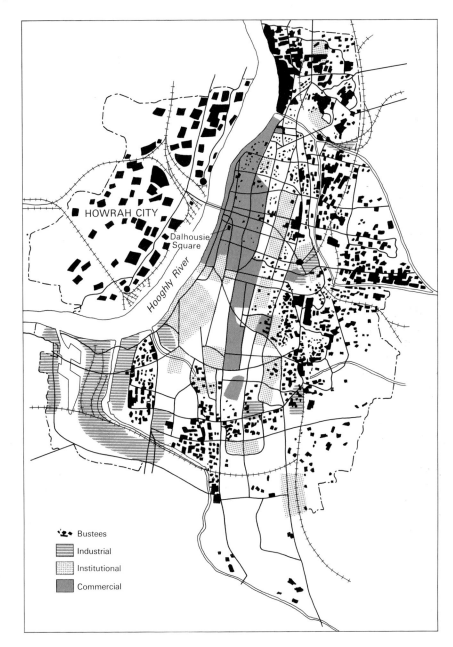

Figure 7.12 *Calcutta: dominant land-uses and the location of bustees (after Berry and Kasarda)*

the creation of the bustees they occupy was not one of orderly choice in an ethnically governed market framework but rather one of often illegal occupation of 'empty' land at the urban periphery by poor farmers. There they erect a shack and attempt to survive.' Thus, in many ways, poverty over-rides ethnicity.

But the second feature is that of ethnicity, for the varied populations migrating to Calcutta have brought about a wide range of populations of different languages and religions. Figure 7.13 portrays some, certainly not all, of these contrasts. From it one can note that the upper class (or high caste) Benghali-speaking Hindus occupy a relatively central position (Figure 7.13b). They have moved there from an earlier concentration to the north by taking over the former Anglo-Indian and European residential area which had been located in close relation to the *Maidan* (marked on Figure 7.11a and b), a large park stretching along the banks of the Hooghly River and extending southward. There the Europeans lived in very large houses with extensive gardens which are now being acquired by both Benghalis and Non-Benghalis who can afford to pay. But even though there is a general coincidence, differences can be identified between the Benghali concentrations and those of the commercial and bureaucratic classes of other ethnic backgrounds (Figure 7.13c). The Benghali poor show a marked contrast with those of higher social status and the correspondence with the areas of bustees (Figure 7.12) is clearly apparent. But there is also a contrast with the Non-Benghali poor, the immigrants from Bihar, Orissa and Uttar Pradesh. In short, in this highly complex city, there are contrasts in terms both of socio-economic status and of ethnicity.

It is perhaps improper to include South Africa under the heading of a Third World or less developed country. But many South Africans will speak of their country as at the interface between the two, as being a developed economy confronted by Third World problems, especially in the realm of urbanisation. The influx of black populations is regarded as the direct parallel of the large scale migrations to Third World cities. In many ways apartheid was designed to meet that problem by ensuring the maintenance of cultural identity. But in its abstract form that went beyond the black-white-Indian-Coloured separation. Figure 7.14 is a plan of an ideal apartheid city, that is one constructed according to the principles set out in the Group Areas Act (compare with Figure 6.12). Note that the various black groups, based on language, the Zulu, Xhosa, Sotho and Tswana, are all allocated separate areas. These represent ethnic segregation of immigrant black populations. As indicated in Chapter 6, this was attempted in the structuring of Soweto. The basic problem is antagonism between the various groups which, in Durban for example, has led to serious disturbances. The basis for ethnic separation is largely the same as in western cities but it can be very complex where states encompass widely different ethnic groups.

OTHER USES

Two other types of city land-use have experienced significant development since the Second World War.

1. Industry. Western cities were transformed by the growth of industry in the nineteenth century and in consequence the location of industrial land has been a significant factor in the organisation of urban land-uses. However, in cities in the less developed world there emerged what has been called the *incomplete metropoles*, that is large cities which lack important elements in their functional make-up. The most crucial of these was factory industry since these settlements were usually relegated to the role of assembling and exporting raw materials to the homelands of the colonial powers where manufacturing into

Figure 7.13 *Calcutta: Benghali and non-Benghali population (after Bose) (a) Benghali poor (b) Benghali speaking Hindus of upper, middle and artisan classes (c) non-Benghalis of commercial and bureaucratic classes (d) non-Benghali poor*

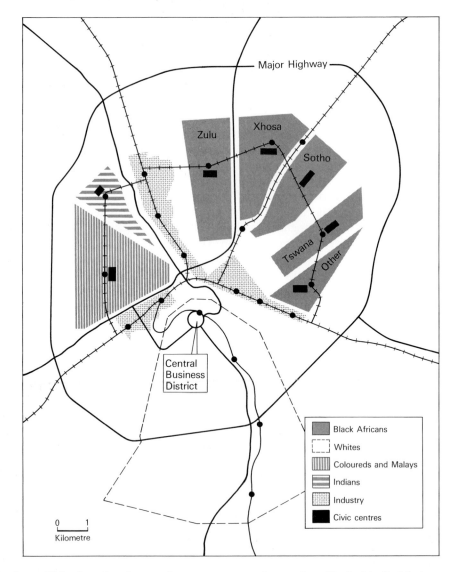

Figure 7.14 *An ideal apartheid city (after Western). This is a model derived from the legal frame of apartheid and of the Group Areas Act. Compare with Figure 6.12 which is derived from the actual pattern within the South African cities*

finished products took place. This situation has greatly changed in the last twenty-five years. The high cost of labour in developed countries has led to what has been called the export of jobs, and low-cost labour countries have taken the opportunity to promote their own industries. This has been accentuated by the conditions of political independence. Countries such as Hong Kong, Taiwan and South Korea are the best known examples. The result has been the growth of distinctive industrial zones within the cities.

Since becoming a republic in 1965 Singapore

has concentrated on what Drakakis-Smith has called 'an aggressive export-based industrial growth financed by foreign investors' (Drakakis-Smith, D. 1987 *The Third World City*, Methuen, London). He goes on to point out that the growth has been based on substantial financial incentives and the guarantee of a cheap and controlled labour force. The money, mainly from the USA and Japan, has been used to promote a variety of industry including petroleum products, ship-building, plastics and electronic goods. Figure 7.17 indicates the extensive areas set aside for industry in Singa-

Figure 7.15 *Township housing, Soweto, Johannesburg. These photographs show the extremes.*
(a) Shanty-type accommodation which is put up by newly arrived immigrants from the rural areas.

(b) Private housing in the area of Soweto known as 'Hollywood'. Township housing is not all of the same quality and wide variations occur

pore which has included the building of a new town at Jurong where some 60 per cent of manufacturing jobs are located. There is a major container dock adjacent. There is also a national science park.

These large scale developments are generally restricted to the major cities and national capitals. Elsewhere industry still retains its older twofold distribution being either in the form of small craft based establishments in the inner city or larger scale factory activity on the docksides of the ports.

2. Administrative uses. Independence for Third World countries has meant an emphasis on national identity. Many have sought to epitomise that identity by building monumental administrative centres parallel to those of western nations (Washington, Canberra). Even in the example with which this chapter began,

Figure 7.16 *Singapore, craft-workshops. Although cities in the developing world, like Singapore, are creating large scale modern industries, some of the old activities still remain although in the process of being removed. Cycle repairing is a typical small scale workshop activity carried out in old, limited premises. But note the highrise building in the background.*

Cape Coast, it was noted that the clearance of a central area was being followed by the replacement by administrative buildings. But the two best known examples are Brasilia, the new capital of Brazil, and Chandigarh built after independence to be the new capital of the Indian part of the Punjab, the former capital of Lahore having been assigned to Pakistan.

The idea of a new capital for Brazil can be traced back to the eighteenth century and it was specifically noted, immediately after the foundation of the republic in 1889, in the Constitution of 1891. The present city is the product of the ambition and initiative of President Kubitschek who was inaugurated in 1956 and in the same year announced an international competition for the design. The competition was judged by an international panel and was won by Tricio Costa. The plan is made up of two axes crossing at right angles, in the sign of the Cross. But in order to adapt to the terrain one of the axes is curved and the other was conceived as a mall. Without entering into detail, two critical points can be noted.

a) Brasilia is an international city in the sense that it has little about it which is specifically and uniquely Brazilian either in its design or its architecture. Perhaps the most distinctive attempts to develop an architecture and an urban ambience different from that of the west is to be found in the oil-rich Arab states where design is related to aspects of indigenous culture.

b) When Brasilia was being built a virtual shanty town, then called Cidade Livre, was developed to house the workers. Initially it was to be demolished when the work was complete but it has become a permanent feature, now renamed Nucleo Bandierante. This is characteristic of the widespread development of squatter settlements about Brasilia with the contrast between the monumental core and the lowest quality periphery indicative of those general patterns which were noted earlier on in this chapter.

Inevitably controversy arose over the massive expenditure on Brasilia, the parlous state of the Brazilian economy and the poverty of many of the people.

CONCLUSION

The brief consideration of Brasilia is an appropriate note on which to conclude this chapter for the countries of the less developed world are quintessentially caught between the ambition to modernise and urbanise and the major problems which the process inevitably brings. Indeed, at the broadest scale, urbanisation and modernisation are regarded as implicitly meaning westernisation and hence inducing critical social and cultural, as well as economic, change. Hence some countries, such as Cuba, have attempted to adopt policies to resist excessive urbanisation.

The most general interpretation of the present process of change, however, is that of

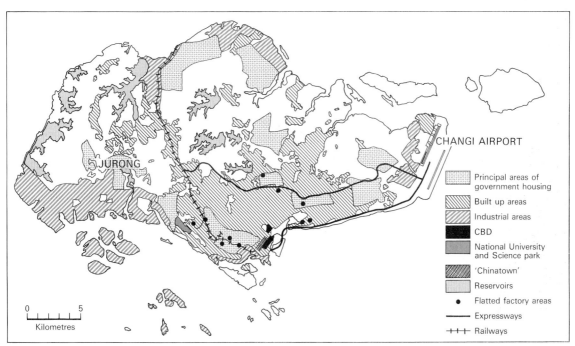

Figure 7.17 *Singapore: major land-uses (after Drakakis-Smith)*

the superimposition of those processes, and their physical consequences, which have created the western city, onto the underlying, indigenous form of urban development. Along with that goes the additional feature of the creation of peripheral shanty towns which are the consequences of urbanward migration. The result is a complexity far removed from the simplistic concepts of concentric zones or sectors which are specifically related to industrialising American towns in the period between the wars.

ASSIGNMENTS

2. Locate Cape Coast on the map of Ghana and compare its situation with the three larger settlements. Can you discover why the British shifted their centre of administration from Cape Coast to Accra in 1877?

3. Perhaps the classic case of contrast between the old and the new is that between Delhi and New Delhi in India. Attempt to develop a study of Delhi similar to the one on Rabat above. If possible consult King, A. D. 1976 *Colonial Urban Develop-*

opment, Routledge and Kegan Paul, London. If you find material on New Delhi difficult to obtain, select another city where you can identify the same contrasts.

4. a) If the explanations given above are applicable to contemporary cities in the less developed world were they in past times applicable in the West?

   b) Is a central London address important to the various British elites (political, literary, media, entertainment) at the present? Is there any comparison to be made with Third World cities?

5. In February 1988 mudslides caused extensive damage and caused many deaths in the '*favelas*' or squatter settlements of Rio de Janeiro. Look up the newspaper accounts in your public library and relate the events to the conditions, physical and social, which are discussed in this chapter.

6. The diagrams in Figure 7.18 on p. 150 all refer to Manila. They come from the ESCAP Report referred to in Assignment 1, p. 125. Consider the problems that arise from these data for urban planners in the city.

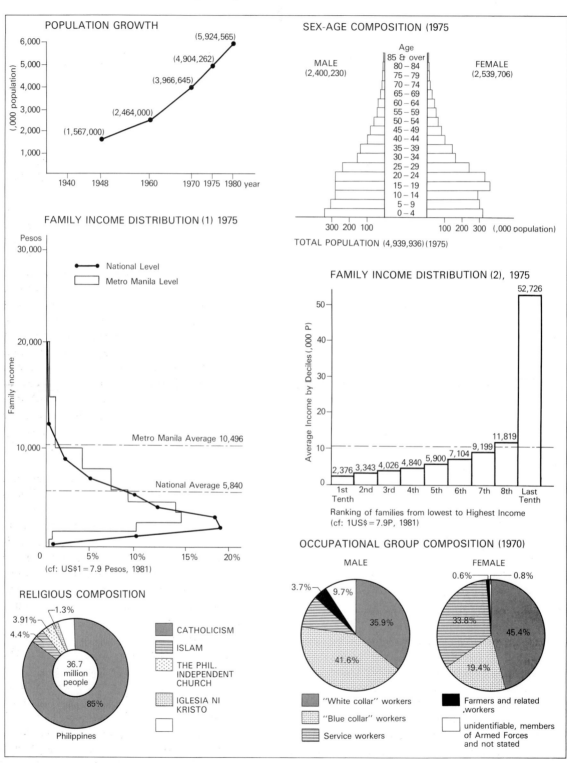

Figure 7.18

8

The City in Socialist Countries

INTRODUCTION

When, in Chapter 1, the characteristics of urban populations were considered it was indicated that, although a division into the developed and the less developed worlds was critical, there were also contrasts between socialist and non-socialist countries. Thus both the nature of the growth and the internal configuration of cities can be thought of as brought about by two opposite sets of conditions. The first set constitutes the free market. Within the law, individuals bid for land which goes to the highest bidder who puts it to any use whatsoever. Normally one would expect the most profitable use but that is not necessarily so. If the decision is a poor one and financial losses ensue, then the successful bidder can be forced to sell and the process is repeated. The city is the product of the set of conditions which constitute the market economy. In its extreme form there are no limitations or constraints at all, such as on the creation of pollution or similar environmental problems. There are no necessities to house, or consider the physical or social welfare of, the poorest, the least able to compete. They are relegated to building whatever shelter they can on whatever ground can be taken over. Hence the emergence of squatter settlements, or of people sleeping rough. There are, however, as noted above, legal restraints which prevent the descent to the ultimate condition where the deployment of force or violence becomes the arbitrator rather than the deployment of money. Even so, many books and films have been based on attempts by individuals or groups to gain control of land by illegal means, usually threats of violence. It is a stereotyped plot frequently exploited.

The second and opposite set of conditions can be thought of as absolute central control by the state. All aspects of the city including its size, function, layout and internal organisation are determined by the authority of the state and are planned centrally by the state, or by the municipality to which powers are delegated. The individual has no freedom to do as he or she wishes. Absolute control over migration by means of internal passports or pass books directs population movements so that pressure on urban facilities becoming too great is prevented. Rural disadvantage remains rural disadvantage; it is not transferred to the towns. Work and housing are allocated, of whatever nature and in whatever location authority determines. In extreme cases banishment to the distant country can be decreed. Everything about the city is planned, therefore – nominally in favour of egalitarianism.

Now, it must be already perfectly evident that neither of these extreme sets of conditions operates in an unconstrained way in any country. Thus, although in Britain the individual is 'free' to buy a house wherever it is desired, as long as the money is to hand or can be borrowed, the actual building of houses, both in terms of where they are located and the minimum standards to which they must conform, are controlled by planning regulations, development control as it is called, on the one hand, and by housing by-laws on the other. Likewise in socialist cities the controls are seldom absolute. Writing on housing problems and policies in socialist cities of Eastern Europe and the USSR, Hamilton and Burnett assert that 'evidence suggests that social strata "sort themselves out" among housing types and zones according to: their priority status for inexpensive state housing; their incomes which may permit them (or not) to rent or purchase better private (villa-type) housing or to become owner-occupiers of co-operative flats; and aspirations which shape their preferences' (R. A. French and F. E. Ian Hamilton (eds.) *The Socialist City*, Wiley, Chichester, 1979). Again, *The Sunday Times* noted in April 1988 that the Politburo has decided to allow tenants to form co-operative groups to buy state-owned apartment blocks. Until then such groups have been permitted to build flats but not to buy properties. Co-operatively owned housing constitutes below 10 per cent of the total housing stock but is preferred because of its higher standards. Like the British decision to sell council housing, the decision seems based on the principle that housing in private hands is better looked after, one that departs considerably from socialist theory. The very terms 'private housing' and 'owner-occupier' are completely at odds with the purest extreme of central control. It is a mistake, therefore, to consider the socialist city as totally and fundamentally different in kind, as this separate chapter implies. Beyond the inevitable national differences which engender contrasts between, for example, British and French cities, there are only differences of degree, considerable though they may be.

Perhaps the most obvious, significant and, indeed, symbolic way in which the differences between capitalist and socialist cities can be seen lies in the character of city centres. Thus, in the USSR, the centre is dominated on the large scale by those instruments of power and coercion which represent state control, and on the smaller scale by those functions devoted to social welfare such as clinics and medical centres. Red Square in Moscow is associated physically with the Kremlin, government buildings and the tomb of Lenin and functionally with displays of national unity and strength. In marked contrast, Times Square in New York's Manhattan is the high point, in all senses, of commercialism. The towering skyscrapers of New York are private commercial structures. This may be regarded as an unfair comparison for the centre of American government, the ceremonial centre, is Washington where The Mall could fairly be set alongside Red Square. But the skylines of New York and London are created by the buildings of companies and finance houses. The skylines of socialist cities are dominated by public buildings and huge blocks of state-provided flats. This contrast, above all others, indicates that there are substantial contrasts between the cities of different economic systems.

ASSIGNMENT

---

1. Debate the issue of whether housing should be a commodity for sale as any other commodity (say a car, or furniture) or a service provided by the state, and the state only, dependent on need, as for example health and education in socialist countries where there is no private medicine or private education. What about the car and the furniture?

THE SIZES OF TOWNS

In the introduction above it was noted that the actual growth of a city, at least in so far as immigration is concerned, can be controlled by central government. F. E. Ian Hamilton writing on Russian cities notes four ways by which such control can be achieved:

1. The direct designation of administrative status. Clearly, the choice of capitals for regions, sub-regions and local areas will have a substantial impact on growth.
2. Central decisions on economic policy and the provision of infrastructures. The decisions as to where development is to be encouraged and the infrastructures to support it, such as roads and railways, will greatly influence the growth of towns.
3. The identification of tributary areas. This is applicable both in the administrative and economic fields since the area to be served from a centre can be formally defined rather than develop 'naturally'.

Figure 8.1 *Highrise in Moscow*

4. The laying down of norms by central ministries. These norms, such as the living space per person to be provided, can markedly influence the expansion of a city.

The control over the natural increase of the population is very much more tenuous. Certainly propaganda for large families, together with a variety of financial incentives, can increase the population. Campaigns for limiting families backed by an opposite package of incentives can be also undertaken by government. But to arrange these to operate differentially between cities is extremely difficult.

As was suggested in Chapter 1, in absolute, theoretical terms one can put forward the presumption that an urban hierarchy cannot exist in a truly socialist state. As Chapter 4 explains, a hierarchical ranking, indeed any ranking system, is the product of competition and a measure of success or failure. That is anathema to the egalitarian principle of socialism. An urban hierarchy, that is towns of different sizes with some offering superior facilities, means that equal access as a basic tenet is lost; some citizens have advantages derived from more accessible locations. Ideally, although even such an arrangement does not solve the problem completely, towns in socialist systems should all be of the same size and equally spaced so that no differential advantages occur. Nothing like this, however, is achieved; it is not even sought. In Poland at the end of the 1960s, criticism arose of urban policies which were designed to favour the smaller as against the very large cities. Three Polish geographers reviewing these discussions noted that, 'Two radical proposals, one based on linear settlement running continuously in several parallel lines from the north to the south, another advocating the concentration of population in cities of a similar size, were rejected as running counter to the real possibilities of economic growth and social development.' A specific socialist solution was turned down on grounds of practicality – 'the real possibilities' in the quotation above. Once again the contrasts between capitalism and socialism are those of degree rather than of kind. Thus if reference back is made to the four ways of achieving control put forward by Hamilton, then the first two have manifestly been employed in western capitalist countries under the form of regional development policies, the direction of industry and office employment away from certain areas by means of development certificates and central decisions on infrastructures such as motorway building, rail closure and railway electrification. A change of emphasis has certainly taken place in Britain since 1980 with the demand for economic benefit or profit replacing regional equalisation or social need. Even so, there are still many decisions which have been taken centrally and the whole issue is one which dominates public discussion.

An analysis of the city system in East Germany, the German Democratic Republic (GDR), has been presented by Frankdieter Grimm in a book, *Urbanisation and Settlement Systems: International Perspectives*, edited by L. S. Bourne and others. A brief review of it will give some indication of the general perception of the city system in socialist countries. Perhaps the first comment to make is that it

reads more like a piece of propaganda, a statement of national intent, rather than an objective, critical study. Grimm begins by dividing the national settlement system into two. The first is what he terms the B (*Bedurfnisse*) system which aims at fulfilling social goals, the other the E or *economic system* with economic aims. The division itself is an interesting one attempting to divide the general area-serving functions from the more specialised industrial functions.

The classification of the B-system proposed by Grimm is set out in Table 8.1 and the centres are mapped in Figure 8.2. The basic

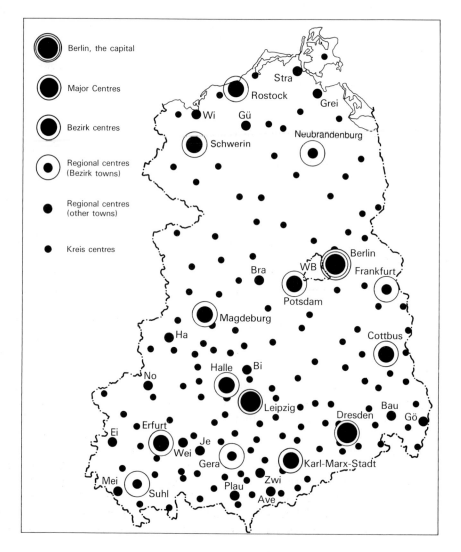

Figure 8.2 *The German Democratic Republic (East Germany). The classification of settlements according to their importance to their hinterland (after Grimm) See also Table 8.1*

154

administrative system of the country is used, the centres established being first the central settlements of the *Kreis*, the lower level administrative division which may be very crudely compared to the British District. There are 191 of them in the GDR. The second level is the *Bezirk*, again roughly equated with the British County. There are 15 of them. Above these, of course, is the national level based on Berlin as capital. The lowest level is called the 'Kreis' town with a population of under 20 000, the Kreis being the smallest administrative area. The paragraph on the Kreis town is worth considering in some detail. Normally a Kreis town can be easily reached by all the citizens living in that Kreis. Every community is connected to the Kreis town by public transport, mainly by bus. Grimm contends that 81 per cent of the population of the GDR lives either in or within 40 minutes travelling time of Kreis towns. They are, therefore, the centres of every-day life with political and trade union offices, schools and adult colleges as well as banks and insurance offices. There is a local newspaper for each Kreis published from the Kreis town where also sporting and cultural events are located. Grimm concludes, 'the present administrative division of the GDR has led to a stable, well balanced integration of settlement systems within the Kreis framework. The even distribution of towns promotes the equalisation of working and living conditions in accordance with the political and social aims of socialist society.'

The last sentence is particularly noteworthy since it makes an explicit claim of a socialist basis to the system.

When he deals with the larger settlements Grimm finds it more difficult to sustain his argument of evenness and equality. The 14 Bezirk towns – the Bezirk is a higher and larger administrative area – vary in size from 570 000 (Leipzig) to 40 000 (Suhl) which is an immense range. These towns are the locations of such organisations as governing assemblies, the central bodies of the Socialist Unity Party, Courts of Justice and Planning Commissions. That is of a whole series of higher-order, higher-

Table 8.1 *Types of towns according to their importance for their hinterland (see Figure 8.2)*

Type of town	Description of hinterland
1. Berlin the capital	many highly specialised functions extend over several *Bezirks*
2a. Major centres	many highly specialised functions extend beyond their own *Bezirk*
2b. *Bezirk* centres[1]	many specialised functions extend over their own *Bezirk*
3a. Regional centres	several specialised functions extend beyond the area of a *Kreis*
3b. *Kreis* centres	many functions and relations extend over a *Kreis*
4a. Partial *Kreis* centres	some functions and relations extend over a *Kreis*
4b. Local centres	functions and relations extend to neighbouring communities

[1] There is a strict distinction in terminology between *Bezirk* town (administrative centre) and *Bezirk* centre (administrative and complex social centre). The same applies to the distinction between *Kreis* town and *Kreis* centre.

threshold and wider-ranging functions. But the wide size range is brought about by 'specialised functions on a macro-regional or national scale in industry, research and information, education and trade'. In other words, the underlying economic variation, represented by the E system (Figure 8.3), completely distorts the ideal socialist condition of equally-spaced, equally-sized towns and the end result is not greatly different from the systems in capitalist countries. The pattern in Figure 8.3 demonstrates the regional variation brought about by industrial development and the dominance of the Leipzig-Halle agglomerated region, the name used by Grimm, together with Magdeburg and Dresden-Karl Marx-Stadt.

The conclusion to be reached from this brief survey is that the city systems of capitalist and socialist countries do not differ fundamentally in their nature. But clearly, contrasts will emerge between a free market system where gross inequalities will necessarily develop as the price of maximising economic growth, and a completely planned system where services are allocated to centres in relation to the population as it is distributed at the time, with the danger either of introducing a freezing of the economic system or of establishing a system unrelated to rapidly changing needs.

ASSIGNMENT
---

2. To what extent do you think the system of cities in Britain differs in principle from that of the GDR as set out by Grimm? Are the differences of kind or only of degree? How would it be possible to introduce greater control into the British system of cities?

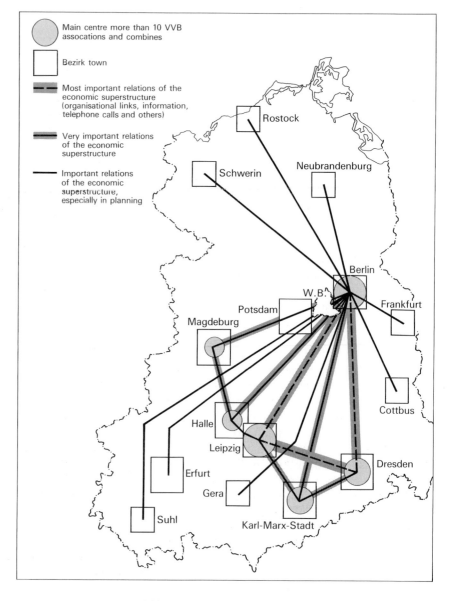

Figure 8.3 *Economic interruptions in the settlement system of East Germany (after Grimm). In VVB association and combines, VVB is Vereinigung Volksseigener Betriebe or nationally owned enterprises*

THE INTERNAL STRUCTURE OF SOCIALIST CITIES

F. E. Ian Hamilton, whose work on socialist cities has already been noted in this chapter, has also presented a model of an East European socialist city (Figure 8.4). From the centre out he identifies as many as eight zones. These are:

1. The historic core. Few city planners can begin with a cleared site and rather than destroy the old cores most countries tend to conserve them as part of their cultural heritage. Thus, much of Warsaw was rebuilt after the destruction of the Second World War precisely as it had been before.

2. Central Business Districts. This also is part of the inner commercial and industrial areas inherited from the pre-socialist era.

3. A zone of socialist transition or renewal, where modern reconstruction is partially and progressively replacing older inherited features. These older features are:
a) former upper and middle-class housing, and
b) former working-class housing (Figure 8.4). Part of this process includes the construction of a new city centre more consonant with the character of the new regime and with its emphasis on political and administrative rather than commercial buildings.

4. Socialist housing of the 1950s. This was generally in the form of unprepossessing apartment blocks, the highrise buildings which play such a large part in the visual townscape of socialist cities (Fig. 8.1).

5. Integrated socialist neighbourhoods and residential districts of the 1970s and 1980s. As in the west, there was a reaction to the large expanses of highrise blocks lacking in essential services. These have been replaced by neighbourhoods planned to have all the necessary services (see service nodes and secondary centres on Figure 8.4) so that population movements are minimised.

6. Open or planted 'isolation belts'. These are the equivalent of green belts to contain the built-up area.

7. Industrial or related zones. There was a conscious attempt to locate industry at the city margins, thus minimising the commuting problem by taking pressure off the central areas, whilst

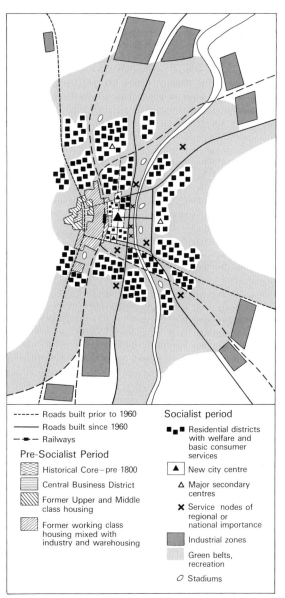

Roads built prior to 1960
Roads built since 1960
Railways

Pre-Socialist Period

Historical Core – pre 1800
Central Business District
Former Upper and Middle class housing
Former working class housing mixed with industry and warehousing

Socialist period

■▪■ Residential districts with welfare and basic consumer services
▲ New city centre
△ Major secondary centres
✗ Service nodes of regional or national importance
▮ Industrial zones
Green belts, recreation
○ Stadiums

Figure 8.4 *A model of the growth of an East European socialist city (after F. E. Ian Hamilton)*

isolating possible causes of pollution away from residential areas.

8. Open countryside. To some extent health and recreational complexes have been built in the surrounding countryside.

A Russian city which can be set against the background of the model is Kiev which has been the subject of a study by A. R. Walker (Urban development and town planning in Kiev. *Bristol Polytechnic. Town and Country Planning Working Paper* **No. 7**). The city as it was at the beginning of the socialist era in 1917 is shown in Figure 8.5. The centre was dominated by a series of boulevards laid out in the later years of the Tsarist era. The focal point was the *Kreshchatik*. Here were the shops and banks and commercial establishments as well as the fashionable apartment houses. Also within the central area was the dominant ecclesiastical core about St. Sophia cathedral. In contrast was the absolute poverty of the working class districts, such as Podol (literally, suburb) where there was neither water supply nor sewage disposal. This was a classic pre-industrial pattern with the well-off at the centre exercising complete control, and the poor at the margins, although there was considerable mixing.

The subsequent development of Kiev is divided by Walker into three phases.

1. 1917–1940. Immediately after the Revolution and the Civil War which followed and between 1920 and 1925 some 25 000 new houses were built. But in the 1930s redevelopment of the centre began with the Dynamo Stadium (1934–36), the Kalinin Administrative Building (1936–39), the Building of the Central Committee of the Ukrainian Communist Party (1936–39) and the Museum of Ukrainian History (1937–39). The emphasis on public buildings is quite clear and the construction of new residential suburbs was undertaken in the form of five-storey blocks of flats forming new suburbs on both the right bank and, for the first time, the left bank of the River Dnepr. Names, identified on Figure 8.6, were Karavayevy Dachi, Pervomayskiy, Belici and Puscha-Vodica on the right bank and Levoberezniy, Staraya Darnica and Osokorki on the left.

2. 1941–1958. Wartime destruction was enormous. The city's population in 1940 had reached 930 000, in 1945 it had fallen to 180 000. Some 42 per cent of the housing stock was destroyed. But revival and reconstruction was rapidly achieved, especially between 1948 and 1954. The Kreshchatik was rebuilt in a monumental style with a new City Soviet Building. But, due to the effort devoted to the symbolic centre, the urgent housing problem was met by building what Walker calls cheap, utilitarian and unimaginative five-storey apartment blocks.

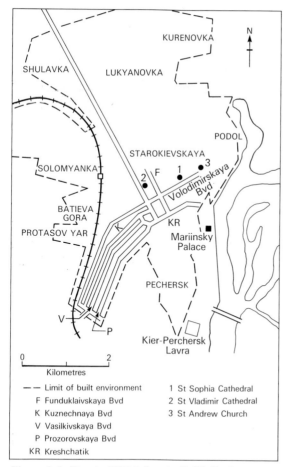

Figure 8.5 *Kiev in 1917 (after A. R. Walker)*

3. 1959–1986. The city grew rapidly to some 1 million in 1959, 2 million in 1976 and 2.63 million in 1983, becoming the third city in the USSR. Again there is a significant comment from Walker, 'During this period of rapid demographic growth, the main task for the city's town planners had been to direct urban growth into new, peripheral residential and industrial districts laid out according to the prescribed norms of Soviet land use planning.' Vast new residential districts with blocks of flats of up to 20 storeys were developed. Examples located on Figure 8.6 are Academmistechko (1962–1975) and Obolon (1974–1981) on the right

bank and Rusanovskiy and Komsomolskiy (1965–1975) on the left bank.

This brief account of Kiev demonstrates clear links with the model set out earlier. Future planning envisages an axis of leisure development along the river itself, a series of satellite towns beyond the surrounding green belt and extensive redevelopment of the centre, including replacement of the early five-storey blocks of flats. This series of measures includes one of the standard Russian measures to control city growth, the dispersion of population into carefully engineered satellite towns. Around

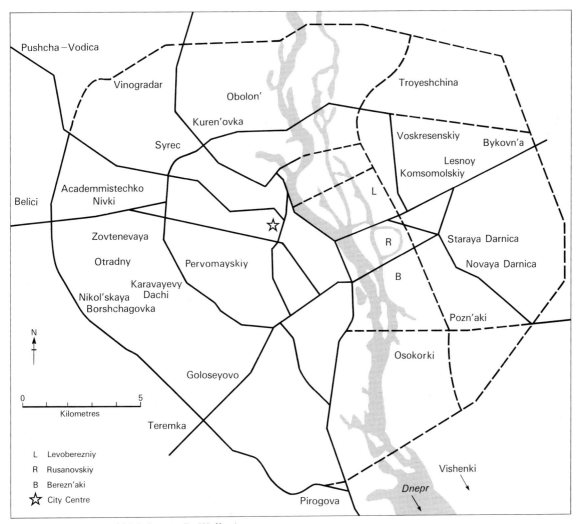

Figure 8.6 *Kiev in 1986 (after A. R. Walker)*

Moscow these *goroda sputniki* are particularly significant. Even within them the main central areas are dominated by buildings associated with welfare, such as health clinics, culture of a Soviet kind and sport. Shopping facilities are less significant in sharp contrast to equivalent developments in capitalist societies.

From these characteristic features of socialist cities another distinctive feature follows. With industry largely located on the outer margins and limited commercial attraction at the centres, both commuting and sprawl are avoided – only in part it is true. There is a limitation on mobility. It is not surprising, therefore, that to a large degree residence at the centre is still preferred and the contrast of the elite at the centre with the mass of population in the 'integrated socialist neighbourhoods' reflects the nature of the society. The real problem, of course, is that it is impossible to obtain the sorts of highly detailed data on a fine grained spatial basis on which western city studies rely. Two examples, however, can be given. The first dates to 1968 and was an examination of the town of Ufa in Bashkir. This suggested that although there were no exclusive social areas there were contrasts (Table 8.2). When the locations of occupation groups are considered, it is apparent that the intelligentsia, as defined in the USSR, corresponding to those with higher earning power, lived more frequently at the centre whilst artisans, the workers,

Table 8.2 *The social configuration of Ufa districts in 1968 (after Fenin, as reproduced by M. Mathews, 1979)*

Occupations	Percentage resident in areas		
	Central	Newly built	Outskirts
Workers	33.5	47.1	57.4
Employees*	9.0	17.8	12.2
Intelligentsia A*	12.0	10.9	6.2
Intelligentsia B**	32.4	14.9	11.8
Pensioners	13.1	9.3	12.4
	100.0	100.0	100.0

Note: * Mainly low grade non-manual
      ** A Mainly engineers and technicians
         B Others

dominated the outskirts. Figure 8.7 maps the distribution of those with higher education in Warsaw in 1970 and again the same general pattern appears.

The final point is that given such a situation those highest in the social scale, that is those with the greatest political influence, do seek to emulate western dispersal by means of the week-end or summer retreat, the well known *dacha* in the USSR. The reaction is to try to prevent such developments and the individualism they represent, for example by prohibiting the construction of dachas in the green belt about Moscow and providing a variety of public facilities such as hotels and camp sites, with extensive ranges of services, linked by rail to central Moscow.

ASSIGNMENT

---

3. Why do you think that in capitalist countries, where private interests are paramount, there is more public information available in censuses, than in socialist countries where public interests are paramount? What are the consequences of such contrasts for geographers, other students of the city and public servants?

CONCLUSION

This has been only a brief survey of the characteristics of urbanisation in socialist cities. But it has been sufficient to make it clear that the simple antitheses that can be argued in theory do not appear in real world terms. The force and complexity of urban growth makes its own patterns. Moreover, the reactions within nation states and socio-economic systems vary widely. Britain during the 1980s has been much more committed to what are called free and unconstrained market forces than it was immediately after the Second World War. It is not without significance that a geographer with clear left wing views has published (1986) a book called *Whatever Happened to Planning?* (Peter Ambrose). In contrast contemporary USSR under Mr Gorbachev is also moving

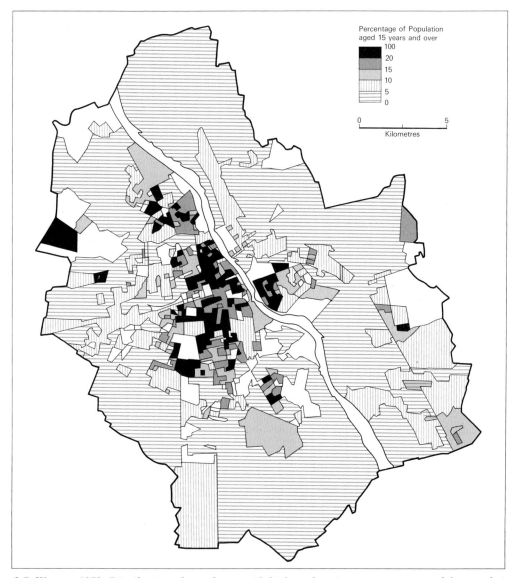

Figure 8.7 *Warsaw 1979. Distribution of population with higher education as a percentage of the population aged 15 and over.*

away from the totally planned and regimented system of the post-war years in Russia and towards a system which envisages competition and the private ownership of land and property, though not without opposition from those most closely concerned with political dogma. Thus, even within capitalist and socialist systems, there is room for wide variation in the degree of central control exercised. Even so, the socialist city is distinctive and has its own characteristics. In part it reflects the centralised control of a highly constrained system, although in part the distinctions may be as much those of culture as of economic order. The real assessment of comparisons and contrasts must await the time when data are equally reliable and abundant under socialist systems as they are under capitalist.

9

Town Plan and Townscape

INTRODUCTION

In Chapter 2 some consideration was given to village form and it is appropriate that parallel study should be made of town plan which is the direct urban equivalent. For a number of reasons, the examination of town plan has played a less prominent part in urban geography in recent times than it did in the period immediately after the Second World War. These reasons are not difficult to find. Emphasis in the geographical study of towns has switched to the social aspects as exemplified in Chapter 6. Even when the physical fabric of the town *is* considered, social aspects, such as the inadequacy of housing in amount and quality, still dominate. It is unfortunate that such a change has taken place; it certainly results in an unbalanced study of towns. The first impact a town makes is through its plan and the remembered means of finding one's way around. The first thing most people do when they find themselves in a strange town is to buy a map – a town plan. Again, along with layout comes an awareness of urban scenery – the townscape – for in reality the two dimensional map is translated into the three dimensional array of buildings. Moreover, those buildings reflect the dates when they were built, so there is also the fourth dimension of time. Elements of the townscape are used to find our way around; we call them landmarks although the word originally comes from seafaring. One landmark can symbolise a whole city, a situation which is widely exploited by film makers. The Eiffel Tower means Paris is the scene; Big Ben, London; the Bridge and the Opera House, Sydney; the Kremlin or St. Basil's Cathedral, Moscow.

It is possible to argue, therefore, that town plan and townscape are the most central aspects of urban geography, certainly the most obviously apparent. The journey to work or to school, whatever the mode of transport, is accomplished by following elements of the plan, and with regard to certain landmarks even if we are no longer consciously aware of them. The quality of the visual scene, of townscape, is, therefore, a crucial aspect of a town, even if our perception is dulled by familiarity. But the controversy generated by change, by new buildings, is an indication of the strong feelings which can be aroused when those perceptions are awakened.

Before reviewing methods of plan analysis there is one very important point to note. There need be no historical or contemporary relation between plan and townscape. Thus, for example, in the early seventeenth century Dutch settlers had established the first European settlement on Manhattan Island. It was called New Amsterdam. In 1633 a wall was hurriedly built due to the threat of English attack. A map of 1660 shows a street following this wall from Broadway to the East River. After the English take-over and the change of name to New York, Wall Street remained as a plan element. It still does. But although the plan line dates to 1633 the buildings are, of course, twentieth century skyscrapers and the name has taken on a wholly new significance.

ASSIGNMENT

---

1. A well known American urbanist (Kevin Lynch) has written a book called '*What time is this place?*'. How would you interpret the title and can you apply it to a town known to you?

What landmark(s) would you use to epitomise your nearest town or city? Try to discover a recent controversy over the replacement of an old building or the redevelopment of a part of a town. Elucidate the bases of the arguments which were developed.

METHODS OF TOWN PLAN ANALYSIS

Having briefly reviewed the place of town-plan studies in urban geography, it is now appropriate to consider the various methods which can be used in such studies.

Historical narrative

This is the oldest, probably the best known and the most widely used of the methods. It is the one basic to a number of books which present the history of town plan and town planning. The two best known in English are *History of*

Urban Form, by A. E. J. Morris, and G. Burke's *Towns in the Making*. There are, however, two contrasted procedures within the general process of a narrative of form development. The first takes a whole city as the basis of study and shows how it is made up of a succession of growth phases each of which has made a distinctive contribution to present layout. The second identifies general phases of town plan development common to a large region. These phases are then illustrated by a number of characteristic examples from many different towns. There will be obvious variations depending on the size of the settlement in the first case and the detail of the study in both cases.

These two approaches can be briefly exemplified by considering the growth of Paris. Here the scale is clearly large and accordingly the treatment general. Later in this chapter, in reviewing other methods, we will change the scale to look in more detail at a very much smaller settlement.

In most cases the analysis of the specific city begins with some consideration of site, for the

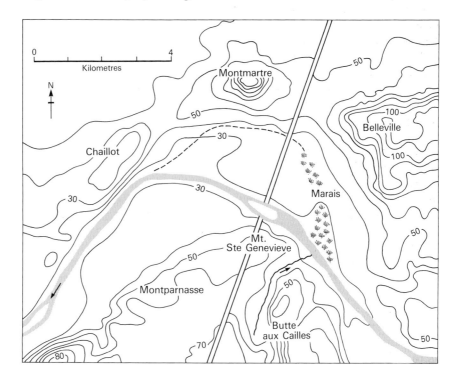

Figure 9.1 *The site of Paris*

physical bases exert considerable influence upon growth patterns. Paris is located at a point on the River Seine where there is a series of islands; the most significant is now called the Ile de la Cité. It offered a much more feasible crossing point and determined the specific location. The Seine has eroded into the plateau of Tertiary rocks which constitutes the central part of the Paris Basin. The process of incision has produced lower spurs which flank the main plateau remnants (Figure 9.1). These elevations are widely known as Montmartre to the north and Montparnasse to the south. Immediately to the north the river has cut across an old meander spur bringing dry ground close to the river, another feature fixing the location. But the old river channel was associated with poor drainage giving rise to the area known as Le Marais. To the south, the land falls off gently in Mont St. Genevieve.

Initially the site was the basis of the central settlement of a Gallic tribe called the Parisii and was confined to the island. With Roman occupation, and in what are usually called Gallo-Roman times, the settlement became the centre of a unit of administration called a *civitas* and was known as Lutetia. It was a relatively insignificant centre within the urban hierarchy since the core of Roman development lay to the south. The Roman town was laid out on the south or left bank where site conditions presented a gentle slope to the river and more room for development than on the small island. The major axis – represented in present day Paris by the Rue St. Jacques – was directed to the river crossing and about it a characteristic Roman grid plan was established. The role of the Ile de la Cité is less clear, but possibly it remained a 'native quarter'. There was little development to the north apart from some villas on Montmartre.

In 275 AD the Franks crossed the Roman frontier and invaded Gaul. It was during this period that the Roman urban system collapsed, partly due to physical destruction, partly due to the disruption of the economy on which it depended. At Lutetia this was marked by the decay of the left bank settlement and a re-version to the pre-Roman situation with the Ile de la Cité forming a residual core. The Roman grid was largely lost though its main axis was preserved. It was during this period too that the Latin name became disused and the name derived from the small Parisii tribe took its place. Its population was probably no more than 2000.

From this lowest point in its development, Paris began its growth to become one of the world's great cities, initially under the Counts of Paris and subsequently the French kings, for with the Frankish invasion the centre of power moved northwards and away from the dominance of Provence and Lugdunum (Lyons). As it grew, Paris became made up of three elements which constituted its layout and are still significant.

The first of these was the small Ile de la Cité, linked to the north bank of the Seine by the Grand Pont (now Pont au Change) and to the south bank by the Petit Pont. It contained the major elements of secular control, the Palace initially of the Counts of Paris, and of religious control, the cathedral of Notre Dame. To the north and south gradual extension took place, especially around the monasteries and abbeys usually developed about the burial place of a martyr, for burials within city walls were forbidden. These, like St. Germain des Prés, became small suburban nuclei. But the major contrasts were to be derived from different functional bases.

To the north, on the right bank, the main concentration of merchants took place about the Place de Grève at the point where ships using the river landed their goods. Commerce abandoned the island, therefore, and became the instigator of right bank development. This was formalised when, sometime before 1137, the market was transferred to Les Halles. It was to remain there until it was removed in 1969. Municipal government was closely associated and the Hôtel de Ville, or city hall, was also located on the right bank.

To the south, on the left bank, a contrasted quarter developed. At first scholarly enquiry was associated with the island and Notre Dame but the location was physically and intellectually constraining and so a move began to the open land to the south. The most significant was that of a teacher called Abelard. At first these were all independent teachers with their own students but at the beginning of the thirteenth century they became associated in an 'Universitas' given its statutes by the Pope in 1215. Thus started the great 'left bank' tradition.

These three parts were eventually physically united by King Philippe Auguste when he undertook the walling around of the city between 1180 and 1210 (Figure 9.2). Contemporaries wrote of the 'ville, cité et université de Paris' stressing the three parts. They are quite clear on early maps such as that of Braun and Hogenberg in 1572 (Figure 9.2). It is estimated

by that time the population was some 50 000.

The growth of Paris continued apace, indeed it was the most rapidly growing European city. Only a century and a half later, therefore, about 1370, when the population was about 70 000 the King, Charles V, built a further wall. The major impulses to growth had come from commerce, and the addition of royal administration from the small island northward. Hence this wall was restricted to the right bank. A distinctive plan feature of many towns which once had walls is the street or avenue which follows their line. Since building near the wall was forbidden in order to preserve a field of fire, wide strips of land were available and these carried the name *boulevards*, derived from the same source as bulwark. It was this line of walls, modified by later work it is true,

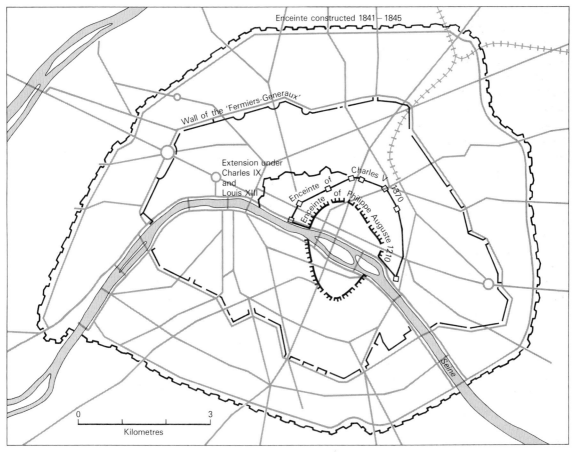

Figure 9.2 *The growth of Paris*

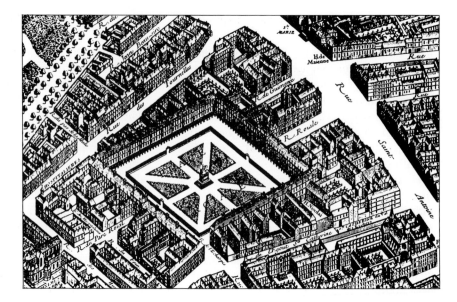

Figure 9.3 *La Place des Vosges (originally La Place Royale)*

which became the Grands Boulevards, one of the most distinctive features of central Paris.

Between 1610 and 1643 there was a further extension under Louis XIII. It was limited to a western extension on the north bank and was partly related to the growing domination of that area by the royal palace and associated buildings, especially the major development of the Louvre under Francis I (1546–1578).

Two further walls were to give structure to central Paris. Between 1784 and 1791 the wall called that of the 'Fermiers Generaux' was built. The 'farmers' in the title refers to farmers or gatherers of taxes and it was a 'customs' boundary rather than a military one and related to special taxes levied on certain goods on entering Paris. Between 1841 and 1845 a further defensive wall was built, and, indeed, fortified structures at the time of the First World War played their part in the way the city grew.

This has been a very general examination of the growth of Paris dealing with the broad structure of the central part. But these features are evident on a map of present day Paris and, in spite of massive rebuilding and redevelopment, they are still fundamental to understanding its layout.

The second approach within the general method of historical narrative was noted earlier as based on the identification of periods of urban development which produced characteristic elements of town layout which are exemplified from different cities.

The standard periods as far as western Europe is concerned are Greek, Roman, Medieval, Renaissance and Baroque, Industrial, Modern and Contemporary. In this book it is impossible to review them all. Indeed, it is only possible to present a very brief indication of procedure by considering the Renaissance.

It is axiomatic that the Renaissance was characterised by new art forms and amongst these were new ideas about town plan. The critical innovation was that of perspective. Along with it went the idea of the aesthetic pleasure to be derived from townscape; that is, the visual scene was to be a work of art with a depth of perspective. At the same time political power was being concentrated in the hands of princes; it was an age of absolutism. Accordingly, there was a strong tendency towards order and balance, replacing the elaborate disorder of the medieval Gothic. Out of all this came one universal form, the city square or '*place*' to use the French word. It began in Italy, was widely used in France and eventually was the basis of the westward expansion of London.

Thus a large number of examples could be chosen in illustration, amongst them the first to be built in London, Covent Garden in 1630. But Paris provides an equally large number, the best preserved being the Place des Vosges (Figure 9.3). It was originally called La Place Royale, the name being changed at the time of the French Revolution. The decision to build the square was taken in 1605. It was to fill a rather indeterminate space in Le Marais, the marshy area referred to in the description of site. The work was carried out very rapidly and it was probably complete in 1609, certainly in 1612. It displayed absolute geometric regularity, it excluded traffic and it was clearly a single entity in design and execution. All the houses had identical façades although there were variations in the roofs and to the north and south the symmetry was broken by two buildings, one for the King, the other for the Queen. Unlike similar squares, there was no central statue as a focal point, part of the emphasis on the control of the monarch or aristocrat who built it, until Richelieu in 1639 had one of Louis XIII installed. Here, then, is an example of a part of town plan widespread in Europe throughout the period. It can be found in most large European cities with a pre-industrial history; it can be found in greatly modified form in small towns.

The real difficulty with this approach is that it is difficult to limit. The brief consideration given here has looked at but one example from one period in the history of plan development. Perhaps the best known general work is one in French by Pierre Lavedan called *Histoire de l'Urbanisme*. It runs to four volumes and a total of 1664 pages. Another well known book by Leonardo Benevolo, *The History of the City*, contains 1011 pages. This is the inevitable consequence of a method which is descriptive and chronological.

Description: verbal and numerical

This second group of methods is also descriptive but it ignores chronology or history and attempts to classify plans according to their predominant shape. Thus when we use the term 'grid plan' we are identifying a particular shape on the ground by its individual geometry. It is here, of course, that many of the difficulties arise because the descriptions are too imprecise. A true grid is like a chess board with streets of the same length intersecting at right angles and at the same distances to produce a series of '*insulae*', the name given to the areas between the streets, which are squares of the same size. But very few towns, indeed, are so rigidly laid out, they may be rectangular but they are not true grids. But the terms 'grid plan' and 'rectangular plan' have become interchangeable. A scheme of classification produced in 1954 is set out below.

Tricart's (1954) scheme for the analysis of town plan

1 *Homogeneous towns*, i.e. towns with a unified structure[1]
   a *Planned towns*[2]
      (1) Rectangular plans
         i Linear
         ii Ribbed
         iii Parallel
         iv Grid
      (2) Radial concentric plans
         i Star[3]
         ii Circular[4]
   b *Unplanned towns*, i.e. towns of natural growth[5]
      (1) Fortress towns[6]
      (2) Star shaped towns[7]
      (3) Irregular plans[8]

2 *Heterogeneous towns*, i.e. towns with a complex structure[9]
   a *Replanned towns*[10]
   b *Polynuclear towns*[11]
   c *Net pattern towns*[12]
   d *Globular towns*[13]
      (1) Concentric
      (2) Radial

1 The essential feature is that the town is

made up of a simple plan unit, a situation which is unlikely in any area of strong urban growth.

2 Allowance has to be made for alteration of the planned core by later growth under changed conditions.

3 The radials dominate.

4 The concentric roads dominate.

5 These display less systematic forms but possess a homogeneity often dependent on continued adaptation to a dominant feature either physically derived, such as an aspect of site, or culturally derived from the past.

6 This is an odd class since it is designated by function rather than by shape. The implication is that form is dominated by a strong focal point.

7 Created by free outward growth, particularly where there have been no walls.

8 Irregularity of plan is often a consequence of site conditions but the same conditions mean that the town develops as one unit.

9 In this major category the towns are made up of more than one plan element giving a richer and more varied class but one which Tricart argues is not as numerically dominant as might be expected. A transitional class is suggested where a town is made up of a series of clear geometrical elements but these have no relation to each other; Los Angeles is the example proposed.

10 A new planned section is often added to an older irregular core.

11 Made up of juxtaposed but contrasted elements, such as ex-colonial towns with their European compounds contrasted with the native quarters.

12 This is near to the original meaning of 'conurbation', being made up of a series of separate nodes connected by transport lines. A mining area is suggested but presumably the classic 'dispersed city' would be of this form.

13 The diverse elements here show one of the emphases noted in 3 and 4 above.

Essentially, what this method attempts to do is to identify geometrical forms within town plan. Accordingly, within the field of quantitative geography, attempts have been made to use more precise numerical description, largely by studying and measuring the relation between street lengths and the number of intersections. This treats the plan as a linear network. But it must be admitted that the results have been disappointing and the work has petered out.

Socio-cultural approaches

These have provided the most promising bases for interpretation, certainly the most interesting. The crux of the socio-cultural principle is that a city is created in the image of its founders; that is, it will epitomise in bricks and mortar – or perhaps in concrete terms is the apt expression – the predominant social characteristics and cultural traits of the people who built it. The most effective example is Washington, DC. The layout of the city, as it was originally planned, is shown in Figure 9.5. In the descriptive terms of the second approach above it consists of two superimposed systems. There is an underlying grid and placed on top of it is a modified radial-concentric scheme with avenues focussing on the major buildings such as the Capitol and the White House. It is interesting to consider the background to the creation of this capital city.

The American Continental Congress had been peripatetic, since its establishment in 1774, moving from city to city. But in 1787 it decided that a seat of government was necessary and debate in 1789–90 led to the Residence Act by which the President was authorised to select a site not exceeding ten square miles on the Potomac near to the existing settlement of Georgetown. This had been done by 1791 and subsequently two commissioners were appointed to carry out the actual design. One was Andrew Ellicott and the other Pierre Charles L'Enfant. Their plan was submitted by 1791 although subsequently L'Enfant fell out with the government over the sale of land and was dismissed, Ellicott becoming solely responsible.

Underlying the plan was a regular grid of

Figure 9.4 *A model of Central Washington. The mall and the radiating avenues are clearly identifiable, Pennsylvania Avenue is the diagonal to the right. The main buildings of government are grouped about the Capitol in the foreground. The planned line of monuments, including the Washington and Lincoln Memorials, dominates the central access*

streets based on the Capitol, numbered to east and west of it and lettered north and south. This was totally in keeping with emergent American tradition. Under the 1785 Land Ordinance of the Continental Congress, all the public domain was divided into six mile-square townships which controlled the whole of the way the USA west of the Ohio was to develop. The grid can be taken as symbolic of American equality and democracy. It is an even division, suggesting lots of land available for all, and is the most appropriate basis for easy commercial transactions. It was proper, therefore, that Washington should show those qualities in its layout. Note also the names – First Street, Second Street or A Street, B Street indicating the rejection of names associated with an aristocracy such as the names of the London squares referred to earlier (p. 167).

But Washington was to be something else. It was to be symbolic of the federal and United States of America, and that, too, needed to be shown. L'Enfant was the son of a painter at the Court of Louis XIV at Versailles and there urban design had a very different purpose, to demonstrate the omnipotence of the sun-King. 'I am the state', said Louis, and Versailles was the physical demonstration of that belief, in complete accord with the principle that plan represents social structure. It was accomplished by means of centring all the streets or avenues of a city upon the royal palace so that the city itself was a sun-burst. L'Enfant brought these ideas to the planning of Washington and it was evident how the federal principle, the principle of all the States belonging to one nation united under its president, was accomplished. Radiating avenues were introduced, significantly named after the uniting states such as Pennsylvania Avenue, concentrating on the Capitol, the centre of government, and the White House, the President's residence (for it was never to be thought of as a palace). Washington, therefore, in its layout at once symbolises the democratic principle in its grid and the federal principle in its radiating avenues. The city symbolises the social beliefs and cultural bases of the nation.

It is appropriate here to refer back to Rabat

Figure 9.5 *Washington DC 1791. The plan as developed by Andrew Ellicott.*

Figure 9.6 *Central Washington. This is a view taken from the Washington Memorial looking towards the Capitol. Refurbishment was in progress at the time, part of the continual operations to enhance this centre of the nation. Note the number of new buildings between the time of the photo (1968) and the model (1988)*

which was introduced in Chapter 7 (Figure 7.5). The two sections of the town clearly reflect the cultural contributions of the two peoples. The Medina represents the traditional Arab way of life, the later town the French way of life; the two parts epitomise the contrasted contributions to city growth.

This socio-cultural interpretation of urban plan is by far the most fascinating, breathing life into the rather arid descriptions of plan and providing an over-riding theme for the purely historical narrative approach. Lewis Mumford, one of the most stimulating students of urbanism, wrote in his book *The Culture of Cities*, that 'the city represents the maximum possibility of humanising the natural environment and of naturalising the human heritage: it gives cultural shape to the first, and it externalises in permanent forms, the second'. That is the heart of the approach.

Structural approaches

The basis of the historical approach, the first of the four being discussed, is that towns grow in a simple additive fashion; that is, contributions or accession from various historical periods are just added on and can be interpreted in that way. Structural approaches refute that concept arguing that it is necessary to disentangle the structural components which make up the present town. Of these components the one which has been most widely considered, and which has been most rewarding, is the *fringe belt*. The concept of the fringe belt derives from the assumption that a town does not grow steadily and uniformly throughout its history. Rather it grows by a series of stops and starts, the one correlating with phases of economic depression, national or local, the other with periods of economic boom. During the phases of depression, of *still-stand* to adopt a term from geomorphology, the edge of the city will be marked by a *fixation line*. This can be a natural feature, such as a river or a steep slope, or it can be a human feature, such as a town wall or even a property boundary. It is contended that two different

plan structures will be developed, one inside the fixation line, the other in the fringe belt which lies outside it. Within the fixation line there will occur the much denser sub-divisions of land related to intensive urban use, outside there will be much larger and less dense sub-divisions associated with primarily non-urban use. Moreover, these more open areas will be used for extensive purposes generated by the city, that is those uses which arise in the city but need large land areas. Examples are water works and sewage farms, cemeteries, and recreational uses, such as golf courses. In earlier times the defensive outworks of the city occupied these areas. There is in consequence a contrast both in the nature of land holding and in land-use. Subsequent growth may well transform the fringe belt, absorbing it or translating it into the city, but its lineaments will still remain. As one fringe belt is translated, so another is created and hence the structure of the town can be conceived of in the form of nucleus together with a series of fringe belts. An illustration can be provided by using the small town of Aberystwyth in Dyfed.

The physical structure of Aberystwyth during the nineteenth century can be related to the existence of two fixation lines and two fringe belts (Figure 9.8). The inner and first fixation line was that of the medieval town walls, together with the physical limits of the small, extra-mural bridgehead settlement of Trefechan (literally 'little town'). Apart from Trefechan, no houses were built outside the walls until late in the 1790s, although minor encroachments had taken place during the eighteenth century. The medieval, inner or first fixation line lasted, therefore, for some 500 years.

To a large degree it remained inviolate because the town itself was but a skeleton of streets, and a good deal of open land remained within the walls, even in the second half of the nineteenth century. Beyond this fixation line lay the *inner fringe belt*. It was composed of the extra-mural common lands of the borough, which were made up of three tracts of marshland which surrounded the small hill on which

Figure 9.7

Aberystwyth North Parade. The contrast in the width of these streets at the site of the medieval town gate, epitomises the difference between the narrow internal streets of the medieval town and the wide parade (the militia) of the early nineteenth century. These contrasts are widely found in European cities

the town had been established in 1277. These were Morfa Swnd (Sandmarsh), Morfa Mawr (Great Marsh) and Morfa Bach (Little Marsh). Since there was ample intra-mural space, little specifically urban use was made of these lands, other than the location of the cattle market, the pound for straying animals and the town gallows! Fringe uses, therefore, did not characterise them in any distinctive way, other than by the manner in which they contributed to those agricultural activities in which the burgesses themselves were involved. For small, remote towns in a period before effective transport, the provision of food can be regarded as a distinctive fringe use, although the conventional view of such uses is one which is dominated by the growth of nineteenth century urban institutions.

It was not until 1813 that these lands of the inner fringe belt were formally divided and leased. In that year an entry in the Court Leet recorded, 'we the jury direct the part of the waste land called Morfa Swnd be mapped and divided into convenient spots for buildings'. The trigger for this decision was the demand for land brought about by growth as resort, port and market centre in the early part of the century. Morfa Swnd was enclosed, divided and leased, as was Morfa Mawr, but the latter remained in agricultural use.

With the extension of the town in this manner, a new and second fixation line was created. This was at the limit of borough common land, which had previously been classed as marshland, and which was clearly marked by the steep slopes of the Rheidol Valley sides both to north and south. Beyond this line, land was in private hands, mainly

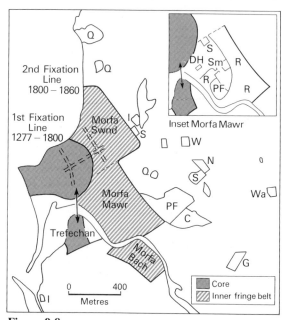

Figure 9.8

Aberystwyth: its structure and fringe belts

172

those of two prestigious local families, the Pryses of Gogerddan and the Powells of Nanteos. It is also interesting to observe that at two points a use, derived from the seaport role and demanding extensive linear land areas, marked the new fixation line, for ropewalks had been established along it. To the north of Morfa Swnd, land use and sharp breaks of slope also contributed to the emergence of this new fixation line which was to last from the early nineteenth century, when the development of the inner fringe belt first began by encroachment, until the 1870s when, after the coming of the railway in 1864, the second phase of population growth and physical extension pushed settlement beyond it and into the *middle fringe belt*. This middle belt, beyond the second fixation line, was formed during the middle and later part of the nineteenth century when, related to a whole range of social legislation, towns were generating a variety of associated institutions. It had, therefore, to a much greater degree, the characteristic uses of a fringe belt. It was dominated by a series of quarries (Q) worked into the valley side and developed as a source of stone for the phase of building after 1813. It also included the Union Workhouse and a militia barracks from the middle of the century and, by the end, an infirmary (I), gas works (G) and the town cemetery (C), as well as schools (S) and playing fields (PF) (Figure 9.8). After 1880 these were interspersed with the extending frontier of house building, as sites on the northern valley side were used.

It is difficult to place Morfa Mawr (Figure 9.8 inset) in this context. Physically it was part of the inner fringe belt, but it remained undeveloped until the later part of the century, when it was characterised by middle belt uses, including recreation grounds (PF), railway yards (R), the smithfield (Sm), a drill hall (DH) and a school. To the south of the river the situation was simpler, for the very steep Rheidol slope meant that the first and second fixation lines were coterminous; there was no distinction between an inner and a middle fringe belt.

It has been possible to characterise this process simply by reference to one easily accessible reference in the records of the Court Leet, two early nineteenth century maps (1809 with additions, 1834) and one late nineteenth century map from which land uses could be traced, and yet the analysis adds considerably to the understanding of the process of extension and enables a wide variety of both sources and controls to be identified.

From this brief analysis it has been possible to characterise the structure of the central parts of the town. These are quite distinctively apparent on the Ordnance Survey map where the intricate and complex infill within the former town walls contrasts with the grid street plan of the inner fringe belt and the linear extensions which succeed it in the middle belt.

ASSIGNMENTS

2. a) Obtain a general tourist map of central Paris. To what extent are the features which have been discussed in this chapter still apparent?
   b) When and by whom were the major modifications made?
   c) Les Halles Centrales were removed from Paris in 1969. Why? Where were they moved?
   Can you cite and compare parallel examples in Britain?

3. Attempt to apply the classification given on page 167 to towns, or parts of towns, known to you. Do you think it is possible to use it? Do you think you gain any understanding by its use?
   '[T]he city represents the maximum possibility of humanising the natural environment and of naturalising the human heritage: it gives cultural shape to the first, and it externalises in permanent forms, the second'.

4. The quotation above maintains that:
   a) The city maximises the humanising of the natural environment giving it cultural shape.
   b) It naturalises the human heritage externalising it in permanent forms.
   Prepare brief exemplifications of these using specific cities or parts of cities.

CONCLUSION

The last of the four approaches, the disentanglement of the intricate and interlocking structure which constitutes the morphology of a town, is certainly the most promising from the viewpoint of the advancement of understanding. It is best seen in the work of Dr J. Whitehand and especially in his monograph, *The changing face of cities: a study of development cycles and urban form*, which was a special publication (Number 21, 1987) of the Institute of British Geographers. This is where research is carrying forward our comprehension of the nature of town plan. However, for purposes of understanding townscape the other approaches all have their own values and their own contributions to make and for the beginner in the study of town plan they are the most appropriate. They are mainly descriptive and only partly analytical but they are especially important in the building up of the basic information which is essential before research work can begin.

ASSIGNMENT

---

5. Four ways of undertaking the study of town plan have been outlined in this chapter. Attempt to use these four different ways in the analysis of a British town which is well known to you. Which of the methods do you consider the most rewarding?

Settlements of the Future

INTRODUCTION

A concluding chapter on the geography of settlement must surely concern itself with the future, an extrapolation from what trends can be observed now into what is likely to be. Once more the complexities of First World as against Third World, and of capitalist as against socialist systems, arise, but for simplicity's sake the discussion in this chapter will be confined to what can be called the Western World.

THE FUTURE OF CITIES: THE URBAN IDEAL

There are two quite opposite trends which can be identified amongst western urban theorists as constituting a move towards the ultimate urban ideal. These two visions of the future can be called *concentrated* or *claustrophilic*, and *dispersed* or *agoraphilic*. They can be considered in turn.

Concentration or claustrophilia

Claustrophilia means a love of enclosed spaces. It is derived from the word for a monastic cloister, and, therefore, associates the ideal structuring of a town with that of the monastery. That linkage was made quite explicitly by one of the leading and most well-known advocates of the concentrated town, the Swiss planner and urbanist known as Le Corbusier.

This view of the town as concentrated, compact and lively has been inherited from the reality of the free-standing town of pre-industrial times. Such settlements are seen as having had lively communal traditions expressed in colourful rituals. These still survive in

sporadic form in mayoral processions and carnivals. Modern street theatre can be considered as a revival of these older activities. The stress in those earlier times is seen as having been on communal rather than private living. At its extreme the attempt to reproduce the social condition of those forms is represented

Figure 10.1 *Marseille. Unités d'Habitation. This is Corbusier's block which contained all the essential elements of the city within it. Its external appearance is disappointing since now highrise blocks are so common that this one appears completely unexceptional. But it was the beginning of a world-wide building style*

Figure 10.2 *Corbusier's Ville Contemporaine of 1922. This was Corbusier's vision of a city adjusted to contemporary life. It consisted of 12 commercial buildings and apartment blocks. It avoided sprawl which was seen as the main evil of the time and in contrast it was to be compact, concentrated and lively. The eventual result was to be very different*

by Le Corbusier's *Unités-d'Habitation*. These were single large blocks within which all the essential urban functions were associated – apartments, shops, banks, restaurants, theatres – so that, in effect, the whole town was contained within one building, as the name itself implies. There lies the parallelism with the monastery noted earlier, for the cell maximises individual privacy when it is needed but there is communal living and co-operation in all the daily activities.

It has been unfortunate that in practice the most widespread derivative from these ideas, the tower block for mass housing, has proved such a disaster. Many of the highrise blocks built in the 1960s in Britain are now being removed and an extensive critical literature has grown up condemning their lack of human scale and clearly defined family space. The latter sometimes referred to as '*defensible space*' refers to the private and particular area owned or controlled by a family as opposed to public areas under no-one's special supervision. But such tower blocks are a travesty of Corbusier's concept for they lack those communal facilities essential to co-operative living and they were built to minimal standards of comfort.

The ideal of the concentrated city still remains, therefore, in spite of criticisms of its actuality. It is constantly revived in visions of the future. Science fiction usually portrays the settlement form of the next century in this way. One example is the floating space station, the so-called *plug-in city*, where a compact settle-ment built up from a series of standard units orbits in space. Also in such fictional characterisations of the future, the space traveller frequently materialises on a plain of aridity and desolation with the walls or defences of a compact city rising in the distance. Seldom are there suburbs, for there is a reversion historically to a hostile physical and human environment. The advanced and civilised (and consider the origin of that word) live in a nucleated settlement of cells and corridors, the monastery emergent once again. And note also that whether it be the concentrated pre-industrial town, the floating space station, or the city of the future on a devastated plain, or the first settlement on another planet, there is a common control in the hostility of the external environment taking us back to the very heart of geographical study.

Dispersal or agoraphilia

In order to avoid what is a widespread misconception, it must be noted that agoraphilia, or the love of open spaces, is derived from the Greek word *agora* meaning a market place, that is an open space in the city, and not from the Latin word *ager* meaning a field. In this concept of the city of the future the stress is placed on low density and wide dispersal. It is inherited mainly from recent suburbanisation. In its development, as well as in its idealism, a push-pull process is entailed.

The push has been derived from the pollution, noise and congestion of the concentrated city, and, indeed, from its physical danger for muggings and personal attacks are perceived as frequent and the night-time city not as a place of communal ceremony and enjoyment but of violence and danger. The vulnerable, such as the elderly or women, do not venture out at night for the city streets are places to be avoided. This is the complete antithesis of the pre-industrial, even of the science fiction, city, where danger, the threatening environment, lay without the walls and security was found within them.

The pull comes from the deep seated anti-urbanism which has been characteristic of the western tradition. This is a complex idea but it can be most easily identified by the way in which evil is so often identified with the city, good with the countryside. It is part of the biblical inheritance as in the cities of the plain, Sodom and Gomorrah, destroyed because of their degradation. Or much later, in the words of Cowper:

> . . . proud and gay
> And gain-devoted cities; thither flow
> As to a common and most noisome sewer,
> The dregs and faeculence of every land . . .
> God made the country, and man made the town.

More specifically, however, the pull is part of the romantic search for rural serenity, the desire to 'get away from it all' epitomised in contemporary counterurbanisation.

This ideal, like that of the compact city, has degenerated as it has become transposed into the mass market. The wealthy were always able to enjoy the best of both worlds with a city apartment and a country home, with a weekly or seasonal movement between them. But for the mass of the population the reaching for the ideal produced extensive areas of low density suburbia, *subtopia* as it has been called, which provided few of the advantages which are supposed to accrue to dispersal. It, too, has its place in visions of the future, and in science fiction, though usually in a literary rather than a visual medium for, by its extensive nature, it is more difficult to portray in striking physical

terms. Even so, the usual depiction is of the single nuclear family living in isolation in rural tranquillity, but with all the modern conveniences provided by automatic communication systems and, if necessary, with rapid physical communications available too. Here is an extract from Simak's book *City*. 'For what need was there to go anywhere? It all was here. By simply twirling a dial one could talk face to face with anyone one wished, could go, by sense, if not in body, anywhere one wished. Could attend the theatre or hear a concert or browse in the library half-way around the world. Could transact any business one might need to transact without rising from one's chair.' That was written in 1952: now it has virtually all come about.

ASSIGNMENTS

1. Why are there such social problems associated with highrise blocks of flats when some of the most expensive and exclusive apartments are also in tower blocks and the penthouse suite is always associated with wealth and luxury?

2. There is a great deal of information as to attitudes to urbanism to be gained from literature.

   If you are also studying English literature, what was the attitude of the English Romantic movement to the city – and why? Wordsworth is a good poet to study. Read the Prelude, Books VII and VIII. If you like science fiction consider what sort of future settlement is implied in the stories you have read – and why.

URBAN IDEALS AND THE REAL WORLD

Having identified two apparently opposite scenarios, a term beloved of those who indulge in futurism or write about possible futures, the question must now be asked as to which of them is most likely to prevail. An examination of current trends will leave little initial doubt for the census data in most western countries show a faltering or decline of the old metropolis, and the ever-widening extension of suburbia (see Chapter 1, Table 1.3). Two technical innovations have served to eliminate the friction of distance which once held outward growth in check. The first was, of course, the motor car, the impact of which is now well-known but that impact has been progressively increased by the construction of urban motorways. The second can be called the micro-technology of computer linked communications and is only now beginning to show its effects. Already banking and shopping can be done from home – as already noted, Simak's envisaged future is already a reality. Dispersal has become characteristic of all city land-users. Residence pushes further and further out. Industry follows both managers and skilled labour and it, too, locates at the margins where land is available and where the intersection of motorways and ring-roads provides nationwide accessibility, once the prerogative of the city centre-based railways. The old sites of heavy industry were some time ago replaced by industrial estates. Those estates now are being superseded by science parks where open and attractive environment is a significant control of location. Retailing follows population and out-of-town shopping centres, with vast parking lots, arise in competition with city centres. Office parks bring another city centre land-use to the periphery.

It is evident that all these developments are fundamentally changing the very nature of urban settlement itself, a point which has already been made at the outset of this book in Chapter 1. The single, separate free-standing city as the characteristic urban settlement has long given way to organisation on a regional scale. The various chapters have attempted to demonstrate the consequences. Thus, in the consideration of suburbanisation in Chapter 1, the nature of development on the metropolitan fringes of St. Louis was introduced (p. 11). In Chapter 4, the transformation of conventional notions of the urban hierarchy was followed through in considering the city system in England and Wales. In Chapter 3 the metropolitan village was identified as the result of the extending impact of the city. In Chapter

6 the way in which patterns of social welfare have been brought about by these changes was indicated.

The major point of conflict between concentration and dispersal in strictly urban terms comes in the well publicised issue of use of Green Belt lands (see Chapter 1, p. 13). The statutory Green Belts were established after 1955 when the then Minister of Housing and Local Government asked local authorities to consider the establishment of clearly defined belts of open country about cities into which urban expansion would be prevented. London's Green Belt, however, goes back to an earlier date, to the 1920s in concept and to 1938 in practice with the passing of the Green Belt (London and Home Counties) Act. In his 1955 circular the Minister put forward three reasons for the identification of Green Belts. They were:

1. to check the growth of a large built-up area;
2. to prevent neighbouring towns from merging into one another;
3. to preserve the special character of a town.

None of these, as such, is now particularly significant and two rather more general bases are at present more relevant. The first is to prevent low density sprawl and the second is the aesthetic objection related to the need to preserve the countryside, as well as to provide recreational land. There is also a third reason more in the background, the hope that by the inhibiting of development at the periphery developers will be forced to invest in the inner city where there is a great deal of land available, but seldom as the large, open blocks which are to be found at the city edges.

The counter-argument put forward by developers is that dispersed developments are needed and that Green Belt land should be brought into urban use, in order to prevent demand for land in short supply leading to absurd prices for building plots and very high house prices. In brief, metropolitan regional systems make demands which have to be met. Two examples can be introduced to illustrate the issue and bring these generalisations down to the ground.

Figure 10.3 is a map of land-users in what the Americans call a *suburban mini-city*. Note that it is some 20 miles from Philadelphia and a characteristic representative of developments in the former rural fringe. King of Prussia has grown gradually rather than in a completely fixed or planned form from the outset. It has, therefore, a somewhat heterogeneous collection of land-users, but their character is unmistakable. There is modern industry related to high-tech research. There are administrative functions in the American Baptist Convention headquarters. There is a range of amusement, recreational and residential functions. And these are not local or small scale: the Valley Forge Music Fair is of a national significance. As these sorts of developments push further out from the conventional city they form the constituent elements of the metropolitan region.

In Britain Consortium Developments, which is a grouping of some nine of the largest house builders including Barratt and Wimpy, proposed the building of what would have been essen-

tially a new town, a potential mini-city, at Tillingham Hall which is a 790 acre farm in Green Belt land in Essex (Figure 10.4). It would have had some 5100 dwellings and a population of 14 000. Land would have been set aside to provide at least 2000 jobs together with shopping and community facilities with a wide-ranging attempt to landscape the area both with parks and water features. Consultants to Consortium Developments wrote that 'the group is committed to financing the development of the new country town, including capital contributions towards education, health care and community uses. A ten-year programme of investment will complete the phased development of the town, to be achieved by the principal developer undertaking the infrastructure and environmental works to provide serviced parcels of development land for acquisition by member companies, local builders and specialist developers'. As can be easily envisaged, this proposal brought forth a mass of objections and the proposal was rejected after a Public Inquiry. The major bases of objection

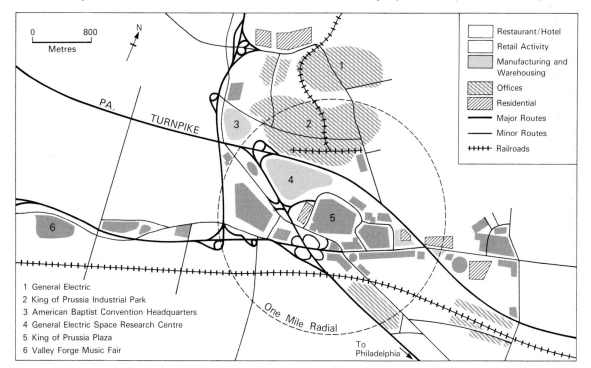

1 General Electric
2 King of Prussia Industrial Park
3 American Baptist Convention Headquarters
4 General Electric Space Research Centre
5 King of Prussia Plaza
6 Valley Forge Music Fair

Figure 10.3 *King of Prussia, Pennsylvania: an American suburban mini-city (after Muller)*

were that permission to develop would open a period of general attack on the Green Belts and would initiate a new era of urban sprawl and of threat to rural environments. In addition, taking up a point which occurred in Chapter 6, these developments would do nothing to alleviate the problems of the inner city where it is argued the members of Consortium Developments should be concentrating their efforts in order to up-grade derelict land. To reinterpret this conflict on the broadest scale brings one back to the two tendencies which were called claustrophilia and agoraphilia at the beginning of the chapter. At Tillingham Hall they were in direct opposition. They still remain so, and the controversy over development of housing in what is now referred to as Roseland (the rest of the south-east, that is the area outside London) has become more pointed. There is a joint interest between Conservative voting residents who wish to retain the rurality of their environment (development anywhere but 'not in my back yard') and Socialist demands for policies to promote regional development in the north. As always the determinant of land-uses is not simply the market, but market forces constrained by political decisions.

Lest it should be assumed that there is a simple antithesis between what are quite erroneously called natural forces but which are in reality the forces of the free, competitive market, and the constraining forces of social control and planning, it is necessary briefly to indicate that there are also natural trends apparent of what can best be called a move back to the city, towards concentration. These trends are strongly linked with the assemblage of attractions offered by the city core, its theatres, cinemas and restaurants, its museums, art galleries and concerts, as well as its shopping. Two major themes are inner city and city centre *rehabilitation*, and gentrification, the latter having already been discussed earlier. Inner city rehabilitation relates to the very determined efforts being made by many cities to refurbish their central areas and to make them more attractive in order to offset the pull

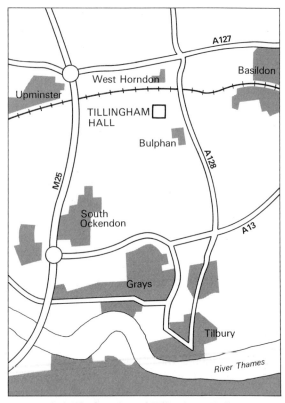

Figure 10.4 *The location of Tillingham Hall*

to the suburbs. Most often such improvements require large amounts of money and are undertaken as joint ventures between the local authority and a commercial developer. Some of the most spectacular have been in the USA, such as the Baltimore Inner Harbor Project or the Point Park and Gateway Center at Pittsburgh. Even the most modest cities can boast similar schemes which have created large city centre shopping malls and pedestrian precincts with theatres, concert halls and restaurants (see Chapter 5, page 95). In some cities improvement has been accomplished by lifting pedestrian circulation to the first floor level, as in Cincinnati's 'skywalk', or, because of climatic reasons, putting it underground, as in La Ville Ste. Marie at Montreal.

Undoubtedly, the largest British project is that for the development of the former London dockland where some 8.5 square miles of near derelict land is being totally transformed

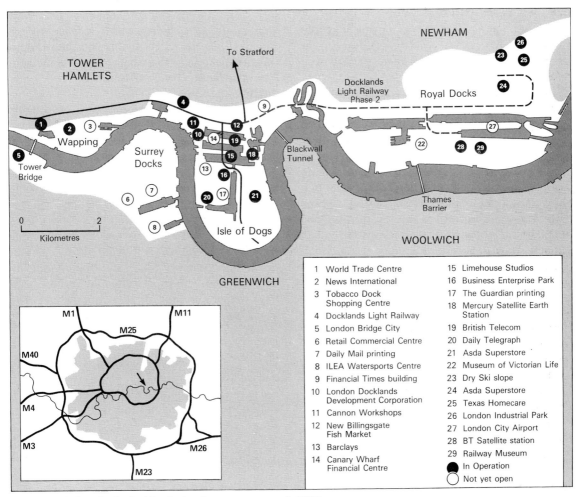

Figure 10.5 *London's dockland: development proposals 1986*

(Figure 10.5). It is characteristic that public and private finance is involved, some £300 million from the London Dockland Development Corporation (LDDC) but £1.4 billion from private sources. Since 1981 about 400 businesses have moved in creating 8000 jobs. Nearly 3.5 million square feet of office space has been constructed. A 4.7 kilometre Dockland Light Railway has been opened and there is prospect of the transformation of Canary Wharf into a major new financial centre of 10 million square feet. In the summer of 1987, a new city airport, the so-called Stolport, an abbreviation derived from 'short take off and landing', opened. The Chief Executive of

the LDDC talks of the success of the whole enterprise in terms of pulling the whole of London eastward and thus reversing a trend which has been in operation since Tudor times. Many British towns can show equivalent developments even if on a much more modest scale.

Gentrification has already been discussed in Chapter 6, where the attempted improvement of the inner cities was also introduced. Both inner city rehabilitation and gentrification are closely connected. Thus, in addition to the developments noted, some 9000 homes have been built in the Dockland. Land costs have escalated. In 1981 the LDDC sold its first piece of land for £33 000 an acre: in 1986 a prime piece of waterfront land went for nearly £4 million an acre. Flats have moved into the £100 000 plus class, whilst penthouses in specially favoured locations have reached well over the £1 million mark.

The conclusion from this consideration of inner city rehabilitation and of gentrification is that the forces of concentration and dispersal are both in operation and the present urban landscape is a product of their operation. The towns of the future will be characterised by the impact which these forces make, and although this consideration has been limited to the western world the cities of the rest of the globe will also be subject to their interaction.

ASSIGNMENT

3. For any town with which you are familiar examine:
   a) Out of town shopping developments and their impact.
   b) Attempts at inner city rehabilitation.

   Do not make the mistake of thinking that such developments are to be found only in large cities. Even the smallest towns will provide exemplification. You will obviously have to adjust the scale of your study to that of the settlement you are examining.

THE FUTURE OF THE VILLAGE

Having considered the future of the town, it is appropriate to review the future of the village or, indeed, to include the single farm, of rural settlement in general. Again, across the world the prospects vary so greatly that only the western areas can be considered.

One of the predominating themes of this book has been the gradual disappearance of the simple division of settlement into two contrasted types of area, one called rural, the other urban. It follows that the one time clear distinction of the village is no longer tenable. That vast increase in accessibility which has led to the spread of urbanism has also led to the substantial modification of the village. Rural settlement has, therefore, been affected by two quite different trends.

The first is epitomised by the term already used in this book, the metropolitan village (Chapter 3). Suburban extension has been accompanied not only by the building of new housing estates in peripheral greenfield sites, but also by the addition of estates to existing villages. But not only the immediate villages are subject to invasion, if that be a proper word to use. In remote villages and hamlets people from the big cities have bought second homes, or summer homes, which are rented out. In addition, those retiring from jobs in the towns have bought houses in the countryside. The character of the village has, therefore, greatly changed and there are few settlements now which are solely inhabited by those engaged in farming or providing services for those so engaged.

The second trend, noted as quite different, is that towards decline and decay. In an age where the economies of scale are seen as a prime objective, and when agriculture itself is highly capitalised, the future of the small settlement is bleak. Chapter 3 demonstrated the loss of services in the smallest settlements. To a large extent the future of the village is closely linked to agriculture itself and with large surpluses and suggestions that land should be taken out of agricultural production and devoted to other uses, the future of rural settlement is even more difficult to predict. Certainly it seems evident that the traditional village, seen as a closed community of people concerned with farming, is already to some degree a feature of the past. In the regional metropoles of the future we will have to abandon long-held traditional concepts of hamlet, village and town and devise ideas and a terminology more adapted to a new situation.

Additional Reading

CHAPTER 1
URBAN AND RURAL POPULATIONS

The basic facts are best obtained from the various annual editions of *The United Nations Demographic Yearbook*.

Most standard textbooks have an introductory chapter on urbanisation. Four books which develop ideas for different parts of the world are:

Conzen, M. P. (ed.) (1986) *World Patterns of Modern Urban Change*, Essays in Honor of Channcy D. Harris, University of Chicago. Dept. of Geography Research Paper No. 217–18. Chicago.

Findlay, A. and Findlay, A. (1987) *Population and Development in the Third World*, Methuen, London.

Santos, M. (1971) *Les Villes du Tiers Monde*, Editions M.-Th. Genin, Paris.

Sarfalvi, B. (1975) *Urbanisation in Europe*, Academiai Kiado, Budapest.

Two books which cover particular topics which arise in this chapter are:

Dwyer, D. J. (1975) *People and Housing in Third World Cities*, Longman, London.

Munton, R. (1983) *London's Green Belt: Containment in Practice*, George Allen and Unwin, London.

CHAPTER 2
RURAL SETTLEMENT: PATTERN AND FORM

The main items are those mentioned in the chapter. The most important is:

Roberts, B. K. (1987) *The Making of the English Village*, Longman Scientific and Technical, London.

The other major references are:

Jones, G. R. J. (1953) Some medieval rural settlements in North Wales, *Transactions of the Institute of British Geographers*, **19**, 51–72.

Lewis, G. J. (1979) *Rural Communities*. David and Charles, London.

Rapoport, A. (1969) *House Form and Culture*, Prentice Hall, Englewood Cliffs, N.J.

Thorpe, H. (1951) The influence of inclosure on the form and pattern of rural settlement in Denmark, *Transactions of the Institute of British Geographers*, **17**, 113–129.

An outdated book, but worth consulting on this topic, is:

Houston, J. M. (1951) *A Social Geography of Europe*, Duckworth, London.

Whilst much more recent general reviews are:

Gilg, A. (1985) *An Introduction to Rural Geography*, Edward Arnold, London.

Pacione, M. (1983) *Progress in Rural Geography*, Croom Helm, London.

Pacione, M. (1984) *Rural Geography*, Harper and Row, London.

CHAPTER 3
RURAL SETTLEMENT: FUNCTION AND COMMUNITY

The books by G. J. Lewis and M. Pacione included in the suggested reading for Chapter 2 contain much relevant to this chapter. The direct references made are:

Cloke, P. and Shaw, D. (1983) Rural settlement policies in County Structure Plans,

Town Planning Review, **54(3)**, 338–54.

Davies, E. and Rees, A. (1960) *Welsh Rural Communities*, University of Wales Press, Cardiff.

which contains the studies by T. Jones Hughes and T. M. Owen.

The discussion of the impact of settlement size on community derives from:

Wirth, L (1938) Urbanism as a way of life, *American Journal of Sociology*, **44**, 1–24.

It has been reprinted many times, for example in:

Reiss, A. J. (ed.) (1964) *Louis Wirth. On cities and social life*, University of Chicago Press, Chicago.

There is extensive discussion in most geographical and sociological texts, for example:

Carter, H. (1981) *The Study of Urban Geography*, Edward Arnold, London, 31–3.

and

Morris, R. N. (1968) *Urban Sociology*, George Allen and Unwin.

which is entirely based on Wirth's ideas.

A book which adds broader reviews after an initial consideration of Wirth is:

Smith, M. P. (1980) *The City and Social Theory*, Basil Blackwell, Oxford.

CHAPTER 4
TOWNS: THEIR SIZES AND THEIR DISTRIBUTION

The basic work on which the material developed in this chapter is based is, in translation:

Christaller, W. (1966) *Central Places in Southern Germany*, Prentice Hall, Englewood Cliffs, N.J. Trans. C. W. Baskin.

There have been many interpretations amongst which one of the best is:

Lewis, C. R. (1977) *Central Place Analysis. Fundamentals of Human Geography, Unit 10*, Open University, Milton Keynes.

One of the standard books published when central place studies dominated urban geography is:

Berry, B. J. L. (1967) *Geography of Market Centres and Retail Distribution*, Prentice Hall, Englewood Cliffs, N.J.

On the development of central places:

Carter, H. (1983) *An Introduction to Urban Historical Geography*, Edward Arnold, London. 82–113.

Carter, H. (1988) The development of urban centrality in England and Wales, *in* D. Denecke and G. Shaw (eds.) *Urban Historical Geography. Recent Progress in Britain and Germany*, Cambridge University Press, Cambridge.

Robson, B. (1973) *Urban Growth: An Approach*, Methuen, London.

A further general volume with a very wide ranging discussion is:

Eisenstadt, S. N. and Shachar, A. (1987) *Society, Culture, and Urbanisation*, Sage Publications, Newbury Park, Calif.

Other publications referred to are:

Cameron, G. (ed.) (1980) *The Future of the British Conurbation*, Longman, London.

Hall, P. (1973) *The Containment of Urban England*, Beverly Hills and London. Two Vols.

The basic volume on the classification of towns is:

Moser, C. A. and Scott, W. (1961) *British Towns. A Statistical Study of their Social and Economic Differences*, Oliver and Boyd, Edinburgh.

The figures in Table 4.3 are derived from:

McInnes, A. (1980) *The English Town 1660–1760*. The Historical Association of London. Appreciations in History No. 7.

The same period is covered in:

Clark, P. and Slack, P. (1976) *English Towns in Transition 1500–1700*, Oxford University Press, Oxford.

The best source in which to examine a series of rank-size plots is:

Hall, P. and Hay, D. (1980) *Growth Centres in the European Urban System*. Heinemann Educational, London.

CHAPTER 5
THE INTERNAL STRUCTURE OF TOWNS

The two standard sources from which much of the subsequent discussion has been derived are:

Burgess, E. W. (1925) The growth of the city: an introduction to a research project, in E. R. Park and E. W. Burgess (eds.) *The City*, Chicago University Press, Chicago.

Hoyt, H. (1939) *The Structure and Growth of Residential Neighbourhoods in American Cities.* Federal Housing Administration, Washington DC.

Most texts on urban geography deal with the material in this chapter. A useful summary is to be found in:

Scargill, D. I. (1979) *The Form of Cities*, Bell and Hyman, London.

References made in the chapter are:

Davies, W. K. D. (1983) Urban Social Structure. A Multivariate-Structural Analysis of Cardiff and its Region. *Board of Celtic Studies, Social Science Monographs, No. 8.* University of Wales Press, Cardiff.

Goddard, J. (1968) Multivariate analysis of office location patterns in the city centre: a London example. *Regional Studies*, **2**, 69–85.

Stedman, M. B. and Wood, P. A. (1965) Urban renewal in Birmingham. An Interim report. *Geography*, **50(1)**, 1–17.

CHAPTER 6
INEQUALITIES WITHIN CITIES

Since this has been the main focus of research in urban studies over the last decade, the literature is voluminous, and to a degree repetitive. One of the earlier and critical works by a geographer is:

Harvey, D. (1979) *Socal Justice and the City*, Edward Arnold, London.

A well balanced discussion can be found in:

Badcock, B. (1984) *Unfairly Structured Cities*, Basil Blackwell, Oxford.

Two other very useful general volumes are:

Herbert, D. T. and Smith, D. (1979) *Social Problems and the City: Geographical Perspectives*, Oxford University Press, Oxford.

Pahl, R. (1975) *Whose City? And Further Essays on Urban Society*, Penguin Books, Harmondsworth, Middlesex.

There are a number of separate topics included in the chapter. On problems of ethnicity there are:

Peach, C. (ed.) (1975) *Urban Social Segregation*, Longman, London.

And by the same author/editor

Peach, C. (ed.) (1981) *Ethnic Segregation in Cities*, Croom Helm, Beckenham, Kent.

Whilst, although somewhat now out of date:

Lee, T. R. (1977) *Race and Residence. The Concentration and Dispersal of Immigrants in London*, Clarendon Press, Oxford – is a very useful study.

On problems related to housing there are:

Bassett, K. and Short, J. (1980) *Housing and Residential Structure. Alternative Approaches*, Routledge and Kegan Paul, London.

Bourne, L. S. (1981) *The Geography of Housing*, V. H. Winston, London.

Short, J. A. (1982) *Housing in Britain. The Post-War Experience*, Methuen, London.

The works referred to in the text are:

Boal, F. W. and Poole, M. A. (1973) Religious residential segregation in Belfast in mid-1969: a multi-level analysis, *in* B. D. Clark and M. B. Gleave (eds.) *Social Patterns in Cities. Institute of British Geographers Special Publication*, **No. 5**.

Evans, D. J. (1984) The segregation of the New Commonwealth Population in Wolverhampton Municipal Borough, 1961–1981. *Department of Geography and Recreation Studies, North Staffs. Polytechnic Occasional Papers in Geography*, **No. 3**.

Davies, R. (1981) The spatial formation of the South African city. *GeoJournal Supplementary Issue* **2**, 59–72.

Herbert, D. T. (1979) Urban Crime: a geographical perspective, *in* D. T. Herbert and D. Smith (as already referenced), 117–38.

Jackson, G. and Oulds, G. (1984) A Social Area Analysis of Stoke-on-Trent. *Depart-*

ment of Geography and Recreation Studies, *North Staffs. Polytechnic Occasional Papers*, **No. 4**.

Jakle, J. A. and Wheeler, J. O. (1969) The Changing Residential Structure of the Dutch Population of Kalamazoo, Michigan. *Annals of the Association of American Geographers*, **59**, 441–60.

Western, J. (1981) *Outcast Cape Town*, Allen and Unwin, London.

Schaffer, R. and Smith, N. (1986) The gentrification of Harlem? *Annals of the Association of American Geographers*, **76(3)**, 347–65.

Some urban geography texts are directed predominantly to these topics. Examples are:

Knox, P. (1982) *Urban Social Geography. An Introduction*, Longman, London.

Ley, D. (1983) *A Social Geography of the City*, Harper and Row, New York.

CHAPTER 7
ASPECTS OF CITIES IN THE THIRD WORLD

There is a growing number of general works on Third World cities. A recent brief volume is:

Drakakis-Smith, D. (1987) *The Third World City*, Methuen, London.

Also of value are:

Dwyer, D. J. (ed.) (1974) *The City in the Third World*, Macmillan, London.

Roberts, B. (1978) *Cities of Peasants*, Edward Arnold, London.

Santos, M. (1979) *The Shared Space*, Methuen, London.

Much of the published work is concerned with housing. Examples are:

Drakakis-Smith, D. (1981) *Urbanisation, Housing and the Development Process*, Croom Helm, London.

Dwyer, D. J. (1975) *People and Housing in Third World Cities*, Longman, London.

Skinner, R. J. and Rodell, M. J. (1983) *People, Poverty and Shelter*, Methuen, London.

Specific items referred to in the Chapter are:

Amato, P. (1970) Elitism and settlement patterns in the Latin American City, *Journal of the American Institute of Town Planners*, **36(1)**, 96–105.

Abu-Lughod, J. (1976) The legitimacy of comparisons in comparative urban studies: A theoretical position and application to North African cities, *in* J. Walton and L. H. Masotti (eds.) *The City in Comparative Perspective*, John Wiley, Sage Publications, New York.

Hinderink, J. and Sterkenburg, J. (1975) *Anatomy of an African Town*, Geog. Inst. State University of Utrecht, Utrecht.

King, A. D. (1976) *Colonial Urban Development*, Routledge and Kegan Paul, London.

The most accessible source to the material on Calcutta is:

Berry, B. J. and Kasarda, J. D. (1977) *Contemporary Urban Ecology*, Macmillan, New York. Chap. 7, 108–157.

There is a series of volumes entitled *Urbanisation in Developing Countries* published by Cambridge University Press under the general editorship of K. Little. These include:

Costello, V. F.: *Urbanisation in the Middle East*.

Gugler, J. and Flanagan, W. G.: *Urbanisation and Social Change in West Africa*.

Levine, H. B.: *Urbanisation in Papua New Guinea*.

Cross, M.: *Urbanisation and Urban Growth in the Caribbean*.

Lloyd, P.: *The 'Young Towns' of Lima: Aspects of Urbanisation in Peru*.

Butterworth, D. and Change, J. K: *Latin American Urbanisation*.

CHAPTER 8
THE CITY IN SOCIALIST COUNTRIES

Material on socialist countries is far less easily available. The two standard sources are:

Bater, J. H. (1980) *The Soviet City. Ideal and Reality*, Edward Arnold, London.

French, R. A. and Ian Hamilton, F. E. (1979) *The Socialist City. Spatial Structure and Urban Policy*, John Wiley, Chichester.

A work which includes a special section on Settlement Systems in Centrally Planned Economies is:

Bourne, L. S. *et al.* (eds.) (1984) *Urbanisation and Settlement Systems. International Perspectives*, Oxford University Press, Oxford.
The study of Kiev is taken from:
Walker, A. R. (1986) Urban Development and Town Planning in Kiev, *Department of Town and Country Planning, Bristol Polytechnic Working Paper*, **No. 7**.

Lavedan, P. (1960) *Histoire de Paris*, Presses Universitaires de France, Paris.
On American cities, the works of John Reps are essential, especially the general volume:
Reps, J. W. (1965) *The Making of Urban America*, Princeton University Press, Princeton, J.N.
And the one dealing with Washington:
Reps, J. W. (1967) *Monumental Washington: the Planning and development of the Capital City*, Princeton Univ. Press, Princeton, N.J.

CHAPTER 9
TOWN PLAN AND TOWNSCAPE

The two useful histories of town plan are:
Burke, D. (1979) *Towns in the Making*, Edward Arnold, London.
Morris, A. E. J. (1972) *History of Urban Form*, John Wiley, New York.
A volume that is limited to England is:
Lloyd, D. W. (1984) *The Making of English Towns*, Gollancz, London.
Carter, H. (1982) *An Introduction to Urban Historical Geography*, also deals with town plan.
An older but very distinctive book more concerned with townscape is:
Johns, E. (1965) *British Townscapes*, Edward Arnold, London.
Works referred to in the chapter are:
Lynch, K. (1972) *What Time is this Place?* MIT Press, Cambridge, Mass.
Mumford, L. (1961) *The City in History*, Secker and Warburg, London.
Whitehand, J. (1987) The changing face of cities: a study of development cycles and urban form, *Institute of British Geographers, Special Publication*, **No. 21**.
The most accessible sources on Paris are:
Bastié, J. (1984) *Géographie du Grand Paris*, Masson, Paris.
Beaujeu-Garnier, J. (1977) *Atlas de Géographie de Paris et de la Région d'Ile de France*, Flammarion et Famot, Paris, 2 vols.
Whilst an older small volume is still an admirable summary:

CHAPTER 10
SETTLEMENTS OF THE FUTURE

One general volume is most useful:
Blowers, A. *et al.* (eds.) (1974) *The Future of Cities*, Hutchinson Educational, London.
The material on the suburban mini-city is derived from:
Muller, P. O. (1981) *Contemporary Suburban America*, Prentice-Hall, Englewood Cliffs, N.J.
There are a number of relevant chapters dealing with attitudes to the city in the USA and Europe in:
Handlin, O. and Burchard, J. (eds.) (1966) *The Historian and the City*. MIT Press, Cambridge, Mass.
There are a large number of books on Le Corbusier. One general treatment is:
Fishman, R. (1977) *Urban Utopias in the Twentieth Century, Ebenezer Howard, Frank Lloyd Wright and Le Corbusier*. Basic Books, New York.
Two others are:
Curtis, W. J. A. (1986) *Le Corbusier: Ideas and Forms*, Phaedon, Oxford.
Raeburn, M. and Wilson, V. (eds.) (1987) Le Corbusier Architect of the Century, *Catalogue of a Centary Exhibition at the Hayward Gallery, London*. Arts Council of Great Britain, London.

Index

We are grateful to the following for permission to redraw artwork; American Academy of Political and Social Science, Harris and Ullman, *The Nature of Cities*, in Annals Vol. 242 (after Hoyt), figure 5.5; Annals of the Association of American Geographers, Jakle and Wheeler, *The Changing Residential Structure of the Dutch Population of Kalamazoo*, in Vol. 59, 1969, figure 6.6 and Muller, *Contemporary Suburban America*, figure 10.3; Armand Colin Editeur, *Annales de Geographie*, in Vol. XXXVI, 1927, figure 2.4; Bristol Polytechnic Department of Town and Country Planning, Walker, *Urban Development and Town Planning in Kiev*, Working Paper 7, 1986, figures 8.5 and 8.6; City of Cardiff, *Report of Survey and Written Analysis Part 2, 1970*, figure 5.8; Dyfed County Council, *County Structure Plan*, 1978, figures 3.2 and 3.3; Edward Arnold, Gilg, *Rural Geography: An Introduction*, 1985, figure 3.5; Heinemann Educational Books, Hall and Day, *Growth Centres in the European Urban System*, 1980, figures 4.6; Her Majesty's Stationery Office/Welsh Education Office, *Ysgol y Dderi – An Area School in Dyfed* (and based on the Ordhance Survey map, Crown ©), 1976, figure 3.4; Kearsley, *The Upper Ranks of the Urban Hierarchy in England and Wales*, 1971, figure 4.8; Kluwer Academic Publishers, Davies, *The Spatial Formation of the South African City*, Geojournal Supplementary Issue 2, 1981, figure 6.12; Institute of British Geographers, Thorpe, *The Influence of Enclosure and Rural Settlement in Denmark*, in Vol. 17, 1951, figure 2.6, Carter and Aitchison, *The Welsh Language in Cardiff, A Quiet Revolution*, trans in New Series 12, 1987, figure 5.7, Poole and Boal, *Religious Residential Segregation in Belfast in mid 1969, in 'Social Patterns in Cities'*, Special Publication 5, figures 6.8, 6.9 and 6.10, Grice and Drakakis-Smith, *The Role of the State in Shaping Development in Two Decades of Growth in Singapore*, New Series 10, 1985, figure 7.17 and Carter and Wheatley, *Fixation Lines and Fringe Belts, Land Uses and Social Areas: Nineteenth Century Change in the Small Town*, New Series 4, 1979, figure 9.8; Journal of the American Planning Association, Amato, *Elitism and Settlement Patterns in the Latin American City*, in Vol. 36(1) 1970, figure 7.8; Koninklijk Nederlands Aardrijkskundig Genootschap, Keuning, *L'Habitat Rural aux Pays Bas*, in Vol.55, 1938, figure 2.7(b) and Lewis and Davies, *The Social Patterning of a British City – The Case of Leicester, 1966*, in Vol. 65(3), 1974, figure 6.5; Lalvani Publishing House, Bose, *Calcutta, 1964, A Social Survey*, 1968, figure 7.13; Lewis, *Rural Communities – A Social Geography*, David and Charles, 1979, figure 2.5; Macmillan New York, Berry and Kasarda, *Contemporary Urban Ecology*, 1977, figure 7.12; Thomas Nelson, Thorpe, *British Isles – A Systematic Geography*, 1964, figure 2.2; The Open University, Lewis, 'Central Place Analysis', Unit 10, *Fundamentals of Human Geography* Course D204, figure 4.3; Oxford University Press, Herbert and Smith, *Social Problems and the City*, 1979, figure 6.19 and Bourne et al, *Urbanization and Settlement Systems, International Perspectives*, 1984, figures 4.9 and 4.10; Prentice Hall, Rapoport, *House Form and Culture*, 1969, figures 2.13 and 2.15; Presses Universitaires de France, Lavedan, *Histoire de Paris*, figures 9.1 and 9.2; Rowley, *Towns of Wales*, 1967, figure 4.5; Staffordshire Polytechnic Department of Geography, Jackson and Oulds, *A Social Area Analysis of Stoke on Trent* in Occasional Papers 4, 1984, figure 6.3 and Evans, *The Segregation of the New Commonwealth Population in Wolverhampton Municipal Borough 1961–81* in Occasional Papers 3, 1984, figure 6.4; Times Newspapers, figures 6.16 and 10.5; Topografische Dienst Nederland, figures 2.8 and 2.9(b); Town Planning Review 54(3), 1983, figure 3.7; University of Chicago Press, Burgess, *The Growth of the City* in Park and Burgess, *The City*, 1925, figure 5.1 and Murdie, *Factorial Ecology of Metropolitan Toronto, 1951–61*, in Research Papers 116, figure 6.20; University of Utrecht Department of Geography, Hinderink and Sterkenburg, *Anatomy of an African Town*, 1975, figures 7.2, 7.3 and 7.4; University of Wales Press, Davies and Rees, *Welsh Rural Communities*, 1960, figure 3.1; Unwin Hyman, Western, *Outcast Cape Town*, 1981, figures 6.13, 6.14 and 7.14; John Wiley, Hamilton, *Spatial Structure in East European Cities* in French and Hamilton, The Socialist City, *Spatial Structure and Urban Policy*, 1979, figure 8.4 and Weclawowicz, figure 8.7.

We are grateful to the following for permission to reproduce photographs and other copyright material: Ace Photo Agency, page 153 (photo: Marka); Aerofilms Limited, pages 35, 95; J Allan Cash, pages 39, 50, 113; Ordnance Survey for an extract from the Landranger 1:50 000 139, Birmingham. Reproduced with the permission of the Controller of Her Majesty's Stationery Office © Crown Copyright; Reflex Picture Agency, page 98 (photo: Piers Cavendish). The remaining photographs were supplied by the author.

Cover: **International Stock Exchange Photo Library**

Longman Group UK Limited
Longman House, Burnt Mill, Harlow, Essex,
CM20 2JE, England
and Associated Companies throughout the World

© Longman Group UK Limited 1990

Published in the United States of America by
Longman Inc., New York

First published 1990
Second impression 1993
ISBN 0 582 35585 0

Set in 10/12pt Times Roman, Linotron 202
Produced by Longman Singapore
Publishers (Pte) Limited,
Printed in Singapore

The Publisher's policy is to use paper
manufactured from sustainable forests.

British Library Cataloguing in Publication Data

Carter, Harold, *1925*–
  Urban and rural settlements. – (Longman
  modular geography series).
  1. Human settlements. Geographical aspects
  I. Title
  910' .09173

Library of Congress Cataloging-in-Publication Data

Carter, Harold.
  Urban and rural settlements.
  (Longman modular geography series)
  Bibliography: p.
  Includes index.
  Summary: Examines the patterns and functions
  of human settlements and their growth into
  towns and cities.
  1. Human settlements.   2. Cities and towns.
  3. Villages.   [1. Human settlements.   2. Cities
  and towns]   I. Title.   II. Series.
[HT65.C37   1990]   307   89-8318